INSTITUTIONS IN MODERN SOCIETY

THE REYNOLDS SERIES IN SOCIOLOGY

Larry T. Reynolds, *Editor*

by **GENERAL HALL, INC.**

Institutions in Modern Society:

Meanings, Forms, and Character

Jeffrey E. Nash

Macalester College, Saint Paul, MN

and

James M. Calonico

Catholic Youth Organization, San Francisco, CA

GENERAL HALL, INC.

Publishers

5 Talon Way

Dix Hills, New York 11746

INSTITUTIONS IN MODERN SOCIETY:
MEANINGS, FORMS, AND CHARACTER

GENERAL HALL, INC.
5 Talon Way
Dix Hills, New York 11746

Copyright © 1993 by General Hall, Inc.

Publisher: Ravi Mehra
Composition: *Graphics Division,* General Hall, Inc.

LIBRARY OF CONGRESS CATALOG CARD NUMBER: **91–75941**

ISBN:0–930390–06–7 [paper]
          0–930390–07–5 [cloth]

Manufactured in the United States of America

Dedicated to the Memory of
Michael J. Calonico

Contents

PREFACE

Sometimes the most surprising thing about societies is that they work at all. Indeed, when we consider the United States, for example, and the management of some 250 million citizens, day and day, year after year, ensuring their food and shelter, employment, and overall social security, the task seems overwhelming — to say nothing of "managing the planet" of nearly 5 billion people. This is not to suggest that the societies of the world all run as if well-oiled, well-kept machines; but given the task, most run remarkably well. And perhaps the most important reason for this lies in their ongoing social institutions.

For us, these institutions consist of ready-made solutions to everyday social problems, whether these be economic, familial, or political. This means that when, for example, we want to obtain a certain job that requires some degree of skill, we do not usually need to develop our own training program; there most likely is an educational institution with a program already in place to service our need. Or if we want to get married or divorced, or to open a business, or to declare bankruptcy, there are institutions to tell us how this is done.

In the present text, we hope to offer our readers a preliminary understanding of social institutions through a discussion of five basic ones: family, education, religion, economy, and politics. We recognize, of course, that our list is not exhaustive. Some sociologists believe the military, medicine, and the vastly complicated welfare system could be included as separate institutions; others feel the transportation and communication industries qualify. For us, however, more important than being inclusive is providing our readers with a model for thinking about social institutions, one that also demonstrates how we might see ourselves within them.

Whether we work for ourselves or "for the other guy," whether we are in or out of school, whether we are religious, atheist, or agnostic, we must participate in or otherwise be affected by familial, religious, economic, educational, and political institutions. We have two complementary goals in writing this text. On the one hand, we want to deal with the fundamental changes in social life brought on by the changing organization of society. In this regard, the book is about society in the most general sense possible. On the other hand, our perspective is not applied to all aspects of life in modern society. We look at the basic institutions of society because we believe we can better understand change in this way. Our strategy, admittedly, omits many aspects of life in modern society.

Having so confessed, we redeem ourselves by stating our purposes. We organize our discussions around questions that assume roughly the following form: "What is modernization and what relationships might there be between a process of modernization and institutionalized social life?" We build from a body of literature inspired by classic European sociological writings to sketch a concept of modernization and of modern society, and we then explore the implications of these concepts in each of the five basic institutions of society. We know full well that the very process we document and interpret might well transform and supplant the institutions we assume are basic. In a future society, we grant, the five institutions that are the focus of our analysis might not be basic. Still, we write from a conviction that change starts within these bedrock institutions and that while these five institutions change, they do so within functional limits. Family life is radically different in America now than it was fifty years ago, but the meanings of participation in the family still derive from intimate, face-to-face, long-term, and mutually caring relationships. Economic life still deals with working, governmental institutions are control oriented, and education prepares citizens for further institutional activity in society.

Each of the paths to understanding modernization that we averted can, of course, lead to the same end we pursue, and we do not claim exclusive rights on how to understand society. We choose our path because of our appreciation of the canons of sociological literature, and because, as we say in Chapter One, many contemporary analyses seem to us either too specialized or too general and introductory. Our book is introductory, but it is not an introduction to the way sociological inquiry is organized today. It is intended to illustrate and exhibit how basic concepts of the sociological perspective operate in the process of analysis, and it focuses on institutions because so much of classical sociology does. But more than this, we engage in the analysis of institutions because we hope to sketch the broadest possible account of the meanings, character, and forms of social life.

ACKNOWLEDGMENTS

From the outset, we had in mind doing the kind of sociology we had always admired. We thought introductory texts should be more than a review of literature with flashy presentations. We wanted to develop our own version of seeing sociologically, but still assist our readers in acquiring a solid grasp of sociological concepts. While we were impressed by those who do not flinch from the task of assessing a society's character, we might not only have flinched but reeled from the task we set for ourselves had we not received strategic encouragement that we came to think of as small bits of advice and positive evaluation coming right when it was needed the most.

Since this text evolved rather slowly, strategic advice was often needed. We believe in what we have tried to do, and we remain practitioners of a sociology informed by essentially whatever sources help us exercise our sociological imagination. Hence the people we want to thank are the people who, with us, practice sociology that both captures the details of individual experiences and embodies generalizations about society.

We thank first teachers such as Charles M. Tolbert and Harold Osborn, and later teachers and colleagues like Joseph Perry, Richard Ogles, and Henry Pitchford. While each practices sociology differently, they all appreciate analysis with a critical edge, and they fostered in us an understanding of how society works. We were graduate students at Washington State University together, and we owe much of our perspective to those we met and learned from there. Mostly, however, that place, the great wheat country called the Palouse, brought us together, a Californian and an Okie, and we have persisted as friends and co-inquirers through the years.

The last strategic encouragement we received was the most significant and came from Larry T. Reynolds, who, when he read our manuscript, understood what we were trying to do. He offered suggestions that enhanced our purposes rather than transformed them, and he acted promptly and professionally. We are grateful for the chance to publish in the Reynold's sociology series of textbooks.

Finally, Anedith Nash not only listened to us during the times when we met to work on the book but she also persisted with Jeff through the cycles of emotions accompanying his writing. She also has been a source of ideas for more than twenty-five years, and for that no thanks can possibly compensate.

Of course, our acknowledgments do not shift blame for mistakes or errors of interpretations. While we hope our readers do not judge us mistaken or in error, even if their interpretations vary from ours, it is our primary concern that what we have done is solidly grounded and deals with basic issues in the analysis of society. We will not be disappointed if our readers disagree with us. We will be disappointed if they are not provoked to think about why they disagree.

Chapter 1

INTRODUCING INSTITUTIONAL
ANALYSIS

Sociology has been virtually synonymous with the analysis of institutions since its founding by the philosopher August Comte (1853) in early nineteenth century France. Indeed, for some, sociological study is the study of social institutions and the relationships between them. Recently, however, with the increased professionalization of the discipline, studies of particular institutions have become specialties within the field. Thus, sociology of the family, education, religion, and the political economy have their own journals and section memberships within the American Sociological Association. Consequently, there seem to be fewer accounts dealing generally with social institutions.

While specialization of inquiry has added greatly to our knowledge of society, it has also had its costs. With this knowledge has come the proliferation of courses to accommodate each specialty, so now students may have difficulty understanding the whole of society for the range of topics before them. Beyond the introductory course, usually a survey of the subfields of sociology, a student might not have the opportunity to think generally about how society fits together. Furthermore, the different specialists often seem unaware of how they all are struggling to understand the same basic processes. Thereby they risk duplicating one another's efforts or, in the worst case, rediscovering what has already been discovered in another branch of the profession.

Theoretical Perspectives

We think the former problem, of missing the whole, is the greater of the two dangers, especially for the undergraduate student. To restore an appreciation of the scope of sociology, then, we provide both a general introduction to institutional analysis as well as a topical review. The concept of social institution serves us well because it is a central, or "core," concept for a variety of theories of society. For example, Marxists analyze institutions to discover clues about how society is actually "structured conflict."

Structured Conflict: Marxist Perspectives

From a Marxist perspective, institutions, other than economic ones, are part of the "superstructure" of society, accomplishing essentially two tasks: decep-

1

tion and alienation. First, according to Marxists, institutions divert attention from the true structural arrangements of society, for example, religion actually serves to placate the masses by offering them rewards in another life in exchange for their suffering without protest in this one. Similarly, family arrangements function to have an impact on members' personalities and motivations in order to ensure the smooth, trouble-free operation of the economic arrangements of society. That is, economic systems built on consumption need members who view themselves and others individualistically. Thus, in our society, which Marxists say is of this type, we favor the nuclear family with its values of self-sufficiency and independence—as opposed to the extended family, which values cooperation and sharing. In a society where much of the economy depends on the purchase and operation of expensive goods such as automobiles, it is obvious that people taught to share and cooperate are less likely to buy as many cars as people taught to be "independent, and make their own way in the world." As we discuss later in our chapter on modern families, almost all adult members of the American middle class have their own cars. In the typical American city, there are half as many cars as people: clearly, therefore, given that many of these people are children and others who cannot drive, little sharing actually takes place.

Second, according to the Marxist view, institutions reflect the basic fact that society is organized around economic production, so the degree to which an economic system is built on contradiction is reflected in the social institutions that maintain it. Ultimately, individuals who live with the institutions suffer the consequences of these contradictions in their personal lives. They feel separated from one another, lonely among the mass of people, fearful of one another and alienated from the very institutional life of which they are a part. The Marxist studies social institutions and those who inhabit them to discover the consequences of the economic organization of society. Of course, to the Marxist, changes in institutions are tied to economic changes, and, in a sense, institutional analysis is always secondary. But it is still necessary to know how institutions are working and what they teach members of society; otherwise, the task of uncovering the "structure" of society would be virtually impossible.

The Marxist intellectual tradition also underscores the importance of addressing questions about how the order of institutions is maintained. Since economic arrangements benefit people preferentially, the institutional order of society reflects inequalities intrinsic to the social structure of society. Hence, when institutions are examined, they are frequently seen as channels or modes through which injustice, inequality, and exploitation are realized in the lives of ordinary people. Furthermore, since the continuation of capitalistic society requires that people remain ignorant of the nature of their society's organization, institutions such as family, church, government, and education become important agents of social control.

By teaching people how to understand their society and their place within it, the social institutions of society function to maintain the organization of society. Perhaps the most famous Marxist insight on institutions and their role in the maintenance of society is that religion is the opiate of the masses. Of course, this slogan suggests a sociological hypothesis about the consequences of eschatology. People who live in poverty, inequality, and injustice in this society, so the hypothesis goes, may be more willing to accept their lot and cooperate with their oppressors if they believe that obedience will be rewarded in an afterlife. Likewise, governmental institutions are seen, in Marxist relief, as justifications for existing power groups and a reflection of the ideology of the powerful; and educational institutions are viewed critically for their role in simply reproducing the class structure of society. The Marxist analysis of institutions forces the analyst to look beyond the understanding of ordinary people to discover the true structure of society.

Social Forces: Durkheim and Weber

In contrast to Marx, other sociologists approach institutional study differently. For example, Emile Durkheim and Max Weber both saw institutions themselves as primary forces in society. To Durkheim, religious practices, the rituals of family life, and even the most private thoughts of individuals result from social forces existing in institutions. Among these forces, or "facts" as he referred to them, was one toward social integration. To Durkheim, the force of integration is a social condition describing the arrangements of the parts of a social whole— a family, a group, or an entire society. It denotes the coordination and mainte- nance of the relationships among the parts of a social collectivity. Disintegration, in contrast, refers to conflict and the lack of fit among the parts making up social life. To Durkheim, the study of society is the study of institutions and their interrelationships.

Durkheim studied all the basic institutions of society, such as religion, family, economy, government, and education, in terms of their degree of integration and disintegration. He found that institutions in traditional, or nonindustrial, societies were integrated differently from those in industrial or modern ones. In fact, a large part of his work focused on how modern social institutions were in a state of drastic change and suffered from disunity and social pathology. Unlike Marx, however, he believed that the changes had not completely weakened institutions, nor made one institution primary over the others. Each functioned as part of an integrated whole, and with the help of sociological understanding, institutions could work in harmony or consensus for the good of the entire society. For Durkheim, the fate of society itself depends on keeping the institutions of society well integrated both as units and as parts of a whole.

Although Max Weber placed greater importance on changes in the economic aspects of society than did Durkheim, he also believed that institutions could be primary forces in society. His classic analysis of *The Protestant Ethic and the Spirit of Capitalism* sought to demonstrate that the great system of capitalism derives its energy, vitality, and basic logic from motivations that people learn from religious institutions. To him, the particular enthusiasm that men and women exhibit in the pursuit of money and power is more similar to the fanatical religious efforts of early Calvinists striving to work their way into heaven than to the rational, calculating economic attitudes of early capitalists. His thesis, as we see in subsequent chapters, has been important in many areas of sociological analysis. We mention it here to show that Weber's insight was possible because he looked at institutional life as a potential *cause* of major societal change rather than as a reflection of it. Generally, sociologists who follow Weber look at institutions for examples of how society works, and for clues as to how the parts of society are interrelated. They look for influences of one institution on another.

Another form of institutional analysis very much in the legacy of the great sociologists Durkheim and Weber deals with the degree to which the influence of one institution persists when an individual engages in the social life of another. For example, will Protestants and Catholics have differing views on political issues? Are there differences between Protestants and Catholics in the tolerance they have for political and social diversity among others? And, of course, concern with the effectiveness of early learning within the family on the values, beliefs, and behavior of individuals in later in life remains a fundamental question of many branches of social and psychological sciences.

Research into answers for these questions brings up more questions about the power and character of social institutions. Answering a question about the lasting effects of having been brought up Catholic, therefore, requires an examination of the institution of the Catholic church. As Weber and Durkheim taught, institutions provide their members with ways to understand their social worlds, and these modes of understanding can be essential to understanding social life in general. To Weber, the shift from Catholic to Protestant theological world views was fundamental to the emergence of individualistic thinking, which in turn grounded the development of modern social institutions. His and many of the sociological theories we discuss throughout this book regarded this change and its subsequent effects as far reaching. Modern individualism, the theories suggest, is a result of changes in religious institutions and the ways that people learn to think about themselves in relation to others and to God.

The power of some social institutions is surprising. Recently, for example, Greeley (1989) reassessed the notion of the "Protestant ethic" to which Weber attributed supreme importance in the shaping and maintenance of Western culture. Religion, Greeley writes, is a significant institution because it operates as "a collection of 'pictures' thorough which humans organize and give meaning to the phenomena which impinge on their consciousness, especially insofar as these phenomena require some explanation of the ultimate purpose of life" (Greeley1989, 485–486). Once people learn to attribute meaning through the use of these images of God, they have acquired a way of making sense out of their existence that they may use in many, presumably nonreligious aspects of their lives. The question that Greeley addresses is central to the Durkheimian/ Weberian view of social institutions: What is the relationship among the institutions of society? Specifically, for this research, this asks whether differences among Catholics and Protestants persist even in a seemingly secularized, modern world?

To test such ideas about the power of a social institution, Greeley used survey data gathered from several nations of the world. He conducted his research in phases, expanding the number of nations to include English-speaking European nations, West Germany, the Netherlands, and Australia and New Zealand. The data he used assessed many different social values; for example, values about equality versus freedom, work ethics, tolerance of diversity in others, morality (approval or disapproval of homosexuality, prostitution, abortion, mercy killing, adultery), ideas about when divorce was justified—in all, he examined thirty-six different variables.

After he concluded his statistical analysis of the differences between Protestants and Catholics on these basic social values in the different nations, he discovered that many significant differences persist. For instance, Catholics are more tolerant of diversity than Protestants, more concerned with equality and fairness than Protestants. What seems to be a result of life in the Catholic social institution is a strong sense of community that translates into a distinctive world view stressing ordered relationships. Society is "natural" and "good" because it is part of the sacrament of God for Catholics. For Protestants, human society is "God-forsaken," unnatural, and oppressive. The Protestant view is individualistic, and competitive; the Catholic is communal and cooperative.

While the differences that Greeley discovered are not exactly what Weber anticipated at the turn of the twentieth century, it is interesting to learn that differences persist and that the power of a social institution is far reaching, encompassing many areas of social life. As Greeley puts it, the effects of religious institutions

> are, in their origin and their raw, primal power, tenacious and durable narrative symbols that take possession of the imagination early in the socialization process and provide patterns of meanings and responses that shape the rest of life. (Greeley1989, 501)

Symbolic Interaction: George Herbert Mead

Another theoretical approach to the study of institutional social life, often referred to as *symbolic interactionism*, is to focus on the personal meanings social life has for those doing the work of society. Instead of thinking of institutions as forces that somehow impinge on individuals, this approach stresses the creative and constructive roles individuals themselves perform. Hence institutions are the stuff out of which common everyday interactions are made. George Herbert Mead, a philosopher at the University of Chicago in the first part of the twentieth century, taught sociologists to appreciate how individuals could also be a force in institutional life. He argued that individual and society are "twin born" — actually part of a single process, a mental one in which people consider and take account of each other in the routines of daily life. From this perspective, social interaction, in an essential sense, is the outcome of persons thinking about one another.

Society exists in the mind, and social institutions are categories of meaning we associate with particular patterns of life. There is an aspect of this way of conceiving of institutions in Greeley's study, to which we referred above. For Greeley, religion represents, among other things, a mental picture of God and human relationships. He reasons that people who have different pictures of God and their relationship to God will build social worlds that reflect these pictures. Thus, the Catholic picture is of life on earth as analogous to heavenly existence, while the Protestant view of social life is opposed or dialectical to godliness. Simply put, life on earth to the devout Catholic is an imperfect approximation of life in heaven. For the Protestant, life on earth is a test or trial to determine worthiness to enter heaven. As Greeley's analysis demonstrates, these pictures translate into different world views that can be distinguished one from the other on a number of values about social life. While Greeley's research focuses on patterns rather than details of interaction, the approach we introduce now usually deals with close-up descriptions of the practice of social life. Greeley comments on some of these details when he discusses the implications of different world views for college students. He notes that Catholics with advanced education report visiting their parents with greater frequency than Protestants with similar educational background. College administrators, he writes, might want to take this fact into account. He writes, "An increase of freed time for family visits might improve the morale of Catholic students more than the morale of Protestant students" (Greeley 1989, 500).

Following the lead of Mead, analysts interested in the practical dimension of institutional analysis try to gather as much information as they can about how individuals think about themselves and their relationships to others. The goal of analysis is to demonstrate the consequences of thinking about each other in everyday life.

Whenever people marry, for example, they develop ways of understanding each other as partners in life. Of course, the ideas they bring with them to the marriage are influenced by the "pictures" they have in their heads of what marriage is supposed to be. But in this approach the meanings of institutional life, a marriage in this case, emerge out of the actual interaction between husband and wife. While one partner may be very much mistaken about the other, each acts toward the other as if they know what the other likes, believes, and values. Institutional life is meaningful life, and the meanings develop from the consequences of acting on the basis of thinking about the other person.

As Berger and Kellner (1964) suggest, each marriage is a separate and often isolated reality in which a couple understand each other and their respective social worlds. Marriage becomes an instance or enactment of institutional family life. In a highly individualistic (Protestant?) society, these marriages, when considered collectively, may represent a remarkable diversity of intimate meanings. And the order of intimate life, since it is so idiosyncratic, may be quite vulnerable to outside influences, that is, meanings from other areas of institutional life. In modern American society, the birth of a child to a couple often becomes the occasion for major changes in married life. In more traditional societies (Catholic?), the birth of a child is integrated into marriage and, therefore, does not require major changes in the life of a couple. If we consider a young married couple, childless for five years, we can appreciate the changes in store for them in their habits of living on the birth of their first child. In like manner, we understand not just how the addition of a child affects the family but how the family itself carries a whole set of meanings that define the child and that the child will eventually adopt to define itself and the world around it.

The theoretical traditions of sociology are rich and dynamic, and we encourage the interested student to pursue this aspect of sociology in courses devoted to theories. We have sketched three major theoretical orientations to show that the concept of institution has analytic power in each. While different theorists might study institutions differently, looking at different data and relationships, all agree that social institutions are vital to society and that a major part of the "sociological imagination" (Mills1967) should be given over to examining them. Furthermore, the "institutions" concept is linked with many others in sociology and thus can be used to introduce them. These concepts will make more sense and ultimately be more useful to students if they are introduced in the context of analysis, however, and with an eye toward attempting to understand institutional change. We draw from all three approaches in subsequent chapters. But, we are interested in the analysis of institutional meanings and their consequences in everyday life within the context of social structure. To achieve our analytic goals, we must develop a comprehensive concept of institutions as social phenomena.

Institutions as Social Phenomena

One of our goals is to use "social institutions" as a concept that will allow us to examine relationships, some causal, some interpretative, among the elements of society. In order to make institutional analysis once again central, we need to develop a sociological manner in which to think about institutions. We also need to understand what they are, what they do, and what their character is. We devote the next chapter to this task; here we establish our perspective by relating how institutions are social phenomena.

Theories about the nature of social phenomena suggest two possibilities: either they are real, can exert influence over individuals, and must be explained according to principles appropriate specifically to them, or they are social phenomena: simply made-up shorthand ways to refer in retrospect to already occurring sets of individual behaviors. The first position has been referred to as *social realism* and the second as *nominalism.*

In the second (nominalist) view, when we discuss institutions, we are merely, but not simply, discussing patterns of behavior, the things people do in similar life situations. The concept of institution is useful here, but only insofar as it affords us an efficient way to recognize and treat "batches" of things that humans do. In the first (realist) view, however, institutions are seen as active phenomena in and of themselves. They are real and they behave according to principles that may not apply to individuals. An individual may be "outside" an institution, then, in the sense that he or she does not have a family, is without a job, or does not have a religious affiliation. But the institutions, in this example family, economics, and religion, still exist. Of course, individuals are necessary conditions for social phenomena, but institutions are emergent in the sense that they come out of interaction and then exist somewhat independently of individuals. While we greatly simplify the theories when we treat them in this way, we can think of Marxist and Durkheimian theories of institutions as exemplifying realism. Weber and Mead, however, were basically nominalists with respect to their understanding of institutions.

In this book, we are realists in one sense and nominalists in another. Social institutions are real, and are a part of the organization or structure of all known societies. They take on the character of the society of which they are a part, and they help define and continuously redefine that character. Yet social institutions are also names we give to ways of thinking, namely, to customary solutions of the problems of everyday life. In this sense, institutions depend on human thought and emotion, and we cannot imagine them existing without people.

In contemporary sociology, then, we say that institutions are real social phenomena, and as such they exhibit certain features that we can enumerate. First, and this is a major point throughout the text, they are founded on human knowledge. It is the nature of human beings to think, and often we think about the world; moreover, we also think about ourselves and of humankind itself. As a result of all this thinking about people and things, some ideas get put into practice and so become organized. Thinking about the transmission of knowledge, for example, and actually passing it on, result in the institution of education. Organized, practical knowledge is the very basis of social institutions.

While it is individuals who think, knowledge itself is institutional. It might actually be stored in a physical sense, as it is in libraries around the world, or as it exists in the laws, constitutions, charters, by-laws and so on, of formal organizations. It also resides in the memories of people as they apply what they know about the world in daily life. Like all social phenomena, institutions begin from the primary act of thinking about the world.

Sometimes it is difficult to imagine how the institution of knowledge can be understood in terms of social realism, that is, as having existence above and apart from people. But modern technology, especially with the advent of computers, provides us with a metaphor for this understanding. If you work on your school's mainframe computer, writing your own programs or using those "stored" there, you already have a grasp of "institutionalized" knowledge. No single user knows all of what is stored on the computer's tapes; and you may not fully understand even the programs you use to check your spelling, or tabulate an average score. But the capability of the computer to store information, and to retrieve and use it on command, is the means that allows you to do what you want with the machine. Your use of the computer is possible because information is *instituted* in the machine. And, while the computer does not know it — it is not human and does not think about itself — as a stock of knowledge, it is like a social institution. Primarily, then, institutions, like the computer, exist but they are lifeless without someone to operate them.

Second, all social phenomena, including institutions, depend on constant application. If people forget what they know, or choose not to use it, they cannot act socially. There is a sense, then, in which it is true that people can act like animals, not intentionally ignoring but simply not recognizing each other's existence. Many sociologists have written about how this actually happens in hospitals and mental institutions, and in prisons. Schwartz (1976), for example, cited what he calls "existence annihilation," which he observed in a mental hospital. One patient would spread out on the floor of the hospital day after day. With time,

> she blends more and more into the physical environment as ward staff become habituated to her unusual posture and to their avoidance. She becomes a part of the scenery, indistinguishable from other fixtures that constitute the physical context. (Schwartz 1976, 198)

Further, the classic work of Erving Goffman (1961) on stigma documents how classifying a person according to a spoiled identity results in treating that person as less than fully human. The process in question is called dehumanization, and its opposite, social recognition and acknowledgement, tells us what *is* human.

Third, as a consequence of being knowledge systems that depend on constant application, institutions are open to outside influences. Mehan and Wood (1974) refer to this feature as "permeability," meaning that different ways of knowing, and variations on the application of knowledge can change the knowledge structure of social phenomena. Of course, some social phenomena hardly seem open to change. For example, it may appear that ritual life is immutable, or that bureaucracy never changes, but this is simply not true. Different phenomena change at different rates and in different ways, and how they change is often a matter of interpretation. But they do change, even when they are organized with elaborate defenses against any tendency to do so. Governments are in a continuous state of flux; even traditional religions change over time.

Mehan and Wood suggest that what follows from these three features, knowledge, application and change, is a fourth, fragility. Again, they refer to the "essence" or "fundamental character" of the thing itself. So even an institutional practice that has lasted for centuries is still fragile in the sense that it calls for care, maintenance, constant use, and, most of all, a grounding in the cognitive capabilities of the people who enact it. These people must remember it and make it concrete in action. Social phenomena are constructed or built, and like all construction, depend on a foundation. Remove the foundation, or weaken it, and even the best-designed structure becomes vulnerable to change and destruction.

Finally, all social phenomena are reflexive. We have alluded to this feature already. Basically, it underscores our conception of the humanity of institutions, that they are created and maintained by humans and for humans. Specifically this notion alerts us to the reciprocity that exists between our environment and who we are. The word *reflexive* has a dictionary definition of "inwardness, self-reference," — take, for example, the "reflexive pronouns," myself, oneself, etc. — and this is essentially what we have in mind. People who make up social institutions examine themselves — they have the capacity to look inward, to be introspective. Hence people in politics seem perpetually intrigued with questions of how their institutional work goes; and, of course, there is no time in human history when concerns about the future of the family were absent. But reflexivity means more than self-reflection and criticism. It means that institutions are capable of creating and re-creating themselves; by reflecting on their past, they also project what they become, or will try to become in the future. Moreover, the reflexivity of social phenomena has to do with the "constructed" nature of the phenomena themselves. They are made and remade as humans constantly use and think about them. In the very process of being used, they are created and re-created. Of course, the idea of phenomena folding back onto themselves is a basic one in many studies. It is central to any conception of language, and it is regarded as essential to all artistic endeavors. It is even fair to say that institutions are a record of the art of being human.

Sometimes this art is magnificent. Music composed for the European church of the seventeenth, eighteenth and nineteenth centuries we now deem "classical," and the organizational structure of "representative" government forged in the struggle between the elites and the common people of Europe embodies a timeless process of the balance of power. Institutions, however, also reflect the "bad art" of human experience — cruelty, insensitivity, rigidity, prejudice, intolerance, and the like. Given this, it is important to understand how institutions operate to provide one or the other, the "good" or the "bad" art of humanity.

What Institutions Do

What we have discussed up to this point is true of virtually all things social. Thus we need to be more specific about just what social institutions are. First, they are human collectivities, perhaps the most stable and recognizable in any society. As such, each institution is a visual symbol of society. The way people react to and deal with the symbols of institutions, a mother and her child walking down a city street, homeless people, the numerous references to family life and to the meanings of work on television, tells us about the general condition of society. If people effortlessly grasp meanings, easily recognize the patterns of action, and generally agree with the images, then the society may be said to be "solid," possessing a vital stability. But if people ignore, reject, or fail to recognize generalized meanings, their society is probably changing, perhaps becoming stronger and more able to solve its problems. It also may be weakening.

Furthermore, institutions deal with common problems and experiences, so there is a sense in which the study of institutions is the study of triviality. But trivia can be tremendous. Think of how many times you have quarreled with family members over the use of the phone, what's for dinner, toothpaste, how clothes are cared for, or any item on the seemingly inexhaustible list of ordinary things. Institutions are the results of how people think and feel about such routine affairs of everyday life. They are both the building blocks of thinking and the ends of thought. Often they begin with categories of definitions. Fathers, mothers, business people, men and women, masters and pets, priests and presidents — these are but a few categories that represent the origins of social meaning and enter into every social interaction a person experiences. And institutions are about feelings as well. They provide the images of "success and failure," of "good and evil," and the processes of outrage and anger and contentment and peace, of pride and mortification from which we stir, stew, and even explode with the basic emotions of human life.

Institutions deal with life and death, with beginnings and endings. They are markers of social life. Birth, death, baptism, bar mitzvah, getting a driver's license, and graduating from high school are all institutionalized experiences. In many cases, these experiences mark movement from one institution to another, or a change in a person's place and stature within an institution, or within society itself. We often organize the very meanings of our lives around the signal events that stand for our contact with, participation in, and internalization of institutionalized life. We measure our life after graduation, after we converted to a religious faith, after we left the armed services; or we gauge what is to come by entry to college, our first job, our marriage. Funerals, weddings, and graduations are major beginnings and endings in social life and are therefore among the concerns of social institutions.

Institutions also routinize life and, hence, function as stabilizers. William James (1890) remarked that habits are the flywheel of society. Habits are, after all, simply routine ways of doing things. Since James's metaphor may seem a little "mechanical" for our electronic age, we might prefer something like "habits are the operating system (DOS) of society"; nevertheless, his hypothesis still seems valid. When large numbers of people are taught, persuaded, or even tricked into doing the same thing over and over, these things become "practical" and "predictable." Most important, as solution and procedure, they become manageable.

As routines, institutions function like prefabricated sets of instructions on how to do things. When people actually do things in accord with the formula, then we say society is orderly. When people fall in love, and can support themselves, they get married. When they reach a certain age, they earn money and become independent; when they are troubled, they turn to their religious faith, and so on. Of course, the places we turn, the jobs available, and our potential marriage partners, and even the customs of work and marriage, are also matters of institutions.

But while at one level institutions are merely conventions, to survive they must become more. Mary Douglas (1986) suggests that in the thinking of people who use them, conventions transform into analogies, and these analogies are the foundations of institutions. A shared analogy can be a device for legitimating and stabilizing a fragile way of thinking. For example, to help people understand what society is, to justify its organization and operation, institutions offer ways to think about it. In preindustrial societies these models or analogies often are derived from more general cultural knowledge, such as how a people understand the human body. In the Western world, the head controls, the heart feels, and so on.

Some early sociologists, like Herbert Spencer and Emile Durkheim, used this body analogy in their analyses of society, suggesting that society itself is like an organism. Institutions work like organs, each serving a different purpose, according to these early sociologists. While family controls sexual activities and the passing on of titles and privileges, religion answers questions about the ultimate meaning and purposes for a people's very existence. Douglas, in contrast, is no organicist. To the contrary, she suggests that the analogy of the body has often been used to justify "inhuman" social arrangements. This is especially easy to see at the beginning of the twentieth century in America where intellectuals like William Sumner taught that the upper classes were the "head" of society and the "working classes" the "lower organs," doing the mundane, mindless, but necessary acts of society. The upper classes, of course, were supposed to control the lower, making sure that the work gets done because the lower classes do not have full awareness of the importance of their work, or of the necessity of the "upper classes" and, if left to their own means, would not do the work.

Douglas discusses not only these grand interpretations but also the ways that institutions work at the level of the ordinary citizen. In our everyday worlds, we use analogous thinking to interpret and understand our experiences. As our American society became industrialized, the mechanical analogy rose to prominence, and we started to understand our lives and the complex events of our times in mechanical terms. Hence our armies worked like well-oiled machines; problems were seen as due to parts needing alignment, or "fine tuning." Today, as Turkel (1984) has documented, the computer analogy is a major means of understanding for many of us, as we select from a menu, program our day's activities, prioritize our options, and interface with each other. Throughout our work, we allude to the fact that institutions are founded on analogy. We are able to gauge which particular institution is dominant in society on the basis of which analogy allows the comprehension of meanings and the formulation of practical action.

Institutions confer identity, that is, they give people a sense of who they are. Again, we see a difference in this function of institutions depending on the degree of modernity in society. Less modern societies are ones where a person's primary identity comes from family, religion, and perhaps government. Economic well-being, or the lack of it, derives from location and activity in family and religion. In more modern societies, education and rationalized procedures for doing things become dominant; people understand who they are in terms of what they can do. Ralph Linton (1936) referred to this modernization as a shift from ascription to achievement. Institutions still confer identity, but in varying degree and proportion depending on the institution's location in society.

As we later see, the specialization of institutional functions that occurs in modern society shifts the responsibility for personal identity more to the individual. We moderns think we have more control over our identity as we negotiate it for each situation of life we encounter. What this means with regard to institutions is that in any single encounter, in any instance of social life in modern society, an individual may evoke several identities, sometimes playing the role of leader, at other times of follower, and at still other times as observer. In our homes, for example, we may influence brothers and sisters by using intimidation; at school, we shift to persuasion and appeal. In all cases, the means and ends of our action are shaped by the thinking, the models, and the meanings, we have learned from the institutions of our society.

Insofar as they exist in memory or even are written down as laws, institutions are conservative forces in society. They form the foundation for the maintenance of social life; hence, to the degree that people use them, they produce fixed patterns of social behavior. But since they define goals and ideals of social life, institutions also can be forces of social change. It is through participation in institutionalized social life that people become "idealistic." Churches instruct the young in moral behavior, admonishing them to "better themselves and their world." Among the very rich, parents often attempt to instill in their children a sense of obligation, an obligation to "give back" through service and good works some of the rewards they have received. And, of course, schools attempt to pass on the "great traditions of culture" that are typically judged in a positive manner. Today, in our public schools , for example, strong efforts are made to instill in children a sense of racial justice and an appreciation of the great civil rights leaders of the 1960s, men like Martin Luther King Jr. Certainly not everybody agrees with these programs, but through them individuals are exposed to the "idealistic" aspects of cultural values in institutional life.

Individuals also process educational materials and information in terms of other aspects of institutional life. For some, family and religion may reinforce the tolerance of racial differences in people; for others, they may strengthen prejudice. An individual under the stresses and strains of complex and contradictory knowledge may attack or defend "the way things are." In fact, the motivation for attacking social practices is as institutional as that for defending them. Subsequently, we explore how tensions in cultural knowledge and institutional practices can be sources of massive change in society, as some people reject and redefine their social institutions through acts of open rebellion. When institutions do not provide their members with useful habits of thought and practice, new social forms may emerge, and, at least indirectly, the conservative nature of the institution becomes an impetus for social change.

Modernity

Although we are concerned about tradition, our goal is to study contemporary society through its institutions; to appreciate the interplay between individual and collective meanings; to see how doing things in a certain way has consequences for all of us; and finally, to place questions of institutionalization within the context of modern life.. And since we will be using the concept of *modernity* throughout our work, we need to outline its significance and meaning here.

> The question of modernity is also the question of sociology itself. It is not facetious to define sociology as the never-ending quest for a definition of modernity, if by that term we mean the changes in social life that became available for reflection by the 1890's and continue to the present. (Frank1987, 294)

Frank wrote this passage as an opening of his review of recent books on modernity. He took the occasion of reviewing new books to place the literature on modernity in the center of sociology. Sociology as a discipline and perspective is modern, tracing from efforts to understand what has happened to society as a result of shifts in the technology of production. While you might recognize this idea as Marxist, it is actually a basic sociological concept. We leave to others the debate about who first thought of the importance of the relationship between technology and society. But we know that by the time sociology became recognizable through a list of authors and the literature they produced (Max Weber, Emile Durkheim, Ferdinand Toennies, Georg Simmel, Charolette Perkins Gilman, etc.), it had become apparent that when humans change their tools and the basic ways they do things, they also change, whether they intend to or not, their social worlds.

Weber thought something so profound occurred when Western civilization industrialized that it changed forever the history of the world.

Industrialization separated humans beings from the products of their labor, and this separation created social conditions that could be filled only by rational organizations. To Weber, modernization was a process that started in Europe because there the objective conditions of production came together with certain subjective conditions (the ways that people think and feel) to give rise to a new organization and sense of social life.

In modern society, people are welded into groups in terms of mutually conceived interests; they do not know one another in the same way they did in traditional agricultural or hunting and gathering societies. They do not trust each other in the same way since, in a very genuine sense, they are all strangers. So they invent rational procedures to deal with one another. In some cases, people find a kind of secular salvation in their energetic and single-minded approaches to work. Weber's classic *The Protestant Ethic and the Spirit of Capitalism* documents one adaptation people make to the separation of work and product. As he described it, they simply shift the motivational forces acquired from their Protestant religion over to their attitudes toward work. Later in sociology, Merton (1957) refines some of these ideas to talk about ritualism, or what we might call "workacholicism." Weber's great insights help us to see how the fundamentals of human relationships changed as Western societies developed the technologies to exploit the earth. Weber's sociology of modernization is somber and sad, for it tells of gray bureaucracies run by routinized souls who live in a disenchanted world. And it cautions us about the limits of rationality and the costs of secular thought.

Durkheim, Weber's French contemporary, reached different conclusions about the effects of the changes that industrialization wrought. Out of his analysis come two very basic concepts about how societies cohere or stay together. Simple societies are mechanical, with people living in small groups, sharing a collective sense of who they are. Organic social organization, or solidarity is more specialized, more complex, and generally larger. Durkheim saw members of societies bonding together quite differently depending on the division of labor (or set of roles) in the society. If the division of labor was relatively simple and the parts of it fairly interchangeable (e.g. women tend crops and raise children while men hunt and fish) then the problem of keeping people together could be quite serious. Since, within sexual boundaries, virtually everyone could do everyone else's job, there was nothing about the job itself that would bond people together. Such mechanical societies (because the people seem to have been stamped out of the same mechanism or mold) depend on what Durkheim called "restraint" to achieve solidarity. In other words, the people in charge relied on strict laws and sanctions and a common understanding of them to compel people to work. Such societies have very severe punishment for crimes, but they have, generally speaking, little crime.

In contrast, modern society depends on vastly complicated and intricate divisions of labor. In the United States, there are literally thousands of job titles that only gloss over the kinds of skills and specialized knowledge required to do a job. A single automobile has thousands of moving parts, each one manufactured to specifications, and each one relying on interdependent layers of organizations in the form of labor unions, managers, personnel workers, and so on. Such complicated divisions of labor give rise to a new kind of social order, which Durkheim called "organic," by which he meant to underscore the idea of unity in diversity. Modern society, it seems, does not need severe sanctions and restrictive laws. It requires, instead, a well-educated public and fair laws that assure equal distribution of justice and restitution, not retribution, whenever crime does occur. The chief danger of modern society is individualism itself, which can obscure an individual's understanding of his or her place in society.

While we must oversimplify the vast range of both scholars, it is probably fair to say that in Weber we have a negative image of modernity and in Durkheim a positive one. But both agreed that the old world was lost, if it ever had existed. Both agreed that new foundations for social order are necessary and that the institutions of society will shift and change to reflect how far a society has modernized.

We highlight Weber and Durkheim because they, more than any other sociologists, began the dialogue about modernity and its effects. They gave us the language to continue sociological inquiry into it, a language that contains concepts still widely used. We mention early scholars like Toennies, Simmel, and Alfred Schutz and contemporary ones like Peter Berger, Andrew Weigert, and Norbert Elias, who have contributed to understanding modernity, to indicate the range of thinking that exists about it. To set the stage for our examination of institutions and how they have changed, we have distilled the main issues concerning modernity and its effects, beginning with a definition of modernity from Berger, Berger, and Kellner (1974) in *The Homeless Mind: Modernization and Consciousness.*

> Modernization must be seen in close relation to economic growth — more specifically to the particular growth process released by recent technology. . . . We will discuss modernization as the institutional concomitants of technologically induced economic growth. This means there is no such thing as a "modern society" plain and simple; there are only societies more or less advanced on a continuum of modernization. (P. 9)

While this definition may seem cumbersome, it does contain the essential elements of meaning necessary for institutional analysis. First, it acknowledges that a major force of change is technology. Humans are tool makers. We have always relied on our ability to invent new ways to do things to survive. Some societies value technological innovation more than others, however, and modernization is a process that embodies technological change. Indeed, as some critics (Ellul 1964) point out, sometimes it seems that change is celebrated for its own sake. Anyone who has tried to fix an automobile cannot help but notice that automobile engineers constantly change things. For example, there are many variations on the solution to the problem "How to stop a car?" and, at least to the "backyard mechanic," it seems that the motivation for all the variations in braking systems is not necessarily to improve the operation of the automobile.

The definition of modernization also allows us to distinguish between aspects of change directly tied to technology and those not so bound. Weber saw the effect of rational problem solving resulting in bureaucracy, and we can say that bureaucracy owes its form to a particular division of labor. But, we would be far afield if we tried to trace all the activities that take place in bureaucracies to the technologies of, say, text production or the assembly line. As Weber has taught us, there is more to it than this. Bureaucrats may lose sight of the purpose of rational procedures, which is efficiency, and become so rational — that is, require so much justification before an action can be taken — that no action is taken at all which often seems to occur in government. Or, as Durkheim showed, the effect of technologies that have many parts can be positive. His theory of solidarity holds that interdependency increases with the complexity of technology and work and thus new bonds are formed among members of society. Of course, we might not all be in a position to see the connectedness of society, and some of us might even fail to see it. This is a danger of modernity. Still, new rituals emerge to help us understand. The game of football, enormously popular in America, can be interpreted as a setting in which we can see the effects of rationally planned organization, as when teams change sides from offense to defense, communicate with the sidelines, enact a game strategy, and so on.

The literature we draw on to understand modernity is not "technologism" or "economism"; instead, we stress that in all of social life humans constantly interpret technology, and the effects of economics and technology on people are mediated through their cultural knowledge and artifacts. There are many great transformations of modern life, from farm to industry, from village to city, from traditional to civil justice, from production to consumption, and from communication to information; how these affect institutions is a twofold process. The changes affect the institutions, but the institutions also affect the forces of change. We mean that the impact of any change is mediated by the ways in which people enact what they know; and what they know, they get from institutions.

A particularly powerful idea for assessing the reciprocal relationship between technological/economic changes and institutional ones is *adaptation*. Most of us have had little to do with decisions about how automobiles are made and marketed, but virtually all of us use automobiles, and in a variety of ways. Some of us give them names, personalize them, and even live in them. As Paul Simon sang, "If some of my homes had been more like my car, I probably wouldn't have traveled so far."

Our point is that we adapt to change. Sometimes what people do with the innovation of modern technology is not what the innovators envisioned. For example, when personal computers were introduced to the mass market, their inventors thought they would revolutionize home life. People would write programs to do their taxes, turn their lights on and off, and generally computerize their life styles. This has not happened. Most people use computers at home, if they use them all, as advanced typewriters. In this instance, the adaptation to the technology is conservative.

In other cases, technology does revolutionize institutional life. Henry Ford's popular automobiles changed dating and romance dramatically in American society. Instead of encouraging young adults to court in the home where parents could chaperon them, the car became a symbol of freedom, a statement of independence that clearly was a condition for the liberalizing of sexual behavior in society. As a symbol and an object of practical use, the car represents an avenue for social behavior that challenged, as it still does, the stabilizing effect of the family.

Dimensions of Modernity

Modernization is a process of change initiated by technology and furthered by human interpretations of it. The forms that such interpretations assume in the awareness of the members of society can vary greatly, but we can discuss them along several dimensions of the meanings of modernity.

First, let us consider *specialization* and *differentiation*. Durkheim underscored the importance of specialization and differentiation in understanding the differences in types of societies. Now we introduce these same concepts as a dimension of modernity. As society modernizes, there is a tendency for activities to become broken into smaller and more specialized parts. Each part is given a special task (specialization), and each part is supposed to shape its energy and organization to fit the work it does (differentiation). Indeed, most of our daily lives are specialized and differentiated. Our jobs require that we know more and more about less and less. When we want something fixed, we seek out a person who specializes in the kind of repair we need and whose knowledge and skills are differentiated to the solution of our problem.

Of course, the medical profession is the exemplar of these processes. The specialist knows a great deal about a limited part of the human body and possesses tools that differentiate among the states of that part. Some physicians focus only on the ear, for example.

One of Weber's great insights was that these twin processes affect personal life. Today, we know many people because of what they can do for us, and we often relate to one another in terms of how what a person knows fits with what we know. Talcott Parsons, an American sociologist indebted to Weber, referred to this aspect of personal life in modern society as *instrumentalism*.

Ironically, at the same time that modernization clarifies the meanings of problem solving by defining terms more specifically and dividing meanings into smaller and smaller components, the *overall* meaning of social life becomes less clear. This is the problem of ambiguity. Modern life is essentially ambiguous (Levine1985), and people seek to deal with not knowing just what is happening to them in a general, societal sense by inventing for themselves activities that seem to make sense. Some do this by escaping into fantasy worlds (Faberman1980); others try to make their work a central feature of their existence; some play their way into clarity; and still others attempt to bring back or conserve what they believe are the ways of the past. But how is ambiguity organized into modern institutional life?

Modern social life is composed of many different kinds of people and a vast array of ways to make sense of life. One theoretical term frequently used to refer to the features of modern life is *multivocality*. This means that no issue, from abortion to freedom of speech to arms for hostages to military intervention, will be of a single voice. For it is the nature of things that all events, all relationships, and all feeling will be accompanied by many points of view. But, we might say, people have probably never fully agreed with each other. Nevertheless, when we compare institutional life in a less modern society with that in one more modern, we see that official voices of the less modern speak in clearer, more unified tones. In the more modern, voices will clash, official with unofficial, and it will be increasingly difficult to tell one from the other; and the meanings that things and events have for people will be layered and complex, without singular intent.

America has no national policy on family life, for example, whereas many nations of the world do (e.g., United Kingdom, France, Sweden). This is not because we as a people care little about family matters. During Jimmy Carter's presidency, efforts were made in a national conference to formulate a policy, but pro-life versus pro-choice voices plus lay people, blurred into a noise of concerns without focus.

In matters of tastes and the consumption of them, multivocality is the rule in modern society. In fact, as a recent analysis of the growth of the popularity of classical music in America shows, the meanings of Toscanini's music became part of the taste culture of modern society. Herbert Gans (1975) has documented the enormous amount of borrowing that goes on from "high" to "popular" culture. Although this was true even of seventeenth century Europe, what is distinctive about the relations among voices of opinion and taste in modern society is that in their consumption the distinctions among them blur . Hence the "high culture of theater" deals with mass popular cultural themes, like the hippie movement in *Hair*, sexual liberation in *"Oh, Calcutta!"*.

A dimension closely related to multivocality is *fragmentation*, which can best be seen as a consequence of specialization and differentiation. Modern life is fragmented, or so the critics say. It is broken into pieces of life so small that they no longer relate to one another meaningfully. For example, someone's urban, economic life may be only minimally related to his or her family some fifty miles away in a suburb. Many children have never seen where their mothers and fathers work. Durkheim warned of the "cult of individualism," and what has happened in modern society does seem to follow logically his, and particularly Weber's, line of reasoning. The end result of too much modernization is the ultimate breaking apart (deconstruction) of the structure of society. This is the meaning of fragmentation. As a consequence of our lives being so fragmented, so one argument goes, many of us turn back to what we think of as the integrating forces of life.

Hence, in modern America, some people are turning to fundamentalistic religious practices, or continuing to move farther and farther away from the central city in an effort to find a more idyllic life. A recent observer (Nash 1987) of sales of trucks in America has coined the term "symbolic trucks" to refer to small, trucklike vehicles that function more like passenger cars; they are too small to pull or haul, yet they symbolize rural existence. Of course, while the motivation to buy a small truck and operate it in the city might be an effort to unite the fragments of life, in modern society all meanings have elements of ambiguity, and the messages of consumption become blurred.

Obviously, the features we have presented are part of the same interpretative scheme. There are degrees of specialization and of ambiguity, and there are different numbers of voices and fragments. This dynamic of meaning as a characteristic of modernity is perhaps the most important. Modern life is oppositional, and a German, Georg Simmel, was the master of capturing the oppositional nature of modern social life. In his discussion of two modern philosophers, he expresses its essentials. From Arthur Schopenhauer, he takes "the conviction that life is valueless," a monotony of suffering and failure, and from Friedrich Neitzche "the belief that all life is value . . . in the process of realization and being and action" (Simmel 1986, 181).

Simmel summarized the thinking of these two philosophers who grappled with the consequences of modern life. And in opposing one against the other, he discovered the procedure, the means, by which life acquires its meaning. His conclusion: It is not so much that modern society fails to give its members formulas to solve problems, but that many formulas are given and these are often contradictory. One consequence is that the modern citizen often must master emotions by being excited and appearing not to be. Lyman and Scott (1989), in their classic essay, take this opposition of "danger" and "emotional detachment" to be the essence of "coolness in everyday life." Losing one's cool can be understood as one side of the opposing forces dominating the other; excitation overcoming detachment.

According to Erving Goffman (1959), perhaps one of the foremost sociologists of modernity, the modern citizen is supposed to be a master of "impression management." To Goffman, the underlying dynamic of "management" is to "hide" inner conditions. One must appear cool when in fact he or she is "hot," and it is a high compliment when we are told that in the face of tension, we remain "in control."

Of course, the basic idea which forms the framework for understanding opposition is G.W.F. Hegel's concept of the *dialectic*. This German philosopher, whom Karl Marx modified when he formulated his economic theory of modernity, suggested that change is actually the result of opposing forces of human thinking. Hegel conceived of opposition in terms of an idea (thesis) and its opposite (antithesis); then, from the tension of the opposition, there arises a new idea or synthesis. This way of conceptualizing change seems to fit modernity well.

In modern society, people enact diverse, specialized roles. Some role playing they understand all too well; with other roles they enact, they seem not to understand at all. In a similar vein, people might be intensely interested in some of things they do and not at all interested in others. People are free to believe and to a great extent do as they choose. They may espouse any among a wide variety of religious, philosophical, or political beliefs and practices; so it is inevitable in modern social life that people will not agree with one another, that they will express different values and find themselves in opposition to one another. According to Simmel, modern society attempts to transcend the problems of inevitable conflict by establishing forms of interaction within which oppositional forces can play themselves out.

Let's explore a few examples. As observers from Marx to Bell (1978) have pointed out, modern capitalism seems inherently contradictory. The values of products are supposed to be proportional to the labor required for their production. This means that the energies of workers expended in the production of goods should determine the value of their products. But workers are paid less than the value of their labor. Marx referred to this seemingly unfair arrangement as the "iron law of wages." While a modern consumption economy seems to work on different principles, such as those of demands created through advertising, contradictions still abound. Everyone should have a job, but there are not enough jobs for all. People should be able to own their own homes, but the average cost of owning a house in a city often far exceeds what the family living on the average annual income can afford to pay. We live in a society that guarantees its citizens the right to pursue happiness, but does not ensure equal health care for all. We live under the abstract premise of "equality under the law," but we know that people who can afford lawyers receive more humane treatment under the law than those who cannot.

Some of these "contradictions" may be all in the way one looks at them. This is the point about opposition. As Simmel noted, "forms" of interaction emerge in modern society, within which oppositions merge to allow interaction. We greet one another according to forms of polite discourse — "Hi, how are you?" — but we do not usually care about and certainly do not need to really know one another's feelings and thoughts. Even though we cannot afford to own a house, if we act properly, qualifying for mortgage loans, we can act as if we have enough money to buy a house and assume responsibility as a homeowner. Even though we know that members of minority groups make up disproportionate numbers of prisoners in America, we can still believe in the fairness of the justice system by enacting laws that ensure the "fair" application of sentences for wrongdoers. Well-educated people consume popular culture, and they watch television programs, forming part of an audience that cuts across class, ethnic, and gender lines. In fact, television itself is a form within which contradictions abound, where reality is suspended; one would never guess from television detective programs that most police officers draw their guns no more than once or twice in a twenty-year career. And yet, through television, the real world comes into our living rooms.

Daniel Bell writes that modernity is so thoroughly oppositional that clear answers to questions of value and judgments of taste and culture are simply not to be expected. "What, then, is culture? Who, then, is the well educated person? What is the community of discourse? It is in the nature of modernity to deny that such questions have any single answer." (Bell 1978, 101).

While reading the opinions of critics of modernity must result in a kind of sociology that is itself modern, that is, built on the features of modern meanings, this does not mean that the quest for clarity should be abandoned. Instead, in a modern sense, we find the goal in the quest; the clarity in the confusion and unity in the contradictions. In this book we treat each basic institution as a dynamic modern social phenomenon, interrelated with and interdependent on other institutions and on culture itself. And there is a one-sidedness to our assessments of institutions. We write around the idea that the basic institutions of society (family, education, economics, religion, and government) change dramatically as society modernizes. Some of the changes are obvious; others are more subtle. But the overall impact of modernization on institutional social life makes each institution more specialized and increases its dependency on the others, and as we hope is the case with this work, it can foster among the members of society an increased sensitivity to their personal experiences and their interpretations of and reactions to them.

Summary

Throughout this work, we follow a format encompassing a theoretical range that appreciates social institutions as systems of knowledge imparting meaning to everyday life, as ready-made forms of organized meanings and as lived-through experiences. While decidedly Meadian or symbolic interactionist, this approach nevertheless takes into account the forces of organization on individual experience. For some topics of institutionalized social life, such as family, we stress the meanings; for others, such as education, we follow the implications of forms; and for still others, such as religion, we focus on the varieties of experiences.

The perspective we invoke is wholistic, so even though we focus on experience, we see it in interaction with organization and meaning. Similarly, if we select form as pivotal, we see the arrangements of social elements such as authority structures as emergent from systems of knowledge and individual experience of them. Finally, even an underlying knowledge structure is itself an outcome of organization and experience. Our analytic scheme is an abstraction designed to allow us to exercise a sociological understanding of the ways that society changes and remains the same.

The concept of social institution is introduced as central to a sociological inquiry aimed at an understanding of cultural meaning, social organization, and individual character in society. Drawing from the theories of Marx, Weber,

Durkheim, and particularly Mead, we develop the concept of institution that stresses the nature of social phenomena as both collective and individual, real and nominal. Such phenomena depend on human systems of knowledge and interaction. They are reflexive, fragile, and open to influence.

While institutions have all the attributes of social phenomena, they also function distinctively. We discussed institutional process in terms of "what institutions do." They provide solutions to problems of everyday life, function as analogical models for thinking, mark the major events of meanings in social life, and by serving as a procedure for interpretation, generally impart to individuals a sense of knowing what they are doing and being correct in the doing of it.

The focus of this book is modern institutions. Accordingly, we discuss the concept of modernity and identify the major dimensions scholars have attributed to it. There are often complex and variegated ideas about degrees of meanings and action that can be described as processes. Specialization and differentiation, multivocality, fragmentation, and opposition are the major processes we introduce, and these provide for us a way of looking at social institutions as agents of change and changed agents within the larger context of modernity.

Chapter	**2**	SOCIAL INSTITUTIONS: DOING THINGS IN SOCIETY

Behavior is not instinctual in human beings. Birds have nest-building instincts, for example; but it is difficult to imagine how people would build houses and raise children without a great deal of formal and informal learning. Over the many centuries of human civilization, various ways of living in families, running economies, and so on, have been developed and refined, and these have become institutionalized, ready to be handed on to new members of societies. For humans, institutions provide instructions and programs about how to do things—they are the means through which ends are accomplished.

Imagine a society composed of three vital interests: what we have learned (socialization), the values and goals we follow and pursue (culture), and the means we have available for accomplishing valued ends (institutions). In the best of all possible worlds, these would be arranged consistently in our daily lives. We would know, then, the purposes of our existence, what kinds of people we are, and how we are supposed to act. But, the ideal society is a myth. Furthermore, for some of us, the prospect of such consistency in life would surely foretell a boring existence. Nevertheless, it is useful to imagine an ideal, even if we do not really want one, because the logical and practical arrangement of actual social life can be understood in terms of its departure from the ideal.

Societies, of course, vary greatly in degrees of consistency between the socialization experiences of their members, their values, and the channels of action open to them. In some societies, ones Durkheim characterized as "mechanical," people live and move about according to certain traditions, representing or even reenacting customs and values. Their society is "in" them in a direct and often literal fashion, and the extent to which the society is in them represents the degree to which they have become socialized to their institutions. Indeed, some societies are almost totally mechanical. These societies, rare in the contemporary world, are usually preliterate, and nontechnological by Western standards.

Anthropologists have taught us that traditional societies are not necessarily less sophisticated than modern ones. Appreciating what hunters must know and do to feed the members of their tribes, or examining the elaborate and intricate religious beliefs of preliterate people, impresses on us how easily we can misunderstand cultures by assuming that what is modern is complex and that primitive means simple. Actually, systems of knowledge among the people of the world are equally complex regardless of the degree of modernization in society (Spradley and McCurdy 1980; Nash and McCurdy 1989). Still, members of traditional societies do live in a qualitatively different world. They understand themselves and their society in literal and straightforward ways that become apparent when we consider, for example, the difference between a shaman in his ceremonial dress and a punk rocker in hers.

The shaman thinks of his apparel as appropriate to a timeworn tradition, such as the rite of passage by means of which a young boy becomes a man (or a girl, a woman). Becoming an adult and going through a ceremony are consistently related — a match in society between socialization and institution. The boy has been prepared for becoming a man by participating in his society, and he knows that the rite of passage clearly marks a permanent change in his identity.

The punk rocker, in contrast, is simply "into" a contemporary scene. She possesses a high degree of self-awareness about the fact that she is staging her appearance, and her actions may be quite meaningful personally, but they do not carry *institutional* meanings the way a rite of passage does. When we ask her who she is, we are not surprised when she gives us a "put on" answer: "Can't you read the T-shirt? I'm Jackette-the-Ripper." Similarly, we expect that her fascination with punk will change with time. Unlike the shaman or the boy/man, her identity is temporary. In fact, were we to investigate and follow her life's progress, we might discover that punk was preceded by preppie and will be followed by a more conventional attitude toward getting a job. In part, we get the sense we have of who we are from the social institutions in which we participate. Obviously, our shaman and "Jackette-the-Ripper" participate in very different institutions.

Effects of Modernization

Modernization is clearly a matter of degree, representing the "growth and diffusion of a set of institutions rooted in the transformation of the economy by means of technology" (Berger, Berger, and Kellner 1974,9). Obviously, as a society relies more on technology, the kinds of work available to its members change. Societies develop institutions that support the kind of work the society is doing. Therefore, when we refer to "modern society," we have in mind measurable institutionalized changes. In Western nations, these occurred perhaps a century ago, whereas in many parts of the world, they are taking place today. Here we mention one major change, in the nature of the work people do. In traditional societies, most people work "extracting" things from nature. They farm, fish, mine, or hunt. In industrial societies, people work in factories, turning raw materials into "products"; in modern society, most people are occupied in serving one another.

Of course, percentages of workers engaged in different types of occupations vary from society to society. A high percentage of people do cultivating work in Bangladesh, while in the United States, fewer that 5 percent of all employed persons do "farm labor." These differences are interesting in themselves, but they also reflect degrees of modern life in society, and they lead us to ask, "What are the effects of modernization?"

One effect focuses on the elderly. In less modern societies, the elderly are generally more revered and respected than in more modern ones. We would expect, therefore, that people living in societies of differing modernization would differ in how they anticipate old age. To test this idea, sociologist Alex Inkeles analyzed data from six societies. In these societies, samples of adult men were asked if they "looked forward to old age." Table 2.1 shows the results.

Table 2.1
Men Who "await or look forward to old age"
(percentages by occupation and country)

Occupational Group	Bangladesh	India	Nigeria	Chile	Argentina	Israel
Cultivators	32.8	60.5	59.0	16.5	46.5	33.6
Urban non-industrial workers	37.8	46.1	67.5	24.5	16.4	45.7
Urban factory workers	35.8	44.4	77.2	29.7	29.2	35.4
Totals	N = 334	632	527	242	234	239
	% = 35.4	49.1	73.3	27.6	28.8	36.5

Note: Cell entries can be read as follows: Of the total sample from Bangladesh, 35.4% (334 of 943) of the respondents chose the "traditional" response: They look forward to old age.

Source: Inkeles 1983, 286

As is sometimes the case with sociological research, Inkeles concludes that these data do not fully support his expectation. In fact, in four of the six nations we would think of as most traditional, relatively few of the men in the sample said they look forward to old age. We can think of several reasons for this. Farming may have already changed so much that people do not assume that the "old way of life" will sustain them in their old age, or the modern attitude toward aging may already have spread outside cities.

Yet, as Inkeles writes, "societal modernization . . . does seem directly related to the individual's attitude toward aging. Individuals in the three less modern countries (Bangladesh, India and Nigeria) . . . show a greater frequency of looking forward to old age than do those in the three more modern societies" (Inkeles 1983, 285).

In modern societies, institutions emphasize choice rather than obedience, active rather than passive role playing, and individual over collective determinations. Yet, in the modern society, laws are supposed to be applied universally. In short, as several sociologists have put it, modern society is the cumulation of many forces of social change that place the individual in various social relationships filled with tension. A modern citizen shoulders the stresses of decision making, emotional detachment, and living with uncertainty and ambiguity.

If institutions tell us how to do things, then, the institutional organization of the modern world seems to define many different ways to do the same things. The effect is dramatic. In modern society, institutional means become like menu-driven programs for computers: A user selects from an array of ways to do work, and can always return to the main menu to make another choice. But the extent to which an institution may allow selection is fixed. Again like a program, the parameters are set: while one may choose, the things that he or she can choose are predetermined by the programmer, in the case of the computer and by the action of past generations, in the case of institutions.

In this and the following several chapters, we are concerned with the question "What am I supposed to do?" Answers to this question, or *expectations*, come to us in many ways, initially from our parents and other relatives and friends and later from the society at large, for example, from laws. For the most part, however, and especially for sociologists, expectations can be categorized in such a way that they fall into certain common groupings, interrelated ones that form ordered systems of knowledge of the social world. These systems are *social institutions* generally representing knowledge of five different subjects: family, religion, politics, education, and economics.

Within any society, all social institutions are interrelated. Marriage, for example, besides falling within the realm of the family as a social institution, is also governed by laws and thus has a political aspect, and insofar as we might discuss family income, it represents part of the economy.

Understanding Institutions

A social institution, then, organizes for its individual members the meanings of specific activities in the society. Sociologists use a "shorthand" method for talking about this organization when they refer to roles and role relationships. A *role* is an organization of expectations about the proper actions for people sharing a similar identity; for example, students are expected to read books, go to class, party, and so on. *Role relationships* are complex sets of expectations associated with situations in which single persons or groups represent multiple, interrelated identities.

Institutional roles can be thought of as being part of a system of common-sense knowledge that people in a society have about one another. For example, virtually all of us take for granted that we understand the organization of families. Thus we immediately characterize the man and woman pointing out animals at a zoo to a two-year-old boy as an example of family life. This is because this group of two adults and a child live up to one of our expectations of what family life is about. Or again, we see a group of children standing on a corner; it is 7:30 a.m. on a Wednesday, and a large yellow bus stops to pick them up. We "know" they are on their way to school because our observations take on meaning in the context of our knowledge about schooling.

Social institutions rest on knowledge systems generally agreed upon throughout a society. At one time or another we come into contact with all our social institutions. Of course, as members of society we do not participate equally in all institutions; still, we do possess at least minimal knowledge about all the institutional forms.

An institution becomes tangible and thus real through the interactions of socialized persons. Furthermore, given our understanding of institutions as goal-oriented means, each time one person interacts with another, a problem is solved; a task, usually an intended one, is accomplished. Over a period of time, ways for achieving mutually acceptable grounds for understanding, intent, motivation, and style of behavior are proposed, carried out, and shaped in this manner.

As means to achieve ends, social institutions always point to ways of solving the everyday problems of "getting from point A to point B." Each time a problem is solved in a way that allows interaction, the effect, or perhaps better, the side effect of that solution is to produce an expectation that in similar situations in the future the same solution will operate. After the institution exists and we have taken on its ways of thinking, it provides for us ready-made solutions to problems. We then use these solutions over and over, and this is how institutions persist.

For example, even the most mundane acts we perform each day, like moving food from our plates to our mouths, entail solving a problem. We can think of many possible ways to accomplish this task: using our fingers, sopping the food with a piece of bread, wrapping it in a leaf, or using chopsticks. But we need not mentally go through these options each time we eat, and in fact, ordinarily we are not even aware that our customary acts are solutions to problems. We take for granted the "proper" solution — in this case we use spoons, knives, and forks. In the metaphor of the computer program, traditional institutions offer limited menus, and we do not have to deliberate much about which selection to make.

Routine selections across society indicate a high degree of institutionalization and provide for the continuity of institutions and, in fact, of society itself.

No one can say precisely how and why one particular solution prevails over another and becomes institutionalized. In one instance, it might be the easiest way; in another, it might be forced on people. Institutions do support routine solutions, however, and each time a specific solution is enacted the institution derives strength and vitality. Hence, when a couple marries, their enactment of the ceremony symbolically reinforces the institution of family.

The institution of the family addresses such problems as the continuation of society and the allocation of place within it. And we may think of a particular institution as providing us with ways to solve only certain kinds of problems. Economic institutions, to take another example, respond to such problems as the efficient production and distribution of goods and services within society. Educational institutions deal with the training of new members to take their place in the workforce; and so forth.

Thus social institutions operate to define problems as well as their solutions, but they can also create problems. Since an institution as a social reality is reflexive, it constructs its own environment and then operates within it. Thus, without the institution of the family (i.e., the ideas about the nature of a family, what a family is and does) there would be no ready-made solution to the problem of, say, who assumes the responsibility for the care and rearing of children. At the same time, though, the "problem" of illegitimacy would disappear. So, we understand the "problems" of child rearing and illegitimate births among teenage girls relative to our understanding of what the mature family is supposed to be and do.

Another way to understand institutions sociologically is to examine the consequences of violations of, or departures from, the routines, and this involves the question of seriousness. We note, for instance, that where birth out of wedlock might create serious difficulties for the mother, a breach of etiquette by her brings only minor embarrassment and disapproval. The unwed mother must decide "what to do" with the baby; and the authorities responsible for the welfare of children in the community must also get involved. A social worker does not question whether a married, divorced, or widowed mother is caring for her child unless there is some evidence that she is not. Yet that same guardian of children routinely raises questions about how well an unwed mother may care for her child.

This dimension of *seriousness*, the gravity of solutions to everyday problems, was first noted by William Graham Sumner, an early American sociologist (Sumner 1959). He called the less serious institutionalized rules "folkways," sometimes known as *customs*, and the more serious ones "mores," often called *laws*. The violation of a more has profound consequences for society and especially for the individual violator, while the breach of a folkway may simply embarrass him or her. Of course, the relationship between folkways and mores is changeable and often a matter of degree. A person who persists in rude and obnoxious behavior in all the various situations of life may be defined as seriously violating the rules of society. And, an act that is usually considered serious, such as assaulting another person, may not result in serious punishment.

The highly publicized case of Bernhard Goetz, the New York City subway vigilante who shot four youths he believed were about to rob him, raises questions of appropriate individual interpretations of institutions. If the police, for example, cannot protect individuals in public places, what is a legitimate thing for the individual to do?

While sociology cannot answer this question for specific cases like that of Bernhard Goetz, it can sketch the general circumstances in the organization of society that take into consideration problems like the ones the Goetz case raises. Several sociologists (cf. Levine 1985) have characterized the problem of modern social organization as one of ambiguity; for example, for virtually any everyday problem, most of us can think of several solutions. Where there are multiple solutions, there is often a lack of agreement among members of society about which solution is the best or most appropriate. One way to appreciate what Levine had in mind is the use a visual devise (se Figure 2.1) to depict the relationship between formal and informal rules of society.

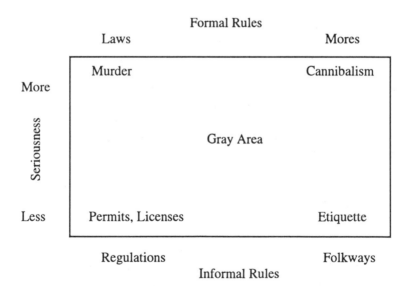

Figure 2.1
The structure of institutional norms

In the figure one, the "gray area" would be larger or smaller depending on the degree of modernization in society. In a modern society, the middle portion of the chart describes a large portion of everyday life. Questions of seriousness, of whether certain behaviors are governed by the informal rules of family life or the formal ones of the legal code of society, are matters of constant negotiation. For example, we really do not know in any definitive way how to specify just when spanking is an appropriate way for a parent, or even a teacher, to control the behavior of a child. Of course, extreme cases help clarify our understanding of these problems precisely because they catch our attention as clear examples. We can understand cases better if they seem simple to us — devoid of the ambiguity that we know characterizes most solutions to our problems.

Traditional societies, of course, also require decision making, and surely there are circumstances under which a traditional person is confused about the correct way to approach a problem. But the chart we would use to depict a mechanical society would need less space in the middle. Life in a traditional society is more nearly black and white, whereas in the modern society life seems gray. Thus, when we "moderns" are faced with a question of the sort "What would you do if . . . ," the answer often begins with "It depends."

Such "variable" institutional answers to everyday problems have become so much a part of life in modern society that several scholars have suggested that we use the term "negotiated order" to refer to the outcomes of problem solving (Strauss 1978). When we look at the process of "getting things accomplished" in modern society, we are struck by the degree to which no typical or "pat" set of procedures fits what actually happens. Instead, we discover a considerable amount of wheeling and dealing, bargaining, compromising, mediating, and exchanging. This is certainly true in interpersonal relationships, and it is also true of legal, bureaucratic, and occupational life as well as of global and political affairs. Indeed, the process of arriving at institutionally meaningful action is a theme not only of understanding how specific actions are understood as right or wrong, just or unjust, but it is also a theme of life in modern society. While it is no doubt true that negotiation plays a part in social life in all societies, the degree to which meaning and subsequent order are negotiated in modern society seems pronounced, and negotiation is a process we encounter throughout our analysis of particular institutions.

Finally, institutions change and influence one another. A folkway may take on the impact of a more, or solutions that once were within the family may be taken over by educational institutions. Also, the meanings of a single act may belong to more than one institution — family, economy, and education, for example — as when a father pays his son to mow the lawn, and the son puts the money away for college.

In sum, a social institution is a body of common-sense knowledge, a shared set of ideas, expectations, and beliefs. It is a social reality representing solutions to kinds of problems we all encounter. In social interaction, specific activities take on commonly understood meanings because we can recognize them as parts of institutional forms. Institutions represent societal ways of dealing with problems, everything from mundane tasks to matters of life and death.

How Institutions Work

People use institutions to get what they want, but they also follow the rules that institutions provide for actions. We see, therefore, that institutions work in two ways. They give members of society meanings for social life, and they guide the interpretations that people make of their actions.

Sociologists usually describe institutions in the abstract — as the family, religion, or the law. But it is at the concrete level of individuals, when people try to act in society, that institutions become real. Of course, people bring with them to any particular act a wide range of socialization experiences. We can, however, talk about the "typical" workings of a social institution, for every institution encompasses a stock of knowledge people can rely on to explain why they think, feel and act the way they do.

Further, we can think of these stocks of knowledge as composed of "typifications" (Schutz 1971), or categories, of people, things, events, and feelings. These typical experiences, or the assumptions people make about them, are used by individuals to make their social worlds manageable. We know what it means, or we think we do, to go shopping, to talk seriously, to joke, to be sarcastic. We understand potential problems in terms or what types of problems people can have and what types of experiences people may have. In this sense, then, institutional meaning is typical, and can be so described.

Without institutional meaning, no single act a person performs can be regarded as "legitimate." There may be others in society who support or agree with an action, but until that action has institutional meaning it cannot serve as a basis for further action. Institutions, therefore, are among the fundamental building blocks of social organizations because they give us reasons for understanding what we have done and the grounds for doing them again. Thus, institutions work to *legitimate* behavior by providing members of society with reasons for it.

If we look at a common practice in society that has ambiguous "institutional" meaning, we can better understand legitimation. The U.S Census Bureau estimates that, in 1987, about 2 million young, unmarried adults of opposite sexes were "living together." Several decades ago, this practice, while not unknown, was uncommon. Now we have a term to refer to it: cohabitation. Even though the practice is a relatively common type of domestic and sexual arrangement, it is not institutional because it is still not fully "legitimate."

For example, in 1986, when the Roper pollsters asked 1470 Americans their opinions about premarital sex, about 57 percent said it was wrong in some sense (29 percent said it is always wrong, 8 percent almost always wrong, and 20 percent sometimes wrong). These pollsters did not ask a specific question about "living together," but we can see that cohabitation as a living arrangement has negative connotations to many. Institutions legitimate behavior, and living together is, at best, only partially legitimate, because its meanings and the rules for doing it are drawn from several sources.

One meaning is derived from what we recognize as the traditional marriage; other meanings for "living together" are adaptations people make to what they see as the "outmoded" character of family. Hence cohabitation has some similarities to marriage: Partners are emotionally involved in an intimate, primary group; they make commitments to each other; and their sexual relationship is usually exclusive. But the partners typically are wary of making the formal commitment of marriage. For some, cohabitation is a "trial marriage," and in this sense it is partially institutional. For others, it is a convenient way to manage "sexuality" in a society with few clear, "legitimate" rules for this area of social life. For this latter group, cohabitation is more like "going steady."

Actually, about a third of all cohabiting couples eventually marry, and we have seen a trend in the American courts to treat such living arrangements as marriage, at least with regard to financial matters. It seems that when one institution (family) does not function to solve the problem of what is legitimate, another (government) will do the job (Blumstein and Swartz 1983).

Obviously, how legitimate and appropriate action is established varies from one society to another according to their degrees of modernization. With regard to sexual behavior and marriage, traditional societies provide for their members clear rules and sanctions for selecting partners and even actual models for how to perform sex acts. In America fifty years ago, marriage was the only social arrangement within which sex was supposed to take place. (Of course, from time immemorial, some people have had sex outside of marriage.) But in America, a society for which we have the most information on these matters, women, and men somewhat less so, usually engaged in sex only within the confines of marriage. Today, while many more options are open to people, marriage is still the modal arrangement for sex. By this we mean that most people who engage in sex in American society are married to the person with whom they are having sex.

But premarital and extramarital sex do occur. According to recent surveys, probably 80 percent of American males have had sex prior to their first marriage, and the figure is about 60 percent for females. Furthermore, the percentage of sexually inexperienced women at the time of their first marriage has been decreasing since the 1940s and may equal that of the males in the future. As Atwater (1987) writes, the same convergence of gender roles is true for extramarital relationships. In her article studying the effects of adding an extramarital role to the marriage, she suggests that as many as 40 to 50 percent of young married women engage in extramarital sex at some time during their marriages.

Can we say, then, that because acts are widespread, they are becoming institutional? They may, if we are referring to typical ways of doing things, to the standardization of problem solving — a key feature of a social institution. Premarital and extramarital sex, and even prostitution, in this sense, are institutional. Obviously, then, there is more to "institutional" acts than their frequency.

We note that, ordinarily, members of society do not call into question the propriety of an activity if it is formally institutionalized. For example, we would not ordinarily inquire about why a woman has sexual intercourse with her husband (Lyman and Scott 1970), for such an activity is legitimate. It is prescribed by an institution; it is what married people do. Institutions acknowledge and prescribe. They symbolize the transformation of two people from single units into a collectively recognizable unit. They tell us what it means to be married with regard to sexual conduct. Such knowledge is necessary to any understanding that the activity is not only allowable within this context but desirable.

Of course, as we have indicated, institutions specify style as well as particular activities. Therefore, a married couple may have intercourse, but not in public, not indiscreetly, not in a manner that comes under the interpretation of some other institution, such as legal statutes of government. For example, in some states, oral and anal sex is illegal even between married couples.

In the case of contradictions between institutions, rules for avoiding open conflict usually develop. Robin Williams (1960) terms such rules "norms of evasion" and refers to established, widely known and utilized procedures for obeying the rules of two contradictory institutions. Thus a married couple will never be prosecuted under the laws of sodomy if their performance of such acts is private, discreet, and unannounced. A law enforcement officer would not ordinarily obtain a warrant to "bust" a married couple in the expectation of catching them in an illegal sex act. Only under circumstances that indicate to the officer that the acts mean more than a courteous evasion of the law might he attempt an arrest. For example, a couple publicly extolling the virtues of oral sex in a conservative community might discover themselves being harassed.

Institutions work, then, by instilling in us a sense of what is appropriate. The knowledge that people have about what kinds of feelings, thoughts and actions go together operates to inform them of what is happening in advance of an event, and during and after it. We may be upset if events and feelings have been inappropriate; but we are satisfied if they have been in line with institutional expectations.

To return to our example of "living together." Many young people cohabit as a prelude to marriage. Thus a woman consents to the proposition of her friend by acknowledging that she might love him. "I wouldn't do that with just any guy, but I think I can really relate to you." According to the couple's expectations of courtship and dating, the essential ingredient relevant to sexual behavior is love, an emotional state associated with a primary group form, a state of tacit, mutual, emotional understanding. Traditionally, our society has legitimated the act of sexual intercourse by joining its performance with an appropriate institutional-ized group form — a nuclear relationship created by marriage. The question of legitimation becomes, "Was this act (of intercourse between the unmarried couple) an instance of a class of acts interpretable as institutionalized?" In "living together," a couple account for their consent by interpreting it as relevant to the potential experience of love rather than to the institutionalized group form. In short, it is legitimate to them because they love each other.

After an act has been legitimated, there is no need for further concern with decisions about whether it should have been carried out or for feelings of guilt about having done it. But legitimation is not a matter of individual rationaliza-tion. It is, instead, a problem of matching with thoughts and feelings action that can be derived from a particular institution — those taken-for-granted stocks of knowledge that guide our actions in society. To institutionalize an event takes care of the reason for doing it: "Everybody knows" that people "in love" have intercourse.

Even with this widely understood institutional pairing of love and sex, there are those who would object to love as a reason for sex. Some contend that marriage is the only legitimate grounds for sexual intercourse; while at the other extreme, we find those who espouse the belief that "if it feels good, do it," that pleasure in and of itself is sufficient legitimation for sexual activity. On the one hand, an institutional procedure in its formal expression (marriage) constitutes the only admissible relevant pairing; on the other, an exaggerated position of what Durkheim (1951) called "egoism" or individualism serves as the minimally sufficient information to interpret what is happening between two people as legitimate. The formal procedure has the effect of rendering the interpretation that the couple who engage in intercourse are married, whereas the individual-ized, informal institutional procedure yields the judgment that they "love each other." Therefore, why have sex? Because of marriage, or because we are in love.

Many middle-aged parents who hold to the first procedure agonize over the behavior of their offspring who utilize the second. The parents know no guilt for their own sexual activities, and neither do the children for theirs; but the parents may experience guilt for their wayward offspring, and the children may feel the need to explain the new legitimating grounds to the parents. And both parents and offspring may condemn those whom they see as using sex for mere pleasure.

This case illustrates two generations for whom institutional meanings are not the same. There can be no understanding between these parents and children unless either the parents convert to the offsprings' point of view or the children renounce their own beliefs in favor of their parents'. What is legitimate to one is illegitimate to the other. We do not mean that neither can articulate the other's view, but that parents cannot take for granted that everybody knows the love-and-marriage maxim. Lively and imaginative maneuvers transpire between parents and children in the conflict of generations, usually resolving into new institutional forms or segmenting into multiple expressions of similar institutional themes.

Legitimation Crises

Within rapidly changing societies such as our own, the continuity of institutional forms may be challenged, as we have seen living together challenging marriage. Whenever it is not possible for all members of a given society to legitimate the same activity in a way that is practically identical, that society's institutions exist in multiforms, disarray and uneven usages. Such a condition amounts to a *legitimation crisis* (Habermas 1975).

For decades, for example, people who have received welfare and other benefits from the government have simply accepted what was given to them. During the 1930s, America's Great Depression years, welfare needs were defined by legislators and professionals and treated formally as technical, not political, problems (Hummel 1987; Piven and Cloward 1971). Thus, the institution of welfare was born. Since the 1960s, however, such disadvantaged groups as the poor and the handicapped have seen their relationship to institutions of government and bureaucracy in a new light. They are now denying the stigma attached to them and calling for control over policies that affect their lives. Ordinarily such demands are not relevant to the operation of a welfare bureaucracy. The recipients' call for participation threatens its foundations and creates a crisis of legitimacy for the everyday operation of the organization. After all, welfare recipients are legitimating their demands with principles of democracy; and the conflict between rational, technical requirements of bureaucracy and the claims for participation that welfare clients are making leaves everyone uncertain about "where we go from here."

An institutional crisis such as this means that no member can achieve the security and self-assuredness that any course of action, belief system, or emotional state he or she may pursue is, without doubt, beyond scrutiny. In its extreme manifestation, a legitimation crisis means that all members of the society live in a constant state of figuring out what they are to do and why they are to do it.

Although institutions work to establish legitimation for actions, feelings, and thoughts, they do not invariably do so in a smooth, trouble-free fashion. Instead, institutions change sporadically; they work in one way for a period of time that may vary from years to centuries and then they change, or perhaps they cease to work at all!

From our example of marriage and living together, we know an institutional means to getting sex involves following set procedures for finding a partner and attributing serious meanings to a relationship. Institutional arrangements for the meanings of sex serve as the background knowledge we use to understand the lyrics of a country song: "Makin' out and makin' love are not the same," we are told, and we know precisely what is meant.

With regard to sexual behavior in modern societies, questions of partners, meanings, and legitimacy are open to a variety of interpretations. The meanings of a sex act, then, are often *ad hoc*, highly situational ("It all depends") and above all else negotiable — even to the point where the act can have distinctively different meanings for each partner.

Of course, all this means that members of modern societies are less sure about what they have done when they have had sex. Have they expressed love, had fun, relieved themselves of biological tension, consummated a relationship, or what? Probably we would not be far off the mark if we said that all these meanings can play a part in the overall meaning of the act. Nevertheless, the freedom of choice that comes from selecting the meanings of acts from a menu carries a price. Whenever individuals are free to choose for themselves answers to "Who am I?" questions, the correlative questions of "What do people like me do?" becomes increasingly problematic. With more choices, there is a corresponding decrease in the consensus that any one way to act has in the society.

General Social Survey (GSS) data can give us some indication of the degree of "crisis" in basic institutions in American society. In a 1987 survey, a sample of adult Americans was asked about their confidence in the leaders of some major "social institutions" of American society. That people may lack confidence in leaders of "institutions" does not necessarily mean that the institution is in crisis, but a lack of confidence in institutional leaders surely does indicate that people do not expect "clear" institutional solutions to society's problems. And if we select the basic institutions we discuss in the following chapters — those related to economics (banks, business, and labor), religion, education, government (the executive branch, congress, and the Supreme Court), we find that most people have at least some ("a great deal" or "only some") confidence in the leaders of these major institutions (see Table 2.2). The percentages range from a high of 91 percent for leaders of banks and financial institutions to a low of 63 percent for leaders of organized labor. But we must point out when we look only at people who say they have "a great deal" of confidence, the figures are different. The high is 34.5 percent for the U.S. Supreme Court, and the low is 8.8 percent for union

Table 2.2

Confidence in Leaders of Major Institutions, by Sex, Age, Income and Race

Institution	Degree of Confidence	Sex		Age			Income			Race		
		Men	Women	Young	Middle-Aged	Old	Below Average	Average	Above Average	White	Black	Other
Business	A great deal	36	27	28	29	36	22	30	46	33	12	16
	Only some	52	60	64	60	48	59	60	45	55	70	68
	Hardly any	10	8	6	8	12	15	6	6	8	13	6
Organized religion	A great deal	30	32	30	28	33	33	29	31	31	30	35
	Only some	47	46	49	49	42	40	48	49	47	48	29
	Hardly any	20	17	19	19	18	22	18	16	18	18	29
Education	A great deal	27	28	32	21	31	28	27	30	27	32	42
	Only Some	60	57	56	65	53	56	60	62	59	55	48
	Hardly any	10	10	9	10	11	12	11	6	11	6	6
Federal government	A great deal	20	17	19	16	20	18	16	25	19	13	26
	Only some	49	51	48	51	50	45	54	48	50	49	45
	Hardly any	29	28	30	30	26	33	27	25	28	31	16
Labor Unions	A great deal	9	8	14	6	7	10	9	6	8	12	10
	Only some	49	55	57	54	48	52	56	43	51	64	42
	Hardly any	41	32	27	37	40	33	32	48	38	17	35
U.S. Supreme Court	A great deal	39	28	42	29	30	32	30	43	34	23	32
	Only some	43	55	44	55	50	50	52	46	50	57	45
	Hardly any	14	11	12	12	13	13	13	9	12	12	6
Congress	A great deal	13	12	17	10	11	15	12	12	12	10	23
	Only some	59	66	63	63	–	60	64	66	63	65	65
	Hardly any	25	19	18	24	21	22	21	20	23	17	3

Source: General Social Survey, 1987.

Note: Percentages do not add up to 100 because we are reporting only cell percentages. Here's an example of how to read the table: 60% of those who regard their incomes as below average expressed "only some" confidence in leaders of Congress.

leaders. Such data present a mixed picture of "crisis" in institutions. Generally, people have only slight confidence in their institutional leaders.

Jurgen Habermas's idea of a "legitimation crisis" is neither proved nor disproved by these data, but they do give us a way to think about his concept more concretely. It seems that Americans are not "overconfident" about the way their institutions are operating. Perhaps most significantly, these data show a variation in confidence, and this variation could indicate that people are choosing among institutional and personal solutions to problems, exactly the condition that Habermas suggests is necessary for a "legitimation crisis."

Institutional Change

In our society, institutions not only have changed over the years but they have also lost power, and we can understand why by applying what we know about how institutions function. The larger the gap between who people think they are and the appropriate channels for action open to them, the less the social consensus and the greater the tension among the components of society. We can think of this imbalance, or lack of fit, as a major characteristic of societies undergoing rapid change. In a traditional society, there is a close match between who people think they are and what they think they should do. In changing societies, there may well be a mismatch. Hence, in nineteenth century America, when the romance novel first emerged, its primary readership was women. When we look at the social organization at that time, we discover that increasing numbers of men were under conditions similar to those of modern life. They left their homes and assumed responsibilities at work that brought them into contact with many different people, often in many different places. Men, especially among the well-educated classes, entered the modern world ahead of their wives, and the increased freedom they enjoyed probably extended to their options for sexual encounters as well.

Women in this society, locked into what some scholars have called a domestic trap, became isolated from the main flow of societal activities. Yet they still developed a sense of who they were within the context of the changing, booming world of new opportunities and new freedom. At least we can say that the changes taking place in society were characteristically understood as progress. Women believed in progress and defined themselves in terms of their relationship to a society to which they did not have full access.

The fantasy novel became one response to this predicament. In the world of fantasy, a woman can be who she wants and do what she wants. She can escape the paradox of being modern in thought and traditional in behavior. In contemporary society, we also see responses to the predicament of defining ourselves as people who have no means to act. Our modern citizen may eschew marriage or the serious relationship, but he or she remains "sexual." So what are the options?

Let us list them on the menu. Marriage is, of course, the legitimate institutional answer. But where does one find an eligible partner? Singles bars, personal ads, and "hitting on" someone in an ice-cream shop are all options. In each option, however, one is likely to find people who are not looking for a serious relationship or who in other ways do not want to have a "legitimate" one.

To be sure, in singles bars there are routine ways to meet, greet, and talk to others. There are also ways to communicate whether one wants to have sex or not. But these rituals, like many of the everyday meanings of modern life, are highly variable and open to individual interpretations. In short, finding an appropriate partner in a singles bar can be very problematic. Likewise, the chance of making a good connection through the personal ads is problematic enough to warrant a movie on the subject. The humorous but painfully accurate *Personals* depicts the predicament of single people in a society organized, by and large, for families (see Stein 1981).

What we discover from our own experiences and from the studies of sociologists is that these social arrangements, while they are clearly rule governed, are not fully institutionalized. In effect, what exists in today's society are very powerful and effective means of telling people they should be sexy, and a very disorganized and fragmented set of behavioral guidelines for doing something about it. The typical advertisement shows sexiness very clearly, but does not portray the details of interaction necessary to act "sexy."

Just as the housewife of the nineteenth century devoured romance novels, so does the "housewife" of the 1990s. But, more important, we are tempted to say that the modal response to the predicament of the failed institutional control of sexual behavior is the proliferation of fantasy. Beginning with *Playboy* in the 1950s and through the vast array of readily available magazines now displaying every imaginable sex act, sex as fantasy has become a major preoccupation of the American people. Some may define these magazines as pornographic, but they are first and foremost a rational, highly organized cultural response to a lack of fit between socialization experiences and institutional means. When one knows who one is sexually, but does not know what to do about it, one can go to the corner drugstore or convenience store and purchase a collective but not institutional solution to the problem.

While it is unlikely that pornographic literature represents a nascent institution, other responses may well be the beginnings of new forms of old institutions or even of new institutions. Singles bars, personals in newspapers, and, perhaps more likely, networking on personal computers may well become a highly institutionalized means of solving the problem of how to have sex. This would be the case if and when people knew how to conduct themselves over a network, for example, from the basic interactional skills they acquire in everyday life. If it ever happens that we communicate primarily over electronic networks with other people outside our immediate living arrangement, then the conventions for conversations that ground everyday life may include means for "contacting" in intimate relationships (cf. Deken's 1982 discussion of the electronic cottage). Also, a full institution is marked by ceremony. While it may be humorous to imagine what kind of ceremony might function to designate the romantic computer "love connection," it is not too far-fetched. In fact, a recent marriage between two hackers was conducted over their respective computers. Other people on the network were invited to the wedding. They watched the exchange of vows on their screens and even "threw" rice at the end of the ceremony by running programs they had written to make patterns of light specks on the couple's monitors.

If you have seen the television show "The Love Connection," you have seen an example of what may well be the institutional response to the "serious relationship" question. Meeting on television and having an audience evaluate the match between potential partners seems to be a consistent step in a direction toward the emergence of a common society wide solution to the problem of how to find a mate.

Other traditional institutions are undergoing change so rapidly that they also are less than complete. For example, Andrew Cherlin suggests that remarriage is an incomplete institution. Consider the question "Are you single or married?" The institutional meanings of marriage are so powerful that they wipe out the identity of being single. If you ask someone if he (or she) is married or single, he will not answer "Both." But if you ask someone who is remarried if they are married or divorced, they may well answer "Both." Residuals of one's first marriage apparently carry over into later marriages.

In the language of family life, we have no standard institutionally legitimate terms for the family composed of a married couple plus children from each of the couple's previous marriages (some popular magazines have recently used the term "blended families"). Nor do we have adequate "kin terms" for the various step-relations that can pertain between siblings living with siblings although they do not share the same biological parents.

The family will surely exist as an institution in the future. The fact that it has lasted through the postwar decades of social change without really developing a vernacular of its own may well mean that it has become a menu selection within which the common vocabulary of social relationships for all members of society functions.

New Rules For Old Institutions

Which responses to "What do I do?" will become institutionalized we cannot ascertain. We can detect trends that indicate the direction of the change. In his popular book *Megatrends*, John Naisbitt (1982) argues that there is a major trend away from individual reliance on societal institutions and toward the development of smaller networks of people and services that allow novel and individually meaningful solutions to the problems of everyday life. If his assessment is correct, while major institutions like the family and government will remain components of social organization, their enactments may well be augmented by "new rules" for coping with the problematic character of social life.

One of the sociologist's tasks is to determine the direction of change and assess the overall patterns of society. Several theorists have captured the character and trends of society accurately. For example, in *The Lonely Crowd*, David Riesman (1950) wrote of his effort to depict changes in the character of modern America. He argued that people were becoming more sensitive to questions concerning what other people thought of them, and most important, they were using the actions and opinions of others as guidelines for their own activities. Hence he contrasted the fierce individualism of the American frontiersmen (what he called "inner-directedness") with the conformity of the gray-flannel generation whose primary concern seemed to be keeping up with the people next door (he called this phenomenon "other-directedness").

Although Riesman's assessment of the rules and institutional strength of approaches to solving the problems of life in a complex, organizational society has been criticized, he was accurate in noting that old ways of conducting life, set patterns of values and experiences, do change. He foresaw a nation of conformity built around a superficial social, instead of a strong individual ethic. We must admit that the remarkable "trendiness" of fashion, styles of talk, and leisure activities such as running, body building, and the like seem to indicate that Riesman's ideas were at least partially correct. For increasing numbers of people, the stress on self-actualization has lead to a curious kind of conformity where people look to one another to learn what the latest form of individual expression is.

Of course, all major social institutional values came under direct attack during the social movements of the 1960s, and several alternative life styles were proposed and followed. Daniel Yankelovich (1981) has since traced the changes in people's attitudes toward women's rights, women remaining unmarried, homosexuality, and other matters of social liberality. Yankelovich discovered that the 1960s had a profound impact on basic institutional values. Generally, people in the 1970s and 1980s have been more liberal in their ideas about sexuality and family life.

Yankelovich and his associates have conducted surveys of the opinions of Americans on a variety of matters over several decades, and his research seems to indicate that we are entering a new era for which norms are just emerging. He writes that, "tomorrow . . . is being shaped by a cultural revolution that is transforming the rules of American life and moving us into wholly uncharted territory, not back to the life-styles of the past" (Yankelovich 1981, 36).

Still, the new rules about which he writes are related to the old. His research gives us some clues about which norms and values are playing a role in the new structure of American society. For example, some traditional norms still command majority assent:

• 90% of those adults who are parents would still have children if they "had it to do over again."

• 87% of adults feel the use of hard drugs is "morally wrong."

• 84% of adults feel it's up to parents to educate teenagers about birth control.

• 81% feel "mate swapping" is morally wrong.

• 79% disapprove of married women having affairs.

• 76% disapprove of married men having affairs.

• 74% want their children to be better off and more successful than they are.

• 77% agree that a woman should put her husband and children ahead of her career.

• 57% agree that its best to demand a lot from children; they have to do their best to get head.

• 55% feel it's more important for a wife to help her husband's career than to have a career herself.

• 51% believe that strict old-fashioned upbringing and discipline are still the best ways to raise children.

In contrast, many norms have changed radically over the years. What follows are twenty major changes in the norms guiding American life. The percentages refer to percentage of the sample from the various studies on which Yankelovich based his figures.

1. Disapprove of a married woman earning money if she has a husband capable of supporting her.
     1938: 75–80%
     1978: 28–30%
2. Four or more children is the ideal number for a family to have.
     1945: 50%
     1980: 17–20%
3. For a woman to remain unmarried she must be "sick," "neurotic, or "immoral."
     1957: 80%
     1978: 25%

4. Would vote for a qualified women nominee for president of the United State.

 1937: 30%
 1980: 80%

5. Condemn premarital sex as morally wrong.

 1967: 85%
 1979: 45%

6. Favor decision making abortion up to third month of pregnancy legal.

 1975: 50%
 1980: 60%

7. Agree that both sexes have responsibility to care for small children.

 1970: 35%
 1980: 65%

8. Approve of husband and wife taking separate vacations.

 1971: 35%
 1980: 50%

9. Agree that hard work always pays off.

 1969: 60%
 1976: 47%

10. Agree that work is at the center of life.

 1970: 37%
 1978: 15%

11.a. Men would go on working for pay even if they didn't have to.

 1957: 85%
 1976: 82%

11.b. Women would go on working for pay even if they didn't have to.

 1957: 57%
 1976: 78%

12. Increase in level of anxiety and worry among young American's 21–39 years of age.

 1957: 30%
 1976: 50%

13. Agree that the people running the country don't care what happens to people like us.

 1966: 25%
 1977: 60%

14. Agree that they can trust the government in Washington to do what is right.

 1958: 55%
 1978: 30%

15. Experience a "hungering for community."

 1973: 32%

1980: 47%
16. American's with a "sour grapes" outlook.
1970: 28%
1980: 18%
17. Agree that it is morally acceptable to be single and have children.
1979: 75%
18. Agree that interracial marriages are not morally wrong.
1977: 52%
19. Agree that it is not morally wrong for couples to live together even if they are not married.
1975: 52%
20. Agree that they would return of standards of the past relating to sexual mores, "spic and span" house keeping, and women staying home and only men working outside of the home.
1979: 20%

Source: Daniel Yankelovich 1981.

Yankelovich's analysis does not lead us to the radical conclusion that we are seeing new institutions in their nascent stages. Instead, his surveys tell us that people have become more interested in the personal meanings of social life, but that at the same time they want to retain the core values of many of society's basic institutions.

Traditionally, Americans have believed that self-denial, sacrifice, and following the dictates of government and church made sense. The modern American, however, is much more critical of the old rules of institutional social life. He or she wants more room for personal choice and seems to be more forgiving of those who innovate and strike out on paths of their own design. The trend toward individualistic and self-serving approaches to problem solving has not meant an abandonment of traditional methods and values. Yankelovich writes that the American people are not saying, "forget the family; to hell with my obligations to others; I couldn't care less about money, status and respectability." Instead, he believes, "People want to retain some elements of family success — marriage and family, material well-being, respectability — but they are also struggling mightily to make room for greater personal choice against institutional encroachments" (1981, 231–232).

According to Yankelovich's assessment, American institutions are adapting to fit more closely the needs of the people in society. He suggests that institutions change, that they prescribe new rules, as it were. Thus in the 1990s we are seeing the consolidation of changes that have been taking place over a fairly long period of time.

Summary

As we have tried to point out in this chapter, institutions are common approaches to problem solving. They are procedures that people can follow to get things done. They exist concomitantly with social identities, and identities are created and maintained in them as well. In some societies, personal identity and means of acting are consistent and the problematic nature of social life is less apparent, at least to the typical person. Societies that are changing rapidly, however, often confront their citizens with a mismatch between who they think they are and what people like them can do.

In American society, this mismatch has stimulated profound changes in basic institutions, especially the family. Here people redefine the means for accomplishing intimate relationships such as raising children and generally having a family. While these changes may threaten the traditional institutional meanings of family life, they do not necessarily replace them. Institutions function, in the first instance, to give people ways to eat their cake. In some societies, institutions tell people how to eat cake they do not have. In others, institutions seem to encourage people to try to solve the problems of everyday life by applying old, often outmoded rules, and so their efforts seem to perpetuate the old problems. Finally, the tensions of inconsistency and social change may stimulate old institutions to change by adopting new rules. Although these new rules reflect profound changes in society, they allow institutions to function in an ever changing larger social world.

Chapter 3

MODERN FAMILY LIFE

Sociologists have very different ideas about the importance of family life in modern society. Etzioni (1977), for one, has written that because of new and alternative institutions, the traditional family has been reduced to a "memory," or "ideology," of how things used to be. He and others suggest that the state, education, and consumer economics have taken over the functions of the family. Other researchers, like Caplow and his associates (1982), believe that families, at least in American society, have not changed much since the 1920s. Accordingly, they suggest that the backbone of society is still the family, the institution that shoulders the primary responsibility for socializing the next generation. What has changed, they argue, is how people think about the family. They point out that people tell stories of the decline of the family to show their understanding of the larger, complex society, and at the same time, strengthen the basis for their own versions of family life. Although such narratives of woe may help individuals think their families are "better off" than those of most people, they do not accurately describe family life. Surely the family has changed, Caplow et al. concede, but these changes have been only superficial and have not meant the weakening of the roles and functions families play in society.

In studying the family in modern society, we confront some crucial sociological issues. If the family is weakened and does not meet the needs of its members or the society, then society itself is, or soon will be, in the midst of a major transformation. Conversely, if the family has adjusted to the impact of rapid change, has modified its structure but still performs an essential role, then we need to reassess not just the vitality of family life in modern society but even the models we have of modern society. The study of the institution of family, then, is first a study of society and second a study of the units that make it up.

The American Family: Middletown And Beyond

In the 1920s, again in the 1930s, and finally in the late 1970s, Muncie, Indiana, came under study by groups of sociologists interested in, among other things, the fate of the family in modern society. Robert and Helen Lynd (1929) approached the families of Muncie (renamed "Middletown" in their research) with the idea that American society was on the verge of massive changes that would render the traditional family obsolete or, at best, under siege. They found

48

that family life was well organized but that forces other than familial ones were at work in shaping the values and behavior of the members of this typical, medium-sized, Middle American community.

In fact, they found a quality of family life that was certainly less than idyllic. They wrote that for most people in their study, marriage was a way of life without "delight, or fresh or spontaneous interest between husband and wife." For many, "marriage seems to amble along at a friendly jog-trot marked by sober accommodation of each partner to his share in the joint undertaking of children, paying off the mortgage, and generally 'getting on'"(Lynd and Lynd1929,130).

The Lynds left a legacy of suspicion about how well marriage and the institution of the family were going to fare in the modern world. Divorce rates did soar in the ensuing years, and major changes are easy to document in the composition and stability of the family. We have in mind increases in families headed by a single parent, the proportion of wives working outside the home, heavy reliance on day care for small children, and so on. To be sure, these changes have been dramatic.

But scholars still disagree about the true state of the family in modern society (Berger and Berger1983). Even the debate about the Middletown families was rekindled by Caplow and his colleagues when they returned to Muncie to repeat the famous study of the Lynds. According to Caplow et al., families have weathered well the many changes in society. They write that there has been

> no appreciable decline in the Middletown family during the past 50 years. Insofar as changes in the institutions can be measured, they seem to reflect a strengthening of the institutional form and increased satisfaction for participants. We have noted the likelihood that the trend for the entire country is similar. (1982, 329)

There is still plenty of room for debate. We start from the following observations, which seem to reflect the "best" information available (cf. Smith1984). People still do marry, and even if they do not have children, they say they want them. Furthermore, most Americans still believe that a strong institution of family life is very important to the well-being of society. Nevertheless, while Americans obviously have not forsaken the family, they have modified their reasons for participating in it. In the 1920s, for example, people believed that marriage and family were inevitable; now, people think that marriage is, and should be, a matter of choice. Both husband and wife choose to marry, decide whether to have children, and, if so, when and how many. They may even try to choose the sex of their children, and, of course, if they discover that their marriage is not what they they thought they had chosen, they may choose to end it.

These changes are especially profound for women. While historical sociologists can trace back changes in how people have thought about the family throughout previous centuries (Gordon1978), we use the Lynds' study as a benchmark. Thirty years ago, women simply assumed they would marry and bear children; they now consider this an option on their life's menu.

This shift in motivation for family life is clearly supported by the strong demographic trends that began many years ago but became obvious only in the 1960s. Families have become smaller. In 1984, they averaged 2.71 members. And there is the equally prevalent trend toward more families headed by a single parent. At present, these families account for about one-fourth of all families. (U.S. Bureau of the Census1987). Moreover, marriage has become unnecessary from the point of view of many single parents, an intolerable condition for many separated parents, and a serial arrangement of mates for the divorced and remarried. Statistics on family size, literature documenting changes in the organization of families, and common-sense knowledge all confirm that the traditional family is no longer a "fact of life."

Family Life as Institutional

The fact that people choose whether to live in families and what kinds of families to have can obscure our appreciation of the institutional character of family life. Any institution can change dramatically but still remain stable and important as a part of the overall organization of society. For example, regardless of form, as an institution the family provides for its members ready-made interpretations for many activities of everyday life. And, like all institutions, the family rests on common assumptions people make about the meanings of social arrangements.

First, in America at least, family life is organized around the assumption that a state of affairs known as "love" can exist between two people. Gordon (1978), tracing the role that "romantic love" played in the organization of marriage from early American history to the present, notes considerable evidence that married people expected to love each other, even when they did not have much control over the actual selection of their mates. Of course, in forms of society where marriage and the constitution of a new family are closely linked to economic, religious, and political matters, love becomes just one among many criteria for mate selection.

As society entered the modern age, people, for a variety of reasons, began to demand more freedom in the selection of marriage partners. We can understand this transformation as a general consequence of the increase of impersonal social interactions that accompany the change to complex, heterogeneous industrial society. In traditional society, where the very structure of social relationships may derive from kinship, to allow marriages to take place on highly individual criteria would have profound consequences for the stability of social order. As the basis for order itself shifts from traditional to modern, though, romantic love becomes a *cover* for a variety of highly individualistic reasons people may have for marrying each other. Herman Lantz and his colleagues summarize the rise of romantic love in American society:

> The data certainly indicate that the romantic love complex was known in colonial America and that, indeed, it may have been a common pattern among large sections of the upper status groups. Thus, with regard to the impact of industrialization, it may well be said that industrialization facilitated the development of a romantic love complex already in existence. Finally, presence of the romantic love complex must be seen in the broader context of the emergence of individualism and the role of personal wishes as an important basis in mate choice. (Lantz et al.1968, 420)

As institutions change, society changes, and people change their styles of thinking, what they are aware of, and what they take for granted. In colonial America, romantic love was just one consideration in mate choice. Now, it is the primary, if not the sole, criterion.

To illustrate our point, let us give an actual example of a well-educated Hindu, an Indian woman, living in America. This particular woman is, in many ways, very modern. She holds a Ph.D degree, teaches at a major American university, is very bright and articulate. Her family life, however, differs in one very important respect from the typical American family — she did not select her marriage partner. Her family, together with her husband's family, arranged their wedding. This means that she did not, strictly speaking, choose to marry her husband. She knew of his family, but she had not met her prospective husband until a few months before their wedding ceremony. In fact, she was a child when her marriage was arranged.

In America, such marriages are virtually unknown. And most Americans cringe when they hear that an intelligent, highly educated woman has been married for ten years to a man whom she did not choose. But this woman tells us that her marriage is successful and she is happy. Her ties to her Hindu religion and Indian society provide her with ways to understand and accept this about her family life. In fact, her "Indian consciousness" may be alien to the mentality necessary to "fall in love." When we asked her if she "loved" her husband, her answer was, "Of course!" But she added that she did not fully understand why Americans make such a "fuss" about "falling in love." This woman may well change if she does not return to her native country. Certainly, her daughter, if she grows to maturity in America, will suffer a clash between the individualism of love and the stability of arranged marriage.

We are focused on marriage and the family as an institution of modern society, one that provides ready-made solutions to some of the problems of everyday life, in this case, to the problem of "How do you know whom to marry?" Some societies, that of India for instance, solve this problem by transferring the decision to persons who have matters of reputation, wealth, and lineage at stake. As we have learned, modern societies tend to shift such serious questions to rational bases. Rationality rests on individual responsibility for assessing consequences and choosing among options. When we see things in this way, we realize understanding love is not automatic, and we are not surprised that people must learn to know when they are in love and when that love is a sufficient basis for marriage.

This task is not a simple one. Judith Katz (1976), for example, notes that love can be understood mostly as a problem of perception. She believes that in their intimate relationships people test the hypothesis "He or she loves me." They judge whether or not a person loves them on the basis of three considerations. First, when we say a person loves us we mean they know us well — our likes and dislikes — and, second, that they will act toward us in unselfish ways. They may sacrifice a weekend to help us fix our car or give up a favorite meal at a favorite restaurant to take us to our favorite place for that "special treat." Finally, acts of love are those we see as motivated by loving attitudes. Katz concludes that the conditions that a person's actions must meet before one perceives them as "loving actions" are contradictory — it is difficult to be compatible with a person and yet sacrifice for them, since both parties like the same things.

In our society, people marry because they believe they love each other. Interestingly enough, love and children are also associated in the common-sense knowledge structure of family life. Most people take for granted that a loving relationship is a solid groundwork for raising children. While the numbers and proportions of married couples who remain childless have increased in the decades since the 1930s, marriage and family are still linked institutionally.

We assume, for instance, that parents, especially mothers, are supposed to know how to discipline, teach, nurture, and love their children. In reality, most of us rely on our own socialization experiences for this knowledge of parenting. Unfortunately, as in the case of parents who were themselves abused, many parents engage in cruel and violent behavior toward their own children, thus creating, or inculcating in them, undesirable behavior without knowing it. But, these "failures" of the family are not sufficient to produce changes in the assumptions that ground family life. Today, most parents do not abuse their children, though in truth, it is difficult, given the current stage of social scientific knowledge, to determine what constitutes "abuse" except in extreme cases.

Family Functions

Since all institutions do certain things for their members, it is appropriate for us to ask what the family functions are. For most people, the core attributes of self are formed within the family, for that is where children first acquire a strong sense of identity and personal significance or insignificance (Mead 1934; Elkin and Handel 1984). The family is perhaps the clearest example of what Cooley (1922) referred to as the "primary group," and is, therefore, an important agent of socialization. Precisely how effective the family is in passing on systems for interpretation of meaning that ground a person's participation in society is an open question. Indeed, specializations within sociology and psychology are devoted to this question. And there is no doubt that influences from peer groups, education, mass media, and other sources have challenged the primacy of the family as a socialization agent. Still, in the long run, the experiences of family life remain as symbolic guides throughout a person's life.

In modern society, the family is also a unit of consumption. Members buy things as representatives of the family; thus there are family living units, such as houses, apartments, and condominiums. There are family-sized and family-designed cars — station wagons, vans, sedans, and wagoneers. Of course, the way items sell may also tell us a great deal about the values of family life in societies. For example, the symbol of American family life, the station wagon, simply does not sell in the European market. There are family boxes of soap, tubes of toothpaste, loaves of bread, and containers of milk. While we have seen significant changes in patterns of consumption in America and Europe as manufacturers tailor their products for couples and smaller, more diverse organizations of family life, the production of "family-sized" items reflects the assumption that families consume.

Family life is further understood as a private refuge from the "real world." A working mother can return to her home in the evening, and, even though she may have washing to do and dinner to prepare, she expects to relax and be herself. In the home, among the members of the family, one can change into "comfortable" clothes and drop the air of formality that must be maintained at the office. The children also can "let off steam" and simply watch television as an alternative to dealing with the face-to-face problems of everyday life. At home, members find a special place where they may retire to their rooms or otherwise pursue personally meaningful activities.

Obviously, the family is the usual context for the procreation of members of society. New members for the society come from the family, and although the medical profession may play a role in the delivery of babies, it is parents in a family who decide to have children. Given the important emotional and economic investments in having children, the primary-group character of family life constitutes the proper background against which such decisions are to be made.

It is, perhaps, a measure of the crisis of family that in many American cities in 1989, a fourth to a third of all babies were born to unmarried women.

Furthermore, one's family is assumed to have something to do with one's place in society. In addition to supplying and socializing new members, the family largely determines one's position in the social world. A person is born, say, into a Catholic family; born rich or poor; born into a minority-language community or with a given ethnic identity. The process of being given an identity by virtue of simply being born into a certain kind of family is called *status ascription*. As the family ascribes identities to its members, it places them into society as kinds of people: black people, Native Americans, poor or rich people.

As we have presented it, people make judgments about what is and is not family life depending on widely distributed and shared knowledge, what some sociologists call *common-sense knowledge systems*. Certainly the institution of family is more complicated than we have indicated. Nevertheless, it derives its meanings from the commonly held stocks of knowledge, the assumptions, that pertain to such activities as we have mentioned.

The Family as a Group Form

Sociologists usually regard the family as a primary group, one characterized by intimate face-to-face interactions. In modern families, however, the degree to which interaction among family members is primary has changed. A British sociologist, Basil Bernstein (1970), observing this change, began a line of analysis that leads to a unique critique of family life. Although the distinctions between traditional and modern families are readily documented (Skolnick and Skolnick 1986), Bernstein's reasoning provides a guide to describing the forms of the family as mixed, with both traditional and modern characteristics.

In contemporary societies, family life may be organized according to the same principles that govern the formal organizations of society. For example, parents may draw up contracts with children, or with each other, and the household tasks may be scheduled into hourly blocks that rotate like shift work from family member to family member. Bernstein suggests that we can best understand the consequences of mixing formal and primary-group forms in the family by examining the ways in which members of families communicate with each other by position or as individuals.

The Positionally Oriented Family

Bernstein's studies and the substantial body of research his work stimulated (see Nash and Calonico 1974; Trudgill 1983) suggest that families seem to follow one of two procedures to create and sustain interaction. The first he calls *positional*; and according to this procedure, control over family members and order in family life is exercised from within, through the organization of the family. Decision making here is made through an order that consists of predefined meanings or roles for the various positions within the family. For example, traditionally a father, because he occupies the position of father, is vested with the authority to direct the behavior of other members of the family — his wife's behavior as well as that of his children.

Other positions within the family also have activities and responsibilities associated with them: The wife and mother has the responsibility for keeping clean and well-mannered children, an orderly household, and a submissive attitude toward her husband, who is known as the head of the household. Children, because they are children, must obey rules of etiquette, curfews, and so on. How legitimate a person's actions are, then, is determined by the degree to which members share assumptions about the distribution of family activities by position, and, of course, by the dispatch and effectiveness of the exercise of authority. One need not fully understand why Dad punished big brother; one needs to know only that the person administering the punishment is a father whose position, in itself, legitimates a wide range of actions for him. Of course, the legitimate use of power and control is well defined and understood among members of the family and those who belong to the larger society that supports it.

Bernstein pointed out that family orientations are created and then maintained by the way people communicate with each other in everyday language, and that when one understands "codes of communications," one understands the heart of family order. The language or linguistic code associated with the positional father he termed "restricted." A restricted language code is characterized by a high degree of tacitness, that is, no one speaks much about it, but everyone knows what it means. In order to understand another person using the code, one must be aware of the context of social life that underlies its usage.

The restricted code is marked by what seems to be elusiveness, but actually, to the users, the context of communications is simply presumed. Hence, when asked to relate an episode depicted by a series of pictures, a group of children from positionally oriented families responded in the following fashion: "He did that and it went in there — boy was she mad — They ran fast from there and she yelled — but they were gone."

Without seeing the pictures, we are at a loss to know exactly what these children are talking about. Generally, the restricted code relies on the use of fewer words and words used in less complicated arrangements than in other codes of communication. As Bernstein (1970, 25–28) is quick to note, however, these considerations alone do not define the restricted code, since it may actually involve an extensive vocabulary in complex usages. What defines the code is its semantic dimension. It is not just what is said, but the way the meanings of what is said are realized that is the only reliable criterion of a code's character.

In the above example, we as readers cannot ascertain the content of the pictures. From what is said, we have only very general information about them. The speaker presumes, however, that the persons with whom he communicates do see the pictures. Hence the realization of meaning through speech is *restricted* to the context of those who actually do see them.

Bernstein discovered that members of positional families employed this kind of shorthand communication, and that the use of this code itself promotes a feeling of "we-ness." In short, to talk to us you have to be one of us, and to be one of us you have to talk like we do. The positional family rests on this kind of tacit, informal communication that depends upon feelings of belonging to a group form and having common experiences.

As long as the common assumptions that attribute meaning to various positions are not questioned, the traditional family operates in a stable manner. Whenever a question is raised, however, it is not merely the topic at hand that is being questioned but the entire form of the family. For example, perhaps a son expresses his feelings that America is not really a country of free men at all and that the founding fathers acted to break from England simply for economic reasons. He first heard this idea from a professor at the local college who told of a theory that so interpreted the Constitution of the United States. The son believes the theory makes a lot of sense. His father, a high school educated heavy equipment operator, becomes enraged on hearing his son repeating this "garbage" from the "intellectuals" at the college. From the father's point of view, such a "theory" questions fundamental issues like loyalty to one's nation, and perhaps even the father's own authority.

In a positionally oriented family, the father and the son cannot simply discuss the theory of an economic interpretation of the U.S. Constitution. What happens, instead, is that the son's disagreement with the father's politics calls into question the father's authority and thus the very organization of the family. In this family, the father has the authority *as a father* to make decisions, and it is this authority which the son inadvertently challenges. In many cases in positional families, arguments such as this result in the father symbolically and even literally expunging his son or daughter from family membership. A father may insist that his biological offspring is not really his son unless the "impostor" dresses more conventionally and changes his mind about the "true" meanings of patriotism.

Within the positionally oriented family, only one procedure for making sense of family-like activities can operate. Individual variations in tastes, language styles, and opinions are not and cannot become the grounds for legitimate action. Thus, needless to say in modern society, the positional family often suffers from complex pressures to change. LeMasters (1975) reports that middle-aged construction equipment operators often blame the problems they have with their wives on television soap operas. They say that their wives used to be content to stay at home, serve their needs, and defer to their judgments about how to spend leisure time and how to vote. Now they have "wild ideas about going back to school, getting a job and setting up a business of their own." Indeed, as the Berger's have written, during the past twenty years, there has been a "War over the Family" (Berger and Berger1983).

The Individually Oriented Family

Bernstein identifies another family form, which he calls individually oriented. In contrast to the primary nature of the positional form, in this form elements of a secondary nature begin to appear. Instead of a common context that grounds interaction being presumed by all family members, the foundations of the individually oriented family are explicated and expressed in detail through each individual's personal "reasons" for action. The "reasons," now expressed in *elaborate* rather than restricted linguistic forms, actually amount to each individual's own version of interpreting and experiencing the world.

Thus, an individual in this family performs the task to which he or she feels best suited as an individual. If the mother seems to have "a good head for figures" and is not particularly upset by the onslaught of monthly bills, she pays the bills, keeps the checking account, and manages household finances. Or, if her individual needs change, and she decides to pursue a career full-time and no longer has the time to pay the bills, the father may assume this responsibility, on the grounds that his "personal situation," his job, free time, hobbies, and so forth, allow the addition of this task.

In the positional family, such matters of personal wants, time demands, abilities, and desires do not operate to define what the members of the family actually do. But in the individually oriented family, the procedures for generating family activities shift to this highly relative, personalized basis. Within the individually oriented family, no single activity, no particular authority, is *necessarily* associated with any one position. A mother may be the chief wage earner, while the husband may do the cooking for the family. What unites the diversified family roles is a procedure decreeing that "everybody in the family knows" that each person does what he or she is best suited to do. The assumptions that underlie the order of this family hold that "psychological," and of course developmental, abilities and potentials ought to translate into family appropriate activities.

Ideally, when a person uses the elaborate code, he or she verbalizes the context of communication as much as possible. Its usage allows a speaker to leave nothing unsaid, for outlining both the environment of the message and the individual's relationship to that environment is the goal of elaborate communication. Thus, when children from individually oriented families are asked to verbalize a story depicted by a series of pictures — the same pictures used with the positional children above, typical of their responses is one like this: "The boys are playing baseball, one hits the ball and it goes through the window of the house. It breaks the glass. The lady in the house yells at them and the boys run away."

In this rendition, little of the experiential context of actually seeing the pictures is presumed. Without having seen the pictures, we still understand what happened. The elaborate-code child, from the individually oriented family, has successfully transformed the experience of seeing the pictures into a linguistic form (sentences relating to the experience). Although people who use elaborate codes typically use more complicated sentences and a larger vocabulary than those who use restricted codes, the definitive characteristic of the elaborate code is in how it requires the transformation of experience into language. Of course, presumptions still underlie the use of the elaborate code, but the nature of the presumptions regarding the socially shared background knowledge is much different.

Individual/Traditional Mix

In the restricted code it is the meaning of the lived-through experience, say, of "being a father," that is presumed. In the elaborate code, in contrast, it is only the specific, delimited meaning of the word that is presumed. Here, "father" simply means male of the household, and more to the point, a "contestant" in the battle to gain control over the family's resources. What this male does, just what his actions mean to him and to others in the family, must be expressed and often "established." Hence, when a person uses an elaborate code, he or she makes the context of a message explicit, and must define for listeners the grounds for each claim being made: "Johnny, will you take out the trash? I'm on the phone right now, and I think I hear the garbage truck." In a restricted code, this message might become "Johnny, get this trash out now!"

To know that a person is the father or mother of a family is relevant information, to elaborate code users, only to the extent that being a parent has to do with the immediate, specific family activity. To know that a judge is also a father or a mother ordinarily would not be regarded as pertinent information to the assessment of his or her legal qualifications or artistic abilities as a cook. Being a judge would become relevant only if we discovered that he or she holds the children in "contempt of kitchen" when they disobey requests to "do the dishes."

Bernstein found the individually oriented family to be more "mixed" than the positional. Its members seem to possess skills in both elaborate and restricted communicative codes. Members of positional families seem limited in linguistic performance to the restricted code. Tying this finding to an hypothesis about the responsibilities that working wives and mothers often have, we might speculate that in mixed forms some people are in a position to take advantage of others.

For example, Berk (1985) asked a sample of husbands and wives, chosen to represent the typical American family, who did what work in the home. She found that women, regardless of whether they were employed, still devoted more time than their husbands to housework. In fact, husbands whose wives were employed full-time did an average of only five minutes more housework daily than did husbands with unemployed wives. Berk concludes that the American household is a *gender factory* in which women are expected to do more than their fair share of the work.

When we learn of the results of studies like this, we can conclude that not all families are "modern"; and, of course, Berk did not separate families according to positional and individual types. If she had, she might well have discovered a more nearly equal division of household labor in the individual family, and she might also have found that it is in families where wives work, but only out of economic necessity, where the "gender factory" phenomenon is at its strongest.

The descriptions gathered by Bernstein and others influenced by his ideas reveal that highly individualistic styles of thinking operate within "modern" families and that these require a linguistic mode of expression specially suited to the task. Thus, just as the contextually *restricted* code both creates and sustains the family form, so does the *elaborate* code, as defined above, function for the individual one.

Tensions in the Mixed Form

There is often a tension between primary and secondary characteristics in social life. To the degree that a relationship is loving and based on trust, whenever competition or even matters of a rational nature, like financial troubles, enter the relationship, there is tension. "You know I love you, but . . . " remarks allude to this tension. Since the positional family is traditional and often primary, and the individual one is modern and rational, we should be able to draw some conclusions about how these respective forms operate and what some consequences for each might be.

First, the positional family, when not challenged by outside forces, operates smoothly, fostering a synthesis between the self of each member and the identity of the family form. Again returning to Berk's findings, in this kind of family we would expect women to do most of the household work. Second, the individual family rests on conflict in which there is a constant negotiation among the members whereby identities are continuously questioned and reaffirmed. In the individual family form, the legitimacy of any act depends on the members' recognition of mutually acceptable rational grounds for the action. This kind of interactional work leads to clever, vocal people whose forte seems to be criticism and scrutiny of fellow family members, as well as a capacity to doubt their own worth and personal identity. Again, we find a situation that might well reinforce a gender trap in the household.

Family Form and the Outside World

Social institutions and even the small social worlds of everyday life do not exist in isolation; instead, they interrelate and are in constant contact with other institutions and other small and large social worlds. In his work on family forms, Bernstein uncovered a relationship between family form and economic well-being. His research shows that positionally oriented families are most frequently found among people whose life styles, occupations and income levels are "blue collar," or working class.

The individual form, in contrast, is most often associated with middle-class segments of society. It is the form of the white-collar worker's family, of the highly educated and professional people in society. Also, people from these segments of society lead lives profoundly altered and shaped by rational or formal organizations. Typically, they are employed in bureaucratic organizations, and even their home lives are ordered by schedules of work and commitments to organizational goals and philosophies. Thus we are not surprised to see a bulletin board in the kitchen of a suburban home announcing whose turn it is to prepare dinner for the evening, who is to take out the garbage today, and who is to mow the yard next. We read also a large note proclaiming a "family meeting" for the expression of grievances, on Monday at 8:00 P.M., in the living room.

Members of the individually oriented family learn to be very specific about why an act must be performed. The five year old's persistent use of the question "Why?" in response to every statement she hears is not only tolerated but might even be answered.

Parent: I'm going to make some coffee now.
Child: Why?
Parent: Because I want some.
Child: Why?
Parent: It tastes good and I'm nothing without my morning coffee.
Child: Why?
Parent: I don't know, maybe it's just a habit or I'm addicted or something.
Child: Why do you have a habit?
Parent: I don't know—I just do.

In a positionally oriented family, a conversation in a similar vein might look like this:

Parent: I'm goin' to make some coffee.

Child: Why?

Parent: Don't ask stupid questions!

Bernstein thinks that the interaction between the first parent and child engenders a character in people better suited to the demands of living in a complex modern world. The second child learns obedience and the first learns inquisitiveness. The second child must either rebel or obey, and the first learns that there is more than one way to get what one wants. Members of a modern family learn from birth a style of thinking they will use throughout their lives, while members of positional families learn a style of thinking and interaction they must either suspend in their dealings with other, more individualized segments of social life or ignore altogether. Positional people must, in effect, be reeducated for modern life, while individually oriented people simply refine skills they already possess.

Typical Family Characters

In the last few paragraphs, we have referred to a concept widely used in the early days of sociology: social character. By character, we do not mean merely the morality of a given person. We have in mind a far more encompassing idea — that people learn to think, feel, and act, and especially interact, with a style and manner that reflects the social circumstances of their family life (cf. Gerth and Mills 1953). Now we address more directly these typical family characters.

In the 1950s, several sociologists thought they saw a significant change in the social character of people who worked for large corporations and resided in the newly emerging suburban areas of the American landscape. In such books as *The Lonely Crowd* (Riesman 1950), *White Collar* (Mills 1951) and *The Organization Man* (Whyte 1956), scholars explored and probed the degree and profundity of these changes, each focusing in a slightly different way on a new American person whose principal attribute seemed to be his conformity. From Reisman, this new social man depended exclusively on the opinions of others to guide his own behavior. He was "other-directed" and drawn toward others who were likewise directed by and toward him. Here we see the image of a new society in which people grope for standards that do not exist and mindlessly follow others who are mostly followers themselves, in an almost robotlike fashion. Mills was the most vituperative of all the critics when he characterized the modern man as soft, without inner principle, and easily manipulated. Whyte also described the thoroughgoing conformity of the organization man and his family to the standards of corporate life.

The 1960s seemed to foster a new social character, one with deep-rooted principles, reminiscent of older heroic types, who were still highly integrated into a social life. Above all else, the response of these characters to authority was rebellion. Newspapers carried story after story of bouts between students and their teachers and administrators, and about the splits between parents and children over ideological issues of war, peace, and patriotism, and, most importantly, about attitudes toward the past and future.

As sociologists and others tried to decipher whether American social character was or was not becoming more conforming and less critical, it became increasingly clear that the family was often at the heart of these debates. The research of some scholars, for example, Keniston (1968), seemed to support the idea that radical students came from radical parents who themselves had been radical as college students in the 1930s. Even if this "pink diaper" hypothesis has some validity, it does not explain the effects of the growing tension between traditionalism and individualism in society. It is that tension we wish to address, and we propose to do this by describing three typical social characters: the traditional, the rational, and the marginal.

The Traditionalists

The positionally oriented family engenders characters "traditional" in the way they organize and understand their own experiences and those of others. In their society, experience is ordered and interpreted via traits of trust, loyalty and camaraderie among insiders; at the same time, suspicion and distrust are fostered for outsiders.

Traditionalists understand new experiences primarily by fitting them into the context of preexisting ones. For them, the purpose of all behavior is the maintenance of continuity, and this is accomplished by interpreting every action as a new manifestation of an old form. A father's child, especially a son, must be prepared by the wife for interaction with the father. Thus the child is taught the etiquette of family, the family heritage, and the significance of the continuation of the family way: Like father, like son. In portions of western Wisconsin, eastern Texas, and other farmlands of America, a family will select one son to take over the farm, and this boy will be groomed to manage it and become the head of the family. He will, on reaching the proper age, accompany his father to the grain store, learn the techniques of heavy equipment operation, help decide which crops should be planted, and gradually become the "father." When he marries, he will bring a new member into the family, just as his father and his father's father did before him . Here the crucial meaning of any activity pertains to the continuity of positionally-rooted procedures, where the organizational principles of social life are constant, or at least that is the intent of the way things are.

This does not mean that innovations in farming techniques are ignored or even that a traditional character cannot deal with outside pressures for change. Of course, there are some extreme examples: The German-speaking Mennonites in Iowa follow a way of life that isolates them from the larger society (Dow 1987). Even here, however, contact with the larger world is unavoidable, as court cases force children from these families into regular schools. We realize that some groups have a remarkable continuity with their heritage, and they are helped to maintain such a linkage by the rigid structure of their family life. No doubt, in some of these extreme cases, the character of members of the "extraordinary group" is fixed.

Most traditionalists are not so completely "authoritarian." Instead, we often discover the traditionalist has already changed considerably from past ideals of family life. A man may no longer farm, having been forced off the family land because a rural bank foreclosed on his mortgage, or a woman may be divorced and working her way up in a large corporation in the city. What defines the traditionalist's character is the quality of the interpretations he or she makes about whether there is continuity in social life. So, traditionalists may act in ways that look remarkably similar to others, but their way of making sense of their actions is distinctively different. Traditionalists may search, in an almost overbearing fashion, for the continuity of social life. When they do not find it, they may use this experience for a critique of what is happening in the modern world, thus helping them support their original position rather than risk any change.

Let us illustrate this important point — that what an individual actually does can vary widely and still be subsumed under the traditional type. In his study of the men who frequented the Oasis Bar, LeMasters (1975) found that the heavy equipment operators derived a sense of satisfaction and self-sufficiency from their work. What the subjects liked about their work was the feeling that they were in control of it. One plumber reported that "unless we run into trouble we might not see him [the foreman] all day" (LeMasters 1975, 22). A crane operator told of surveying the world as he sits atop the crane and of the responsibility he carries for the men working below him. He said, "I wouldn't trade that job for anything in the world." These men also spoke of the integrity of their work, seeing concrete results in buildings they put up, brick walls they laid, and the like. To them, a white-collar job is just not an "honest day's work."

To these men, it is very important to be able to conclude that they are their own men, honest and hard working, and that they are producing something that can be used by others, something tangible or, as they say, "real." Being laid off — without work — can be a disastrous event, often leading to excessive drinking and deep depression.

We have here a depiction of men whose way of seeing their workworld is quite traditional according to the ideals of America culture. The rugged individual, the man who is his own boss. But when we look more closely, we see that these men may find themselves in a bind when it comes to their marriages. Either they may not be able to find the right woman to serve them and have their children or, having tried and failed to develop an acceptable martial relationship, they divorce in order to preserve their ideals of the "proper marriage." Said one man: "Hell, anymore a man can't find a decent woman. They are all uppity and want to wear the pants in the family; my first wife was like that. If I can't find a good woman, I'll just stay single" (LeMasters1975, 55).

Obviously, such men will be counted in divorce statistics the same as will a woman or man who divorces creatively in search of a more meaningful union with a kindred spirit. In this example, divorce, which is often seen as a measure of the breakdown of traditional ideals, may actually gloss over the real clash between traditional characters and modern ones.

For the traditional person, the relationship between who people think they are and the way they judge others depends on the imputation of positional grounds between them. More explicitly, it depends on both members imagining there exists an ideal positional relationship, one derived from the organization of the family itself and on which can be built an instance of family life. In everyday life, though, the roles man and woman, husband and wife, mother and father are synthesized into a single positional arrangement by virtue of organizational principles that underlie the relationship between the individual selves involved.

A man is father, and he has that in common with other men only if he can assume that being a father means the same thing both to him and to the other men. A woman knows what it is like to be a mother and "instinctively" can communicate with other mothers about "love of children," and "women who abandon them to day-care centers," but only if the same meanings of the position of mother are understood by all.

For the traditionalist, trust, loyalty, and friendships outside the family all are related to one's identity within the family. Whenever there is no shared position, whenever a person forsakes or otherwise threatens tradition, communication changes from the likely restrictive code to a combative form, and the traditional person strikes a defensive posture, becoming close-lipped, cold, and formal. Traditionalists know others by placing them within the context of their understanding of the scheme of things. So far as a traditionalist is concerned, who a person is becomes a matter of where a person fits.

The traditionalist's world rests comfortably amid taken-for-granted positional significance. The divorced man and woman understand one another. Through the application of a procedure, they understand that men are of a certain character and that women possess their own unique character. Furthermore, both characters are grounded, for the purposes of marriage, in tacit, mutual understandings of the traditional meanings of the positions of husband and wife, father and mother. An analysis such as this helps us describe a way of taking on identity

— a way in which identities are imitated and carried on from generation to generation.

The Rationalists

Over the past several decades, the change from a positional to an individual orientation within the family has fostered the emergence of a kind of consciousness that is distinctively modern. More and more, people the world over seem to be using this way of understanding what goes on in everyday life. One simple but powerful example is the degree to which people in modern societies believe in the efficacy of science and technology, and in general eschew passivity and fatalism in the face of life's difficulties (cf. Inkeles 1983, 302). Rationalists are clever and insightful in the pursuit of what they think is right and desirable for them as individuals.

In conflicts between what seem to be family as opposed to individual interests, the individual generally prevails; not so much because the individual wins, as in a game or contest, but the family interest simply cannot be ascertained. No one knows what it is, for the family has lost much of its vitality as a social institution in this regard. While people still have families and provide support for them, as the recent Middletown studies demonstrate, often the family is merely a "living arrangement" between institutional encounters.

The typical person in this environment relies not on the endurance of a family reality but on individual resources that, perhaps ironically, have been developed within the family. Thus it appears that the better the individually oriented family operates, the more successfully it inculcates the rational pursuit of self-interest, the less likely is its own survival. The offspring of such a family acquire a character and a typical consciousness that are simply not conducive to marriage, or at least not to long-term familial commitments of the traditional variety. Mary put it this way:

> I am 33, I'm living with a guy now; but I still keep my apartment; gives me a sense of security. I go back a few nights every week or so to sort of get my head together. I don't think I'll marry. My parents always told me that the most important thing was for me to be happy. Well, I'm happy living thousands of miles from them and not being like them. Oh, I've mellowed over the years. We don't fight much, but I still have things to do. I enjoy my independence, I just can't see children and an old man I'm tied to anywhere in my future.

When a person adopts a rationalist stance, this means that all the facilities of that person — intellectual, emotional, and physical — become tools for the achievement of individually conceived goals. Mary's goals are independence and happiness. For her, this means freedom to work at a job she enjoys, to be with people who make her feel good, and most important, to feel that she exercises some control over her own destiny. The rationalist's mind, then, rests on assumptions that a sharp distinction between self and others may be drawn and that the self is the seat of potential control.

To the rationalist, a person's self is the energy source; the nonself, (i.e., the world outside individual consciousness) consists of items (things and people) that have some "use value" for the self. Other individuals and certain material things can be employed by the self for the purposes of gaining satisfaction. Regarding other individuals, there can be no reasonable grounds for the continuation of a relationship that is not mutually satisfying. Such action would be "irrational."

The child who grows up in an individually oriented family learns to expect that every act he or she performs, every relationship he or she has, should be coupled with a *reason*, which in turn should be linked to some gratification. Consider the seven-year-old boy who not only freely and openly inquires of the reasons why he cannot swim in the hot Rocky Mountain sun all afternoon, but even is inclined to disagree with his parents' reason — that he will become sick if he swims for that length of time. For him, the matter is one of doing something he enjoys. Having never experienced sun sickness or not knowing the causal link between the activity of swimming and overexposure to the sun, he understands only one option, that of continuing to swim. The parent sees this confrontation between allowing enjoyment and protection from illness as an opportunity for a lesson. The child may be taught about the "harmful effects of the rays of the sun."

Father: Too much sun, especially at this altitude, can be harmful.
Son: Why, I like to swim here?
Father: It's like an x-ray — the right amount can serve a good purpose, but too much can injure us.
Son: What d'you mean?
Father: Well, it's like eating too much cake. You enjoy it, but later your stomach hurts.
Son: That never happens to me!
Father: It will if you overdo it — I think you should get out of the pool *now*.
Son: OK. But I still don't think I'll be sick.

As you can see in this dialogue, when the appeal to rationality fails, the parent resorts to a positionally based control of the child. But in such a circumstance, the parent usually regards it as temporarily necessary. As soon as the child grows and learns of the truth of these facts of the environment, he or she will then behave appropriately, limiting exposure to bright sunlight. Such occurrences and attitudes enacted daily, thousands of times over decades of parent–child interactions, creates people whose profile we now present.

The rationalist is *instrumental* in outlook, *manipulative* in style, and *hedonistic* in purpose. "Instrumental in outlook" refers to consequences of self-other distinctions that the person makes. When one has no firm commitments to others, the world becomes merely material for one's own use. The materials, in turn, become valuable only as they relate to some goal. Such materials are put to use toward the achievement of a goal as if they were instruments. A "friend" is worthy of time and effort because one can expect that for every personal effort made in the friend's behalf, something in return can be expected. A person becomes known as a friend because he or she has instrumental value toward the acquisition of a goal. For example, Fred has a friend at Flatrock Oil who buys cases of motor oil for him using his employee's discount. Fred, in turn, can get his friend a discount on tools because he has access to wholesale goods as a purchaser for the Clubs Hardware chain. Each man means something to the other in terms of what they can do for one another, not as members of a community or even from shared identities.

When we say the rationalist is manipulative, we have in mind the style and means through which a person interacts with others. If, in order to get a good grade or avoid the rage of a parent, it is necessary to change character, then such action is not only desirable but even totally appropriate. Hence a student repeatedly volunteers to answer questions in a class concerning a subject he or she dislikes. Or a child learns to feign politeness while visiting the family with the cabin and the speedboat on Lake Tanookee. What clues us to the manipulative nature of these behaviors is that they are unauthentic; they are consistent only in that they serve the perceived ends of the person. Our polite child, at home without the prospect of water skiing at Lake Tanookee, suddenly becomes obtrusive and rude, insulting and challenging to his parents in efforts to procure more play time, special favors, or some other activities not desired by other family members. In effect, the nature of the person's character changes, that is, character seems suited to situation. But this does not mean that no central organizing procedure exists. Instead, that procedure may be described succinctly in this maxim: One may change one's own appearance, and whatever else one has control over, for the purpose of achieving a self-relevant end. This is the essence of manipulation (cf. Lyman and Scott 1970).

Finally, by hedonistic, we mean the ultimate legitimation of any action: It must bring gratification to the actor. This version of hedonism must not be confused with selfishness. Selfishness is generally understood to concern one's own interests so much that the welfare of others is neglected. This rendition of hedonism is a principle, holding that nothing better serves the general interests of all than the recognition that really no one can be happy without unfettered opportunity to pursue individually determined goals.

The Marginalists, or Most Everybody Else

Decades ago, a famous sociologist from the University of Chicago, Everett Hughes, encouraged one of his students to study a predicament that is unique to people who find themselves living in societies in which they are not fully native. This predicament is one in which a person is caught between social allegiances to two or more conflicting cultures. To Hughes, it seemed particularly suitable to describe the situation of persons whose parents were of the Old World (European society) and who carry in their appearance and speech marks of this ancestry, while living in the New World of American culture. Hughes and his student, Edward Stonequist (1937), studied Italians who were children of immigrant parents but who themselves were born in Chicago as American citizens.

These people found themselves caught between two cultures. On the one hand, they owed loyalty to their parents' way of life and language; on the other, they wished to be fully accepted as members of the American society. If they ignored their parents' heritage, they ran afoul of their parents and their friends. If they preserved old cultural practices and traits in their behavior, they knew that peers at school and at work would reject them. These people were referred to as *marginal* because, from a social standpoint, they lived on the margin between two social worlds.

This idea has applications to the family life of many members of modern America. The transformation of the family from positional to individual has not been thorough or complete. Many people have family life experiences that are mixed in the sense that the parents may try to operate a positional family while the children are individually oriented. Likewise, a family may be positional, but the school system that educates its children may foster a rational or modern viewpoint. To the degree that positional and individual, traditional and rational, are in conflict and to the degree that people feel caught between these different modes of family life, we can say that their family life is, in fact, marginal.

Individuals can adapt to marginality in several ways. First, they can fully assimilate into the new form, which in many cases means, on attaining adulthood, breaking ties with one's family or using a variety of ways to keep some distance between one's private life and one's family. Second, a person may elect to remain traditional in the face of change. Such a person must choose a marriage partner selectively and constantly guard against the intrusion of modern social forces. Some families do this by banding together with likeminded families in small communities that they carefully isolate from contact with the larger society. This is what the Amish do. Others do this symbolically by imposing strict limits on television viewing and carefully supervising the movies their children see and the friends they have. In short, they attempt to retreat into a social world representing traditional family values.

Or, finally, they may seek ways to integrate the past and the present in their families. So, parents may settle for moderately outrageous clothing on their teenage daughter in return for her regular church attendance. Perhaps the most famous efforts at this adaptation are those of the Osmond family, members of the the Church of Jesus Christ of Latter Day Saints (Mormons) who rode waves of popularity to wealth and fame. Donny and Marie used the appearance of modernity (sex appeal, suggestive music, and the like), yet they voiced a "traditionalist" perspective on family life. They saw no conflict or contradiction in their stance. Instead, they claimed the modern styles suited or served their ends.

As sociologists, we cannot judge whether integration is complete or if the synthesis of old and new actually takes place. We do observe that the people involved in this mixed adaptation act as if there were no contradictions. The Osmond brothers and Marie may find the going rough as each struggles with opposing forces in their lives, but the outcome of their struggle, and those of many others like them, may be the emergence of a new form, for example, the modern Latter Day Saint.

Sociologists have observed that the phenomenon of marginality best captures the experiences of people who live in heterogeneous societies that are changing rapidly. Chicago was clearly this in the first half of this century. Immigrants poured into the city, often from quite different cultural backgrounds. Not surprisingly, the children of these immigrants experienced marginality and had to develop coping procedures for it.

Today, the United States has a much different composition to its population. In large cities, the ethnic identity of neighborhoods changes rapidly and is expressed in subtle ways. In fact, from our perspective, the ethnic and national foundations for family have been superseded by a larger trend. The trend found operating over the flavor and history of local background and without regard for ethnicity is that of the change from positional to individual orientation. Because such change is the common denominator, the family of a successful man of Italian ancestry bears the same characteristics of individually appropriate gratification as does that of the successful black couple. We do not intend to minimize the differences still existing across ethnic and racial boundaries, but we feel it may be even more critical to focus on procedures, for it is at the level of procedure that important similarities are found.

Nevertheless, the transformation of the family into a modern form is not complete, and it may never be, nor has it been evenly distributed throughout society. Ethnic heritage, religious background, and the conservatism of social life still exert influence over the development of individual consciousness. Thus any actual family, depending on the socialization experiences of the parents, many exhibit a mixed form. The procedure for action taught and followed may derive from both positional and individual mentalities. For example, a father may be willing to "explain" certain grounds for discipline and not others; or a mother may generally follow a rationalist's approach to controlling the behavior of her children by "out-talking" them, but at times revert to a positionally oriented approach (e.g., spanking).

In families of mixed social forms and institutionalized functions, marginal conditions very similar to those depicted by Hughes and Stonequist may exist. The child in a mixed family form, for instance, must cope with opposite meanings for actions. The child may mistakenly believe that an act such as questioning authority is encouraged, only to discover that he is rebuked when he tries to do this, or even punished when questioning in certain areas such as family finances. At one time, the parents encourage and are patient with the child's inquiries; at another, they abruptly cut off this line of conversation (cf. Dreitzel 1972,15–17).

With regard to family forms, it is as if we were talking about two warring cultures and the fate of one individual who must deal with both at the same time. Viewed from the vantage of the individual, marginality seems an apt concept. The cultural discontinuities of early generations of Americans have been replaced with culturewide discontinuity and conflict between two very general devices for deciding the meanings of social existence. Marginality is the condition that most clearly captures the predicament of most people for whom the transition has been and continues to be incomplete.

What, then, is the character of the marginalist? Probably the essence of marginality is self-doubt and self-scrutiny. The marginalist, indeed, knows confusion and expresses a great deal of ambivalence toward even the most routine of everyday problems. He or she may equivocate for months over whether to purchase a new car or to save the money and be in need of a new car. The marginalist muses, "What about the symbolism of a new car — its implied support for the coalescence between big government and big business, and what about the effect the car has had on patterns of city growth, dispersing families to the suburbs, breaking up old neighborhood solidarity and giving new freedoms to young people, freedom to 'make out' in the back seat of a car? . . . But, on the other hand, how about the standard of living we all enjoy! That is something in which the auto industry has played a major role. And how about supporting the American worker. But, wait, pollution, what happened to that issue . . . ?

The marginal person invariably turns this equivocation inward. It is the self that lacks clear guidelines, that cannot integrate opposing forces into a course of action. The marginal person is motivated by what seems to be perpetual introspection, shifting in activities from the instrumental outlook of the rationalist to the self-preservation posture of the traditionalist. He or she is often torn between loyalty to a family form and exercising self-serving calculation. Perhaps nowhere is this predicament more clearly embodied than in the "new woman" who believes she can have "it all."

I want to marry and I want to have children, but I just can't see myself as the housewife type. Sure, I want a good job, a real career, and I want a husband who understands all this — who'll give me room to grow and be myself and I want a man who is loving and good with children. Yes, I guess that's what I expect of family life.

Summary

This chapter introduced one of the perennial questions in sociological analysis: What is the fate of the family in modern society? We discovered that there is considerable disagreement among experts. Some suggested that the family has changed so radically that it is just a vestige of its viable traditional form. Others felt that the institution of the family is remarkably stable and adaptable.

We suggested that one way to understand the sociological issues underlying the "war over the family" is to focus on the principles of social organization that underlie the meanings of family life. Following the work of Basil Bernstein, we identified two distinctive organizational forms: the positional and the individual.

In its ideal type, each form rests on and uses a style of communication that, in turn, serves as the basis for interaction within that form. Positional families operate from the restricted code; in individually oriented forms, members selectively shift from restricted to elaborate depending on the circumstances. The elaborate code, however, works as the carrier of the primary meanings of family life.

The two ideal types of positional and individual usually exist in tandem incompleteness in society. Hence most people experience, in varying degrees, what we referred to as "marginality" with regard to the modes and meanings of family life. Marginality is essentially a matter of being caught between two "warring forms."

While each form fosters a type of character for its members, traditionalist and rational for the positional and individual respectively, the mixing of forms that occurs in societies undergoing change creates in families interactive settings in which people become manipulative and aware of self-interests. Hence people whose family experiences do not match their ideals of what family life should be must adapt. Some of the ways people cope with marginality were depicted, and we stressed that the actual biographical experiences of people need not be consistent with the ways they interpret family life.

The family is clearly a strong and vital part of the organization of modern society. Like all institutions, however, it reflects changes taking place in society, and the ways people make sense out of their own experiences and the ideals of form and character will shape the quality of future family life.

Chapter 4

EDUCATION IN MODERN SOCIETY: A CONFLICT OF GOALS AND MEANS

Every society inculcates its young with traditions and teaches them the knowledge and skills required by adult roles. Eskimo boys must be taught how to fish and locate seal breathing holes in the ice; girls learn to make clothes and soften sealskin for boots by chewing it. A Mexican peasant youth learns to prepare the soil, plant crops, and bring in the harvest. In the United States, young people learn to drive automobiles, operate computers, and develop the skills for one or another occupational role.

In any society, the distinction between socialization (early learning that begins at infancy) and education is difficult to make, as all learning takes place within primary groups, usually the family—whether it is learning to speak one's native language or to build a house and earn a livelihood. But in modern society, what one must know to enact the culture is only partially learned in primary groups; thus the educational function of the family has been steadily reduced, while formal schooling has grown to encompass much of our lives. Preschools, grade schools, colleges, military schools, technical-vocational schools, continuing education and corporate training programs—all of these and more transmit knowledge and skills. So much has this trend altered the locus of responsibility for the transmission of culture that one scholar calls ours the "schooled society" (Illich 1971).

In a traditional society, where primary groups are responsible for education, one person recognizes others with special knowledge and skill by acquaintance. Indeed, each member of such a society is presumed to possess certain traditional skills. House building is something all might learn through apprenticeship and participation; and there are people with special knowledge, such as that used in curing the sick, but even their reputations are based on personal acquaintance.

In our society, judging what others know can be problematic. As education has shifted to secondary groups and institutions, there have been changes in the criteria by which we judge the acquisition of knowledge and skills. Judgments are now made on the basis of formal credentials rather than personal acquaintance. Because we cannot possibly know all the people we deal with in a personal sense, we must have some ways to recognize skills and those who possess them. So, we equate skills and knowledge with the possession of a formal credential, and, indeed, the credentialing process has become a necessary prerequisite in all societies where secondary forms predominate (Collins1979).

Now while the credentialing process in modern society is far from perfect, it is effective enough so that we can feel confident that a person with a credential has acquired specialized knowledge and does have a reputation that is authentic. Our focus in this chapter, then, is on formal education in modern society. And since we expect our readers to be college and university students, we look primarily at "higher" education, keeping in mind that what we say can be applied at other levels. Technically, we examine education from three perspectives. First, we explore its foundations as a social institution, and in doing so, describe stocks of taken-for-granted knowledge. Second, we view education as a social form, and this requires that we look carefully at how educational organizations operate. Finally, we discuss the manner in which the institution and its form influence how individuals interpret their own experience with it.

Education as a Social Institution

Every social institution provides ready-made interpretations for specific activities, and we can view the interpretive meanings of educational activities through the five assumptions on which they rest: (1) the need for a the teacher; (2) the instrumentality, or usefulness, of education; (3) the "civilizing" effects of education, that it leads people to behave in socially approved ways; (4) the "moralizing" effect, that education instills higher-order values in people; and (5) the measurability of the results of educational experiences. The interpretations people make of education are grounded in the content they give these assumptions, and we consider some of the possible interpretations here.

The Teacher Assumption. This assumption holds that in order to impart skills or knowledge, one person must assume the role of teacher and the other of student. This means persons are defined in such a way that for certain purposes one is regarded as superior to the other. One is competent, the other incompetent; one informed, the other naive. An implication of this assumption is that mere exposure to information is insufficient for learning. Therefore the teacher not only must possess skills and knowledge about a subject but must know how to teach. Teaching is a defining characteristic of the educational institution. Teachers do certain things: They stand in front of a class; they initiate talk, they elicit questions; they have opinions about students that they need not, and often should not, express except in a standardized procedure of measurement, such as grades.

Although we cannot describe all the substantive contents that may be associated with the role of the teacher (see Cazden et al. 1972; Cicourel et al. 1974), essentially the teacher-student relationship is a superordinate–subordinate one. In any interaction between a student and a teacher (regardless of any other meanings affixed to the relationship), there is a dimension of asymmetry in the influence of one over the other. This is so because no other relationship is possible, given the institutional character of education, for that reality defines the essence of all relationships that come within its scope.

There is, however, some latitude in this institutional meaning. Besides evaluating classroom learning, a teacher may give credit to learning through living. Several colleges during the 1970s and 80s lured students to their doors through the promise of teacherless education. These programs award classroom credits for equivalent experience, for example, course credit in accounting for having worked as an accountant for ten years. Some teachers minimize the asymmetry by becoming "nice," "the human being" on campus. They attempt to equalize the student-teacher relationships with such requests as "call me by my first name." Their homes may be open to students to drop by and chat. They are willing to serve as a confidant, one who will work *with* rather than *against* students.

Nevertheless, schools still belong to teachers. The "nice teacher" is still a teacher, one who holds the knowledge and makes judgments about its use and application. Even in the ungraded classroom (the pass/fail curriculum), little confusion results from an effort to ascertain who is teacher and who is student. The distinction is time honored, and the "battles" that often rage between students and teachers in public schools in large American cities often stem from students failing to accept this distinction as legitimate. These are schools where teachers may be assaulted and where strong controls are instituted to prevent assaults. Of course, one can easily make the case that these schools are not really places of education, and that may well be. We can see what they are more clearly after we place the functions of education into the broadest social context possible.

In higher educational institutions, distinctions may often be blurred by the "self presentations" of professors who dress in the blue-collar style their generation helped to establish. Honorific titles such as professor and doctor can be dropped, students can dress in business suits and teachers in blue jeans, but the essential nature of the relationship remains unchanged. The position or status of teacher is a necessary component of education as a social institution. The teacher is perceived by all involved as the source of information for the learning process and as a channel for control over the student.

The Instrumental (Means-Ends) Assumption. This assumption holds that the materials taught must be have some practical application. Under this assumption, both teacher and student regard the experience as useful. Imparting information, in modern American institutions, is rarely accounted for on exclusively intrinsic grounds. It is difficult to maintain an entire social organization such as an educational institution by justifying its existence solely in terms of "learning for its own sake." Some colleges have survived as "Great Idea" schools (where curriculum is built on the ideas of recognized classics of Western civilization), but even these schools market the outcome of their process as "useful and worthwhile" in some practical sense.

Education within societally appropriate forms is thus justified as a means to an end, and educational institutions may be defined and legitimated according to a wider, societal value of instrumentality. Recently, we have read reports from high officials in government that expose the failures of public schools to prepare students for the challenges of life in the modern world (cf. Bennett 1988). Schools are responding by "returning" to basics in the belief that "essentials like mathematics and reading" will ultimately be useful to society. Institutions of higher learning, in contrast, continue to graduate rather unemployable art, philosophy, and sociology majors on the grounds that, in the future, such graduates may discover new ways to apply what they know.

Higher education, in particular, casts itself in the role of provider for society. Thus a university has value if it supplies engineers for the space program, mathematics teachers for elementary schools, and social workers and clerks for governmental bureaucracies. Specific goals may change; for instance, the space program may be phased out, but the means for achieving overall societal goals remains.

Education as a way of accomplishing society's goals is characterized by both openness and closedness. It is open because its offerings, teachers, scheduling, and naming of what is taught can be reorganized to fit the demands from other institutions of society. For example, chemistry, biology, sociology, and psychology departments jointly support the establishment of a prenursing program in most liberal arts colleges without adding any new personnel or significantly altering curricula. Many campuses have used this model to accommodate student and faculty demands for "minority" programs, such as black, Hispanic, and gender studies. Conversely, education is closed in that its presumptive grounds remain constant. It is a primary source for specifically useful knowledge, and it remains so over time.

Education as an Agent of Social Control. The third assumption of education as institutional knowledge, that there is a need to change behavior, has become a hallmark of many organizations, particularly K–12 schools. In American society, parents expect the school to "shape up" their children, or continue to mold them in ways set up in family life. This behavior modification function of education permits parents a more relaxed, indulgent approach to child rearing. At age five or six, the "spoiled" child must face up to the rigors of a school, and this may represent for many children their first encounter with direct attempts to mold their behavior.

Often there is a dramatic alteration in the styles of control from home to school. In the home, most children have space within which they can play. Some parents rearrange entire households, putting away breakables, blocking off stairwells, and the like, so that their infant or toddler may roam uninhibited and relatively safe. In other homes, the play area may be much more restricted, such as a 4' by 4' area of a discount-store playpen. There are, naturally, great variations in the styles of supervision exercised by parents or caretakers over their young charges (see Bernstein 1970, 41–46). Regardless of this rich variation, most tactics have one aim: to minimize the necessity for adult intervention. When a child is playing safely in a secure environment, parents need not become involved in the play, and can do other things if they so desire.

The school, in contrast, approaches the distribution of play space and the role the child plays in that space very differently. Beginning with the first exposure to school, the aim is to construct an environment that allows the adult (teacher) opportunity to intervene in the child's activities. Authoritarian styles, which some teachers assume, attempt to control virtually all the behaviors of the children. Other teachers adopt styles that allow children free play in an environment planned to be consistent with the idea the teacher has about what constitutes an "educational setting." The authoritarian style may be marked by forced activities, carefully timed: five minutes for blocks, five for sandbox, and so on. The *laissez-faire* approach may entail a "children do what you want" attitude where the things the child can do are "structured" by what is in the room. Creative play toys, reading-readiness color books, exercise climbing toys designed by Ph.D. physiologists, and play therapies to maximize motor development surround the children.

Whether authoritarian or *laissez faire*, the idea that adults must intervene in the activities of children in order to stimulate and influence appropriate growth is a bedrock feature of the organization of the school. Teachers are supposed to possess specialized knowledge telling them how to shape the behavior of children. Some schools demand a submissive, obedient and politely inquisitive attitude from students: others, such as "free schools," encourage or tolerate rambunctious, creative children. While "countercultural schools" still exist in the United States and some European nations, they have been severely criticized because they do not support basic learning practices, which, critics claim, depend on "discipline." Even in these extremes, however, maximum adult influence has replaced the parental ideal of minimum interference. Such "interference" on behalf of the vested interest of the adult version of society is a taken-for-granted feature of any approach to education. It is the disagreement over *what* the vested interests are and not the notion of "interference" itself that generates diversified educational styles . (Even in communes, adult versions of interests dominate children's views. See Zicklin 1973.) .

Higher-Order Values. The fourth feature of education often produces conflict with the others, for it maintains that education functions to fulfill the entire individual. Education, according to this assumption, must first discover the innate, biologically endowed potentials of each child and then develop these potentials to their fullest extent. In short, education is supposed to allow each individual to "self-actualize."

Acting on the basis of this assumption may result in conflict between individuals and segments of the organization of education. As an individual, a person may do well with general learning and be justly rewarded for it, but when study becomes specialized and instrumental, he or she falters. Since the other features of institutionalized education demand specialization and instrumentality, the individual who pursues knowledge just to become a well-rounded person will eventually conflict with organizational tendencies in education.

Self-actualization and *instrumentality*, as meanings of education, refer to different aspects of the institution. Since the first is an individual-level phenomenon and the second societal, if one acts exclusively on "actualization," conflict with the other meanings is inevitable. This conflict between structure and psychology, however, rarely surfaces at the institutional level. What happens, instead, is that the individual begins to define self-actualization in terms of the other features of the institution. We should expect this in any organization that is reflexively built, that is, that creates its own environment. An inventor is "self-actualized" by becoming a technical expert in some field like electronics, an armchair philosopher becomes a generalist and prepares others for specialization by becoming an elementary school teacher or even a sociology professor. Nevertheless, that "self-actualization," or finding oneself, is a feature of the educational institution seems beyond dispute.

Basic, traditional understandings of what a liberal arts education is often stem from some version of self-actualization. For centuries, the maxim "Know thyself" has been a rationale for the time, money, and energy spent on higher learning. But, the style of self-actualization has changed with the decades and waxed and waned with societal changes. Although many students still believe in the importance of developing a "philosophy of life" during their college years, recently the proportion who regard this as the most important reason for college has declined significantly (Katchadourian and Boli 1985, 14), this trend being significant in terms of the tensions generated by contradictions in the institutional meanings of education. .

For almost two decades, self-actualization, as a kind of intellectualism, sought to establish itself as a permanent organizational feature of American higher education. The tensions that resulted were so intense that self-actualizers often simply dropped out. The student's search for a philosophy of life often contrasts with the faculty's emphasis on other institutional features, like specialized knowledge. From Thorstein Veblen (1918) to C. Wright Mills (1951) to Michael

Useem (1989), critics have pointed out that the American university is like a large corporation. It can accommodate the pursuit of self-actualization as long as this pursuit occurs within proper limits and does not seriously threaten the chief purpose of the institution, what we have called shaping behavior.

Thus, a total pursuit of self-actualization may lead to "walking out on the university." Still, since we are discussing the institution, its features and the stresses among them, we must acknowledge that the feature of self-actualization does exist and, depending on application and interpretation, could become either a source for conflict or one for change.

The Measured Progress Assumption. The final assumption of education as an institution is that what is accomplished there can and must be measured. For the elementary school age child in a Montessori program, this measurement may be informal, taking place in "conferences" between teacher and parent where the teacher tells of the child's progress or lack of it. In more conventional settings, the formal report card is the index, par excellence, of measured progression.

For teachers, performance may be measured in committee work, their students' opinion of them, or the way they distribute grades. At the college level, a professor may spend hours out of every day working on publishing research or scholarly articles, which are symbols of measured progress. Education assumes all participants are moving in a forward direction, expanding, growing, and becoming more educated with each passing event. Further, it is assumed, even though the difficulties of this task may be readily admitted, that the movement can be measured. Indeed, standards for the assessment of this movement are, perhaps, the most crucial aspect to understanding the character of any particular educational organization. Tremendous amounts of time and energy devoted to the establishment, evaluation, and reevaluation of standards characterize the educational institution, at least in Western society.

In other societies, where educational organizations often function to provide continuity to the norms and structures of the society, the activities of educators are judged very differently. The master teacher is a person who embodies the traditional wisdom of society and transmits this wisdom to the young. Schools in traditional, or *gemeinschaft*, societies are often only for the elite, however, and do not promise to set the stage for progress. Indeed, as Table 4.1 indicates, there are dramatic differences in literacy rates around the world, and generally whenever a society begins to modernize, it establishes public or mass education. The fact that we use literacy rates as a criterion illustrates the power of the assumption of measured progress.

Not only does accountability seem important when we consider the educational reality of society, but its flavor can be discovered in every activity it generates. A small child's first report card may not be marked by As, Bs, and Cs, but it surely will have such categories of evaluation as "works well with others," "shows progress," and "needs improvement."

Table 4.1
World Literacy Rates by Selected Nations

Nation	Percentage Literate
Australia	98.5
Bangladesh	29
Chad	20
Chile	90
Germany (West)	99
El Salvador	65
Korea (South)	90
Kuwait	71
Libya	50–60
Mexico	88.1
Mozambique	14
Paraguay	81
Poland	98
United Kingdom	99
United States	99
Zaire	55 male, 37 female

Note: The CIA uses a liberal formula to determine literacy. Basically, it means that a person can read simple instructions in the nation's official language. Of course, if one defines literacy more precisely, these rates change. You should be aware that much has been written lately about literacy and its meanings. Generally, as reading becomes more important in society, we see higher standards for defining literacy. Therefore, some recent critics of literacy in America use the term "functional illiterate" to refer to people whose skills do not allow them fully to participate in the information age. Of course, rates of functional illiteracy are much higher than the above table indicates. See Pattison 1982.

Source: Central Intelligence Agency, The World Fact Book, (Washington. D.C.: GPO, 1986.)

Everybody wants to know if the activities of educational institutions do anything, even if what they do is not what educators say they do. Learning, then, as we have seen, must be toward some end, and that end must be a condition or state quantifiably better than the one from which the movement took place.

A sixth grader is better educated than a fourth grader; a high school graduate has progressed further than a dropout; a graduate degree is higher than a B.A. Thus we are describing not just the idea of accountability but also the ideas of progress and hierarchy. The public school system supposedly improves the children who come under its treatment. The university builds on the raw materials it receives from secondary schools. The graduate and professional schools hone emerging talents into specialized skills and performance.

Now we know very little about how educational learning actually takes place, but what we do know is not exactly what one might expect given these assumptions. For example, we know that children who deviate from the norms and expectations teachers have about how normal learning takes place often are classified in ways that influence their entire careers in schools. Rosenthal and Jacobson (1968) showed that the expectations teachers have toward a child, such as whether they regard the child as bright or not, determines even performances on IQ tests. And, Cicourel et al. (1974), studying the precise ways that teachers get lessons done in a classroom, discovered that getting the "right" answer depends on much more than knowing the material. Teachers, it seems, expect students to organize their responses in the "completely correct" form. So, if an elementary school child answers the question "Where is the triangle?" with "Over there" or "It's there," the teacher will regard this "correct" answer as "wrong," until the student learns to organize the response as expected. In this case, according the researchers, the teacher is looking for an answer with the form "The triangle is under the line." It is interesting that teachers seem to be more satisfied with "wrong, but properly organized responses" than they are with answers that are "right, but improperly organized."

Paradoxically, a higher quality of life through better education can be proven "better" only by unambiguous criteria. An A grade on a test not only means that the student receiving the acclaim knows more and expresses it better than the student getting a B, but that the difference is recognizable to all who may be involved in the evaluation.

An application for a job by a graduating senior is accompanied by a transcript that represents the work of teachers who have performed the evaluation, having given grades and written letters of recommendation. These teachers must have taken each other into account in the evaluation process. An A student, a B student, a C student—these labels have meaning to the teachers who made the evaluations, and to the prospective employer, only to the degree that they can be regarded as valid applications of institutionalized knowledge.

Hierarchies of knowledge exist, it is assumed, and these hierarchies are correlated with hard work or a special aptitude, or a combination of both; furthermore, differences between the hierarchical levels are recognizable to all who deal with them; and, finally, such recognition may be communicated in a style true to the intent and purpose of the evaluation. But evaluations are made on subjective grounds, namely assumptions, and a general capacity to take on the attitude of the other. So although the results of evaluations of others are presented as if they were "correct," the "objective" meanings of a grade, they actually derive from institutional assumptions.

As we have seen, the idea of measurement stems, in essence, from the notions of accountability and progress. In the first case, the necessity to show that abstract, even tangible states exist and have consequences in everyday life is the paramount concern of the institutional use of knowledge. In the second, the vital interest is to transform the mundane tasks of control, specialization, and behavior into value states capable of operating as grounds for interpreting social interaction.

A child's work after school in lieu of play, a consistent bedtime on the grounds that children need rest to do well in school, a lifetime of dedication to being a research scientist - - all become "usual" sacrifices when interpreted institutionally. This final feature of institutionalized education, to measure progress, functions to legitimate the demands of organizations charged with carrying out the tasks of educating.

The Social Forms of Education

Distinctive forms of social organization are built on distinctive sets of assumptions. The form of education we allude to in the above discussion is education as bureaucracy. Some critics, for example Illich and Collins, point out that education has not been and need not be grounded on the assumptions we outlined. They call for change. Illich proposed a "de-schooled society," and Collins shows how emphasis on credentialling should probably be curtailed. Our first goal is description, however, and to that end we must deal with how different applications of knowledge gel into forms of organization.

From the first assumption, that teachers are necessary, the asymmetrical form of teacher-student emerges. No activity without such form is readily interpretable as educational. The once popular television show "Welcome Back Kotter" in one episode portrayed a classroom scene in which the teacher and students merged into a single activity. The teacher spoke in the Brooklynese of the students while cajoling them to enact their ideas of what the "Founding Fathers of America" thought about freedom. Of course, right in the middle of a speech by one of the "sweat hogs," the principal walked into the room and could not immediately identify the teacher, or if what was happening was really "educational." Kotter, the teacher, then spends a good deal of time explaining how his unorthodox approaches are appropriate owing to the attitudes and backgrounds of his students. Kotter attempts to show that what he does is "really" a subtle form of the teacher-student relationship and one that is necessary as an adaptation of the normal form, not a radical alteration of it.

Perhaps, the most dramatic illustration of how this assumption generates forms are those situations in which young teachers first begin teaching. Physically, some of the young teachers "look like" the students. Although this is the case, there are often strict rules that the school lays down for the dress and conduct of a teacher. Women, for example, must wear skirts, heels and hose, and insist that students address them in formal terms: Miss, Mrs., or perhaps Ms. One young teacher we know told us that she was severely reprimanded when her principal learned that she allowed students to address her as "Sally" (her first name) after school hours. The principal backed up her reprimand with reasons:

> These kids will take advantage of every inch you give to them. Oh, they're good kids, most of them. But they are always looking for a way to "lighten their load." If they ingratiate themselves with you in any way, they use it. So for your own protection, keep that distance between you and the kids. It'll pay in the long run.

The assumptions of specialized knowledge, instrumental behavior and measured progress all tend to produce a social form that is distinctively secondary in nature. In an educational form such as this, it is the person with knowledge and, finally, the position of authority, in whom power resides. As knowledge becomes more useful and more technological, its transmission requires two conditions (1) the centralization of the resources of the knowledge, and (2) the organization of the knowledge into "teachable" units.

Hence universities operate as elaborate warehouses and distributors of knowledge (Mills 1951, 133). Their very existence requires that the stocks of goods they dispense be administered, that someone or something be responsible for the overall impact the form can have. The administrator symbolizes the transformation of teachers from "personable sage with a retinue" to "experts with a precisely delimited field of knowledge." In the administrator, we see the rationalization of the teacher. His or her expertise is the management of other specialists and the maintenance of the "house in which they live." It is the administrator who must ensure that the assumptions we have outlined actually become an organization of education. In them, their consciousness and action, we see the reality of education as it has been constructed in our society.

A dean of a major university once remarked to us that, to him, a good faculty member is a person about whom he hears only "good things." When asked what he thought was an example of "good things," he replied, "That the teacher meets his class, arrives punctually, speaks primarily to the topic of his class in an overall language that allows for the fair discrimination between students who learn and do not learn the subject matter." Another administrator, speaking to the same issue, said, "The absence of complaints is by far the most reliable indicator that a man or woman is doing his or her job."

The Authoritative Form

We can describe more precisely the forms educational institutions assume. One such form couples properties of bureaucracy with the elitism of the expert. The resulting form we call *authoritative*, and there are many variants of it. Some administrators seem less inclined to "play by the rules," and some often utilize the advice of nonadministrators, but all rely on the secondary form, its rationality, expert knowledge, and elitism

Great individual variety exists within any given organizational form. But when we understand the institutional foundations of the form, we see how specialized knowledge and instrumentality lead to an organization of behavior that is authoritative, that is, individual consciousness is subjugated to form. In order to become a physicist one must think like one, and to think like one, one must, to a certain extent, act like one—work in laboratories, read books and journals, enter discussions with other physicists and the like. Thus, if a student constructs a "theory of molecular structure" in disagreement with the teacher's, the teacher has the organizational power to say to the student, "You are wrong." A student who continually challenges the physics teacher will probably be well advised to change his or her major. What ultimately counts in the authoritative form is the form itself. The organization of knowledge about natural phenomena is a resource for formulating a student's response to questions as either right or wrong.

The Libertarian Form

The pursuit of self-actualization results in forms that are much different from the authoritative. Here, since each self has unique potential, the communication between student and teacher defines the qualities of their relationship. An elementary school teacher may want to discover what a child's interests are, for example, whether he or she loves to ski, in order to get the child to act appropriately. Or she may simply be interested in the child's thoughts as intimate voices of the self. She may reward good mathematics work (the completion of problems in a workbook) with ski tickets that, when accumulated, result in expanded choices for the child during "free time" play activities, or just more play time; or she may simply discuss skiing and skiing trips with the child. In the first case, we illustrate the authoritative form, in the second the libertarian (cf. Dixon 1972).

The libertarian form serves the institutionalized assumption of self-actualization by providing an environment conducive to self exploration and expression. It does this by removing the standards of education designed to assess progress and in their place substituting a primary-like form in which tacitness once again plays an important role. Professors in small colleges who promote this brotherly and sisterly environment in the classroom and outside between themselves and the people they teach are sometimes referred to as "touchie-feelie profs." While "touchie-feelie" professors have been under siege in recent times because they allegedly have lax standards, they still serve a function on many campuses. They often have the reputation of being "sincere," but an easy grade and worth taking only one class from, usually a "sluff" class that one can take together with tougher and more demanding classes.

The libertarian form is easily identifiable. It is family-like in its organization, and class members often develop close and perhaps even lasting relationships. Students simply sit and listen to their professor. They do not take notes. They converse with him or her, rather than ask questions. One asks questions in the classroom to get information needed for testing purposes, and the libertarian rarely "tests." He or she is not concerned with information per se and subjugates other instructional goals to self-exploration and self-realization. The libertarian form makes minimal demands on the student in the traditional sense; however, there may be authority in it. The distinction rests in the forms themselves.

In the authoritative, students are coerced by knowledge. When they select a topic of inquiry, they are subject to what is known about the topic and their thinking about it is controlled by what can be discovered. In the libertarian, since no coercion is involved, the student follows the teacher into a way of thinking, or as we call it, a *Lebenswelt,* or life world. The first instance emphasizes the strictures of the knowledge and its organization. The second involves following a style, assuming a way of thinking about things.

The libertarian professor has a retinue. This "prof" has been able to articulate a perspective that has been "taken on" by others as their own. It further allows both to expand and grow, developing an understanding of who they are and of the nature of the world around them.

The contrast should sound familiar because it is often made between primary and secondary socialization experiences. As an institutional reality, education contains both experiences. Furthermore, these distinctive experiences may be in conflict with a given form, and in the interaction transpiring within the form.

We can illustrate the conflict of forms by comparing two opposite cases. The first we call Grading and the Guru and the second, How to Be Friends with a Biology Professor.

Grading and the Guru. Doctor Franklin, associate professor of English, known as "Sam" to his students, conducts a "loose" class. At the first meeting, he announces to students that he prefers to be called "Sam," in spite of the fact that he is thirty years their senior, and he gives out his home phone number while inviting students to "drop in" any time they feel the need to communicate. He does not talk of grades; instead, he speaks of what he thinks education should be.

I believe in the open and free exchange of ideas. In this class, we are intellectual equals. I have more experience, but your advantage is freshness and energy. Together, we will make this class a growing, vital experience for us all. But you must be prepared to give yourself—your thoughts and emotions. You must overcome any shyness towards ideas you may harbor in your soul, for it is the richness of your soul that I believe in.

For fifty minutes, such exhortation continues. If the student hears this for the first time, the effects can be spellbinding. A sophomore coed remarks, "He is the first prof I've had here at State U who really cares about students as people. I know this will be a great class." Sam speaks fine words. He stresses the "higher values" of education and regards the poets Yeats, Shelley, Bryon, and other great sages of the English language as mediums to the enrichment of human life. He is a humanist, and he declares love for all human beings.

Attending class under Sam's tutelage consists mostly of listening to him talk, writing, and reading the writing of other students in his classes. Since Sam does not require attendance, some students come to class only when they think the topic of the daily talk, announced one class period ahead, sounds "interesting." All students are, however, required to write and to criticize one anothers' work. It is in the situation of criticism that we discover the mechanism of form.

Since everyone supposedly "loves" everyone else, and since no objectively discoverable criteria seem to be available for criticism, when students voice their thoughts about the works of others, they do so in carefully chosen words. For example, "I really like what Jennie's poem tried to say—a separation between who we feel we are and the internal drive for a different experience—man, uh, but if that's what she means, then I think she could have said it better." Or, "I really like what you wrote and think you have good ideas." A student can disclaim her association with what she feels may be an area of potential criticism by prefacing the reading of her poem, "I may have made some technical errors in this, but I really felt the part and that's where the poem is at!" Any student who criticizes on a technical point, then, will demonstrate to others ignorance of the significance of the work (cf. Hewitt and Stokes 1975).

Sam's entry into student exchange comes only when things get out of hand. He intervenes when Jerry remarks that Jennifer's poem not only is poorly written but shows the thinking of a "preadolescent egotist." Sam says, "All human thought is of value, for the task of soul enrichment and some of the most beautiful poems on earth are from the minds of the innocent." He adds, "We are not about the business of slaying the creative potential of our fellow poets; we are here to learn to live, not die." With that, Jerry changes his comments and points out some moving passage from his own work that attempts to express Jennifer's major ideas. Sam's role is to reintroduce the tacit assumptions of criticism for this context, a context he imagines and builds with the student's help.

At the end of every semester, Sam must fill out the grade sheet like every other member of State University faculty. After four and one-half months of the class, Sam knows every student by first name, and all have been to his home at least one time. They have met his family, played with his dog. He does not hide the philosophy of life he attempts to use both at school and at home. His egalitarian views have been espoused repeatedly in spirit and deed. Students select themselves for his classes. They become his followers, at least for the duration of the semester and for the purposes of receiving the "good grade" he invariably gives them.

But Sam confronts the assumption of measured progress. At State University, grades are expressed *A, B, C, D* and *No Credit*. He has seen the "soul growth" of all the students in his class. His goal in teaching is to encourage this growth. He believes he has seen it. But Jennifer does have a problem with grammar and spelling, and Jerry's elocution is without peer, and there were those ten or so students who turned in their poems by dropping them in the campus mail, not bothering to talk to Sam about them. Sam thinks they may have grown as well. They may have been so inspired by the first class that they used all the rest of the semester to explore on their own, in ways not know to him. But they have not followed instructions and Sam must fill out that grade sheet. Once, when he was young, he toyed with the idea of giving all students *As* in affirmation of his faith in egalitarian education, but a senior colleague discouraged him on the ground of avoiding trouble with the dean, who regularly expressed concern over a disproportionately high number of student's on his "dean's list."

So Sam's own formula, worked out over the years, goes like this: *Cs* to those who never attended class, but turned in some work, *Bs* to those whose technical writing skills exhibited fault (this, he noted, was the majority), and *As* to those faithful whose spelling and grammar was impeccable. Sam has been at State University for fifteen years, and neither the dean nor the department chair has ever criticized his way of distributing grades. But the students express widely varied opinions of Sam.

Frank: Sam's an SOB. I believed in him and worked very hard in that class. I would skip other classes and write and rewrite poems. Sometimes I even embarrassed myself by revealing things about myself in the lines of my poems. He always protected me in class. I appreciated that. But after all that work, he gave me a *B*. I'll never take anything from him again.

Alex: A snap course. All I wanted was a *C* and I got it by writing a few silly lines one night over at Joe's bar. Had a pizza in one hand and a beer in the other. I just dictated and a woman in there wrote it down for me.

Jennifer: The kindest man, the most human person I know. He will do anything for a student. When you hand in something written to him, you get back in comments almost as much as you write. You know he cares and I trust his judgment. I have had three classes from him.

Alice: Oh, he's all right; a big blowhard if you ask me. I just went to class and had a good high school English course behind me, so I just wrote carefully and I got an *A*. It was easy.

How to Make Friends with a Biology Prof. Seymour Markowicz has taught biology for almost thirty years at State U. He has published widely in the various scientific research journals of his field, and he has built a reputation as a careful and meticulous researcher. His rank is full professor, and he is the highest-paid professor in this department, if not the university. Students all call him Professor Markowicz, and all but his closest friends on the faculty, administrators, and biology colleagues from other campuses refer to him as Dr. Markowicz. His close friends and department colleagues call him Mark.

Although he teaches fewer course than his younger fellow biology department members, he does teach one beginning biology class each year, and it is mainly through this class that students know him.

Professor Markowicz spends the first class meeting in careful description of the mechanics of his course, such things as the number and kind of examinations, laboratory requirements and hours, the way he expects to curve grades, and reading assignments He distributes a five-page course syllabus, and students read along as he "goes over" the syllabus for that day's lecture. Tests in his class are objective, mostly multiple choice and definitions of terms, and a teaching assistant handles work in the laboratory.

Professor Markowicz gives well-organized lectures. He repeats at least twice the materials that will reappear on examination questions. He has planned, by the week, the topics to be covered, and he coordinates laboratory and reading assignments to classroom lectures. All this material, in outline form, appears on the syllabus entitled Biology 101.

A typical lecture begins, "Good morning, students. I hope you are well prepared for today's lecture. Before I begin, I will entertain questions of a review nature. Are there any questions?" If students ask questions (a rare occasion) the professor reiterates, some say verbatim, the materials previously presented on that particular topic. Questioning is frequently employed by students to fill gaps in incomplete notes or to clarify illegible sentences scribbled while trying to keep up with the fast-paced lecture.

Professor Markowicz makes himself available to students through a widely practiced academic ritual called "office hours." This consists of announcing in class (in Professor Markowicz's case, the information is also on the course syllabus) the specific times he will be in his office and will meet with students. Students are to understand that they may not expect the same attention if they happen to contact the teacher outside office hours. In the allocation of Professor Markowicz's time, scheduling is paramount. He must have time to do research, write, travel to professional meetings, attend to committee work, and, finally, have time for students. Although not always a reliable rule, generally all other times take precedence over time for students.

During office hours, this kind of conversation can be overheard. "Hello, my name is Sally Anderson. I'm in your Biology 101 class, and I would like to talk to you about the next examination." From behind a paper-filled desk, in an office lined with shelves containing a cluttering of books, some upright and others piled on top of one another, all conveying a message of "work in progress," the professor replies, "Good, I'm happy you dropped by. Could you tell me which area of the materials gives you the most difficulty?" Sally: "I don't understand photosynthesis." Professor: "Fine. That process may be defined as", whereon a rendition of the lecture of that day in the language and style most familiar to Sally commences. The conversation that occurs during these office hours amounts to condensed lectures. Students assume a note-taking posture and write during the conversations.

On rare occasions, a student may try to account for his poor performance on an examination by relating a "sad tale" of the death of his grandparent and the insistence of his parents that he attend the funeral in spite of the necessity to study for the biology examination (cf. Scott and Lyman's 1968 discussion of the social functions of "accounts"). The good professor listens politely and then states his policy regarding makeup examinations: "Make-up periods for laboratory and missed examinations will be given once during a regular semester. Each student is allowed to make up three laboratory assignments and one classroom examination. The makeup work consists of related but different materials." The professor says the same thing regardless of the student's account of why he or she missed an examination.

What of this man's reputation among students? He holds a formal dinner once a year at his house, to which all biology majors are invited. Majors report that he is a "nice guy." Nonmajors say he is fair and tough, but brilliant. Few students know him informally, and once a year his appearance as a member of the biology softball team is greeted with silence when he appears attired in Bermuda shorts, a T-shirt and a New York Giants baseball cap, bottomed off with tennis shoes and black socks. The usual tweed sport coat, baggy pants, and penny loafers, replaced by contrastive informal clothing, produces an uneasy feeling among the students, one of whom remarked after the professor fielded a fly ball, "That was a fine catch, Professor Markowicz," to which the reply, "Why, thank you, John," seemed to come from a genuine intent to lessen the distance between student and teacher. The next day in class, John receives the teaching-assistant-graded examination from the midterm. He made a *D+*. John's comments about the test.

> I really screwed up that exam. It's not old man Markowicz. All you have to do is memorize notes from his lectures. He never asks any question not from notes or assigned readings. No trick questions. I just didn't study. I'll work harder next time. I sure hate it. I blew this one.

Kinds of Educational Experiences

Interactions between institutional and social forms result in distinctive kinds of understandings for the meanings of educational experience. Just as we were able to describe typical individual adaptations for general societal trends and for the family (traditionalists, rationalists, and marginalists), so we can identify the manner in which interactions produce individual adaptations for students who live in almost daily contact with the educational reality of our society. In this section, we work from the students' perspective. We chose students, for we believe they best reflect, in the most immediate and dramatic fashion, the impact of education. Of course, faculty, administrators, regents, trustees, parents, and others also feel the import of education, but students receive the full brunt because they typically find that their entire lifetime is defined, directly and indirectly, in the language of the educational reality. Probably only their teachers can even begin to make such a claim. They, however, are professionals "as well as teachers." Their lifeworlds are complex and segmentalized compared to the students.

A simple typology can identify the adaptations individual students exposed to varying levels and intensities of institutional and group phenomena may make. This typology first involves the four educational assumptions (the teacher assumption, instrumentality, social control, and measured progress) emphasizing education as a means—as a device to get something for the individual. These assumptions stress the extrinsic nature of education, which resides in its instrumentality. The remaining "moralizing" assumption, in contrast and often in conflict, emphasizes the intrinsic quality of education defined in terms of the inward development of the person. Together these assumptions configure into two distinctive forms, libertarian and authoritative, and we juxtapose them to the major features of the institutional reality, the instrumental (extrinsic) and the self-actualizing (instrinsic), to complete our typology. As we see in Figure 4.1, we define four kinds of students: activists, fun seekers, careerists, and intellectuals.

Institution

	Extrinsic	Instrinsic
Libertarian	Activitists	Fun seekers
Authoritative	Careeists	Intellectuals

Group
Form

Figure 4.1
Individual adaptations as functions of group form and institutional
meanings

The Activists: Politicos

Activist students have definite goals, but do not like how they must go about achieving them. Since they perceive the overall character of education as instrumental, they often have little patience with classroom organization, professors, and even administrative policy, which kindles the "liberal arts" spirit. Activists want education to "amount to something," and they do not like the strictures of the authoritative types they confront among faculty and administrators. Their response, then, is offensive, one of attack, and they attempt to modify what they see as the "way things are done." They are attracted to curriculum experimentation; they often serve as student members on faculty committees, or are active in student and faculty governing bodies, such as the student associations or the senate of a university.

They may even, on occasion, let their studies "slide" in favor of work on the campus newspaper, the yearbook, or a committee on some campus issue. They see these activities as more relevant to their life plans than course work. On one campus we have described, the activists are called *politicos*. Students at this campus use the term to refer not only to persons active in student government but also to students who feel the institution of education can be better organized. As one student put it, "This is a good school but there seems to be a lot of 'dead wood' around, I mean profs whose teaching and subjects are of no use to what students want, none whatsoever." Better organization seems to imply more direct alignment between form and purpose.

The Fun Collegians: Jocks, Buds and Freaks

The historian Paula Fass (1977), in *The Damned and the Beautiful*, traces to college life the emergence of a distinctive youth culture in American society. She suggests that during the economic instability of the 1920s and 1930s, whenever people of the same age and interests were "isolated" in similar collegiate social settings with the prospect of several years of "preparing" for vaguely understood occupations, they would band together to form a culture. Images of Joe College with his raccoon coat, college pennant, and jalopy are consistent with Fass's depiction of the beginnings of youth culture. And indeed, while appearances have changed, and while the playful segment of students on campuses around the nation varies from campus to campus, no one associated with college life can deny that fun seeking continues to be a large part of it.

In terms of our typology, fun seeking students are nonpurposive in their view of education, but they expect a variety of self-actualizing experiences. For some, it seems that the sole criterion for taking a course, hitchhiking across country, traveling to Europe, or being in college at all is to "have a good time." The meaning of "good time" derives from a tacit understanding that the end result of activity should be fun, though few would venture a precise definition of it. For some it is getting high on grass and coke and having a "real good one-nighter" after a rock concert. For others it is a Zen meditation followed by pizza and beer. It can even be intramural or intercollegiate athletics.

Fun seekers obviously must take classes, and what course they pursue often depends on a complex informational network about professors. They know this network as the "grapevine." So before one actually enrolls in a course, he or she asks fellow fun seekers, "How hard is this professor?" "Does he require a paper?" "Do only politicos or serious students take his classes?" "Is this professor a nice guy?" and so on. Whether the course fits into a curricular plan is of secondary concern. Of course, virtually all colleges and universities require some courses, and to the fun seeker these courses are often regarded as very boring.

Since these students follow both self-actualizing and libertarian assumptions, their adaptation embodies conflict between these two sets of assumptions. Their lives are reflections of conflict between "whether to do something meaningful and enjoyable" or "something individually useful." In fact, studies on the extreme effects of libertarian and self actualizing interactions show that dropping out of college is common.

All in all, the fun seeker possesses a breadth of self-indulgence that covers everything from athletics (jocks) and beer drinking (buds) to Eastern occultism (freaks). She may be into sororities or Zen, or both. He may excel in some courses that "turn him on" and avoid others that do not. He is a modern Joe College. He dons jeans, wears a Greek fisherman's shirt and a captain's hat and reads the literature of consciousness expansion. At least this was a 1970s manifestation that Tom Wolfe observed when he wrote of the intelligent coed who hears and understands the gloomy messages of the bards and sages of the American college lecture circuit. But, to her, "life keeps getting easier, sunnier, happier . . . Frisbee!" She asks, as did one young man of an ecologist's analysis of the horrors of the depletion of the earth's resources, "What I want to know is—how old are you, usually, when it all hits you?" (Wolfe 1980).

The Campus Intellectual

Seeking the authority of the "really good" faculty on campus, the intellectuals, like the fun seekers, decide for themselves the meaning of their educational experiences. The intellectuals seem willing to endure the "tough prof" and the "rough course" if such "suffering" can be related to intellectual growth. Lyle says, "That logic course Professor Smith teaches is the best course I ever had. It was a lot of work, but it paid off in the clarity of thought I believe I now have." Here, the question of the usefulness of knowledge translates into inward development. Something is useful if it sharpens writing skill, logical thinking, historical background, and the like. Unlike the "intelligent coed" who does not attend to the imminent danger of "ozone depletion" or world hunger, the intellectual not only is well versed in current literature but uses that literature as a basis for interpreting everyday life.

As rationalists, intellectuals do not "give up" altogether, they merely eschew the instrumental dimension and turn rationalism into its extreme solipsist form: that is, they develop their minds, like the body builder "pumps iron," for the joy of feeling the blood rush to the exerted muscles, filling them with new strength. The intellectuals "pump" their minds; they fill themselves with information and emulate authoritative sources in their speaking and writing styles.

They are not necessarily ideal students in the conventional sense. They may not attend classes. They may be highly critical of reading materials and teachers who do not measure up as "authorities." Their presence in a discussion class, for example, may be regarded as distracting by teachers and other students. Because the intellectuals must define for themselves what is interesting and what is not, they may dominate discussion topics, introduce issues that are of limited interest or are even idiosyncratic. They habitually name drop, and book drop, prefacing each remark with "according to Sartre" or "I just finished rereading Plato."

A native term used by students at one college we know of denotes the intellectual adaptation. It is *hondo* , and it refers to a person who has been converted to an intellectual zealot, someone who seems to have an interest in a particular course of study. There are poli-sci hondos, anthro hondos, bio hondos, and even soc hondos. These students have located their intellectual work in a particular academic department. They interpret all the other subjects they are exposed to from the perspective of their "hondoism." For example, a political science hondo takes a sociology class to find out information useful to a research project he has under way for a political science public administration course. Or, biology hondos take a required psychology class and attend only to the materials on physiology, ignoring, say, theories of personality.

What identifies the intellectual, then, is the definition of the intrinsic worth they impose on educational experiences. Hondos, for example, may aspire to graduate school, but do not think much about, or at best are uninfluenced by, job market considerations. That political science or history Ph.D.s face a greater chance of unemployment than bricklayers seems to be an irrelevant bit of information to the hondo's version of "mind expansion." What matters is the discernible worth of the knowledge itself; intellectual adaptations turn on a modern version of the adage "Knowledge for knowledge's sake."

The Careerist

In this final adaptation, we see a consonant alignment between pressures from institutions and forms. Just as jocks, buds, and freaks seek "good times" within an environment seemingly tailored for their purposes, careerists find in education avenues directly related to their aspirations. These students are usually premed, prelaw, or business and accounting majors. As a common denominator, they have an interest in getting somewhere. To them, the worth of the education they receive is measured by the extrinsic usefulness of it. A premed major feels no inward joy from analytic chemistry; there is no "inner glow" from the study of biochemistry for these students, the way there could be a warm feeling in such study for a biology hondo. Careerists are simply following necessary steps or jumping hurdles on the route to their selected goals. As such, they represent the most clear affirmation of the instrumentality of education and the secondary nature of its group form.

Careerists stay away from guru types and have "good times" only after examinations, between terms, in the "off times." When school is on, they are too. They are always in class, on time, and attentive to test-specific materials, and often they can be overheard demeaning the "softness" of work required in courses that are not part of their career track. To them, only relevant courses directly tied to their career aspirations make sense. Only these courses merit their full attention and energy.

Of course, most colleges do not exist entirely for the careerist. So this pragmatist may, on occasion, be compelled to touch the "softness" and "freaky types" of the other parts of the campus. When this happens, the student displays a frankness that may be disconcerting to the "intellectual" faculty. For example, a premed student approaches a history professor. He asks of the professor, "I have a tough load next semester, anatomy, analytic and biochem, all together; I've got to have a fourth course and I'm looking for something not too hard. Tell me about your European Ideas class. How much reading do we have to do? What type of examinations do your give? Is it a really difficult course?"

Careerists draw from the educational reality the resources it offers. No matter how distasteful their experiences in the laboratory, no matter how ruthless and aloof the faculty they encounter, the payoff comes in the acceptance letter from the medical or law school, the successful job interview with the corporation, or placement in the management intern program after graduation. Interpretations of the meaning of college life for careerists are prospective, living in the future, regarding the present as a "necessary evil." They are not looking for personal contacts with faculty except insofar as these are necessary for letters of recommendation and tips on the midterm or final. Other students may see them as "groupies," hanging around with only their kind, haunting the labs at all hours of the night, when any self-respecting student would be at the local bar. But their relationships with others of their kind are also instrumental and authoritative. Some hoard their notes, while others help each other study and offer assistance in lab work only insofar as this does not skew the competitive outcomes of a fair contest on the examination. Although rare, there are documented observations of tampering with laboratory experiments, thefts of other students' notes, and other chicanery employed in efforts to achieve a high grade average—a necessary condition for passage through the gates of a profession.

Assessing Education

Probably since education began, the people responsible for it and those involved in it have been preoccupied with assessing precisely what effects education has on individuals and society. The range of this question is overwhelming, and we here attempt to present only two recent efforts at assessment, each representing two poles of sociological research.

The first study helps us tie together our characterizations of kinds of student experiences with larger trends in society. Basically, most studies of the effects of higher education indicate that it has a liberalizing effect on the individual. In fact, while political ideas do not always correspond with intellectual ones, the goals of liberal arts education parallel those of the development of grand ideas in Western society. These ideas are familiar to us by now. They seem to suggest that educated people are able to live in complex social settings, tolerate ambiguity and uncertainty, and, most of all, believe in higher-order human values like freedom, self-determination, and representative government. Whereas learning to read is clearly the first step toward these goals, reading leads to more and more complex and lifelong learning tasks.

The educated person is, in common-sense terms, cosmopolitan and wide ranging in interests. To put the matter succinctly, most of us assume that on the continuum of open- and closed-mindedness (Rokeach 1960), the educated fall toward "open-mindedness." In very complicated ways, this assumption serves to justify the elaborate and expensive institution of education. We have seen how the relationship between educational forms and consciousness is tied into society. What we now learn is that the effects of education on individuals are equally tied into societal considerations.

Frederick Weil (1985) has tackled the question of the relationship between education and liberalism on an international scale. He begins by underscoring the strength of this relationship and cites many studies back into the 1950s showing that education is associated with liberalism. He suggests, however, that most of these studies are of American populations and that cultural or national factors might well change this strong relationship. In other words, he questions whether there is anything intrinsic about education that liberalizes people.

Using survey data from studies conducted in several countries (United States, Germany, France, and Austria), Weil focuses on the variable of anti-Semitism, selecting data that show how people responded to questions on whether Jews have too much power, whether or not they would vote for a Jew for public office, whether or not they think Jews are less nationalistic in their attitudes than non-Jewish citizens, and whether they think Jews "cause trouble." Generally, studies in the United States have shown that negative attitudes about Jewish people are found more frequently among poorly educated populations.

When Weil controlled for factors like the type of governmental regime and the degree of religious heterogeneity in the various nations, the negative relationships we would expect between education and anti-Semitism became much weaker. In fact, when he pooled all the data for all the countries, and used statistical measures of the effects of education on political anti-Semitism, he found, especially for the variable "Would not vote for a Jew," no significant relationship between education and how people answered the questions.

While his study does not contradict absolutely the many other studies that do show an association between education and liberalism, Weil reminds us that the meanings and effects of education are conditioned by social factors. So, in societies that do not have strong democratic traditions and are dominated by a single religion (ecclesia), experiences in higher education may not instill values of tolerance and equality. And, conversely, it may be that educational institutions in democratic and pluralistic societies are not the only carriers of the values of equality. In societies where democratic values are strong and there are many religions to choose from, people may learn equalitarian values from everyday life. Education, then, is clearly not the only agent that promotes "higher-order values."

Indeed, as we have seen, the very meanings of education may be changing in American society. In their four-year-long study of students at Stanford University, Katchadourian and Boli (1985) document the struggle between careerism and intellectualism that students often experience in their four years at college. While the proportion of students who are careerist seems to be rising at Stanford, and perhaps nationally as well, these authors do not come to a pessimistic conclusion about the role of liberal arts. Instead, they believe that a liberal arts emphasis can function as an axis around which can turn activities that help students understand their own interests in fun, in seeking careers, in pursuing intellectual matters, and in engaging in the governing of their school. They call for a recognition of the role that students play in shaping the quality of educational experiences and the tension that often exists between faculty whose aspirations are professional and students whose understanding of education is often far from professional.

In the authors' careful attention to types of students and the dynamics of change on campus is an underlying concern with societal forces that are indeed shaping and reshaping the meanings of education. Education influences people, their knowledge, attitudes, and tastes, but often students' academic orientations "are already well formed by the time they come to college" and "the state of the economy and the political mood of the county are external constraints that also influence student orientations and choices" (Katchadourian and Boli 1985, 253). Education, its functions, organization, and meanings, is a reflection of society as much as a shaper of it.

Summary

Education assumes increasing importance as society becomes more modern. It functions primarily as an agent of socialization and for confirmation of credentials. These functions of education parallel shifts in society from primary- to secondary-group relationships.

Education as a social institution rests on several assumptions: the teacher assumption; the instrumental (means-ends) assumption; the controlling agent assumption; the assumption of "higher-order values"; and, last, the measured-progress assumption. These assumptions underlie the meanings people and organizations give to educational experiences, and they combine to function as the supporting rationale for different ways to organize the experience itself.

As social forms, education divides into authoritative and libertarian, the former activating the assumption of teacher's knowledge, instrumentalism, control, and measured progress. The latter, while drawing from each assumption, emphasizes the "higher-order" meanings.

The bases of education as institution and form are not necessarily consistently related, and any actual educational experience may draw disproportionately on various aspects of the system of knowledge. We illustrate how individuals may construct reality for themselves by way of another typology. Activists, fun seekers, careerists, and intellectuals are the four ideal types of educational experiences we describe.

Finally, we assess education by looking at the consequences that higher education has on individuals. Generally, liberalization, well documented as an effect of higher education in America, varies with other social conditions, such as the form of government and the composition of a society's population. What education does for people seems to reflect the changes taking place in society. As an example, we cite a study of rising careerism among American college students.

Chapter 5

RELIGION IN MODERN SOCIETY

Contemporary sociologists think the feelings people have about deities, the ways in which they worship and regard or disregard them, contain information that is crucial to understanding the character of the societies in which they live. Just as there are "no atheists in foxholes," there are no societies without some religious beliefs and behavior (Lenski and Lenski 1978). Apparently, people find the prospect of "going it alone" unsettling both at the social and the individual level.

Early sociologists, such as Emile Durkheim, Max Weber and William Graham Sumner, regarded religion as a major, if not *the* major, social force in society. Each thinker stressed different aspects of religion and, in given societies, each related religion to different aspects of life. Durkheim (1954), for example, attempted to show, through the analysis of "primitive" societies, that conceptions people have of God reflect the social arrangements of their life. People who depend on nature for existence have animistic religions, and people with a strong and powerful social order that bonds them into a single unit, like the people of ancient Jewish tribes, have monotheistic beliefs. Finally, societies such as ours, which are atomized or which are complexly organized, have individualistic religious systems (e.g., Protestantism). For Durkheim, God, or at least human understandings of God, are made in the image of society.

Weber (1958) regarded religion as potent force in shaping values, which in turn could shape the entire character of a society. Hence Weber analyzed religions of the world to see if he could thereby account for why vigorous forms of capitalism emerged in only select societies. He concluded that the Protestant Reformation was a shaping factor in the development of modern capitalism, for people who live in protestant societies work as if they are attempting to save their souls from eternal damnation.

Sumner (1906) also believed that religious beliefs in society often shaped basic social norms. The origin of folkways and mores, therefore, can be found in religious beliefs that themselves are often responses to fears and unexplainable natural phenomena. Sumner and other nineteenth century thinkers, such as Herbert Spencer, suggested that as people understand more about nature and social worlds, the power of religion would lessen. Although it is true that church membership and attendance do go down in modern societies, religion remains a vital social force, even in highly pluralistic societies like the United States.

For people who define themselves as "religious," religion deals with the ultimate questions of life. As a belief system, it rests on assumptions that give meanings to questions of life that no other institution of society addresses. It defines such things as death, the ultimate reasons for existence, the origins of spiritual feelings, and the meaning of suffering. As such, religion spreads what one authors calls a "sacred canopy" over society (Berger 1967).

In its organization, religion both reflects and influences the dominant forms of secular society. Religious institutions, like all institutions, impose an organization on the experiences of individuals. So religion is a social force on several different levels: as an institution, a form, and a set of individual beliefs.

When someone is confused and angry about the injustice of cancer striking down a "loved one," religion offers a formal, institutionalized solution to this individual's problems. By supplying forms for the practice of a ritual, a prayer, a holy sacrament, or simply attending a worship service, a religion interprets suffering, trouble, and the essential confusion of life and thus meets the needs of its believers.

Religious forms exert uneven and cross-pressures on individuals. Hence, the belief that God cares for His believers may conflict with living in a troubled family, or ones personal convictions may seem contradictory to the practices of ones church. But individuals adapt and make sense out of their predicaments through the application of the stocks of knowledge, or typifications (Schutz1971) that are available to them. In this chapter, we treat the topic of religion from three different perspectives: religion as a social institution, as a social form, and as an individual adaptation. We see that in modern society, religious forces are vital and powerful, even if they are different from the practices one observes in more traditional settings.

The Nature of Religious Institutions

As a social institution, religion is rooted in assumptions that are taken for granted and held tenaciously, though often tacitly. Such assumptions provide the foundation for many different expressions of religious thought, feelings, and actions. These expressions often use the institutional knowledge of religion differently, with distinctions between secular and sacred sometimes becoming lost in conflict and practice. For example, the line between science and religion may be sharply drawn ,as in arguments over "creationism," or it may disappear, as state laws are passed to give tax monies to private schools under a rationale that suspends the church-state separation many protestant religions regard as essential. Within a given society, however, all matters of God derive in some way from sets of assumptions that are, by definition, religious.

The Limits of Human Knowledge

Religion assumes definite limits to human knowledge. A religious belief stems from the acknowledgment that human mental capacity cannot comprehend everything. On this point, religion and science are in conflict, for science rests on the assertion that human intelligence has the capacity to know and control—though not necessarily that any single scientist can know all, or even that science as a system of knowledge, is omniscient. But, theoretically, anything that impinges on human consciousness, any force that enters into a cause-and-effect cycle in the affairs of things, can be known and eventually controlled.

Rather than rest its faith in the ultimate refinement and eloquence of knowledge, religion contends that the limits of knowledge stop at the beginning of faith. This may seem a little confusing, but we are trying to make the same subtle distinction that those faithful to science and religion make. Hence we point out that the two ways of knowing—scientific and religious—function in different ways. For religion, knowledge becomes a testimony of belief. Religious knowledge describes the circumstances for gaining and losing faith; it deals with the operation of faith itself and even, in the more intellectual versions of Protestantism, offers definitions of faith. But all this amounts to knowledge about faith, and faith can never be measured, quantified, or replicated because the source of faith is divine, and the divine, by definition, is unknowable. Thus one may study *about* religion, acquire knowledge of a system of belief, describe the differences between Catholicism and Protestantism and the significance of these differences for the spirit of capitalism. But the religious believer must experience faith, inwardly. Faith, according to religion, is an intuitively experienced state of mind.

Religionists know about the faith of others, but they have experienced only their own faith. There are, of course, individualized and rationalized versions of religion, like Protestantism, and, in contrast, group and emotive versions to be found among fundamentalists and Catholics. Nevertheless, one defining characteristic of religion is the assumption that knowledge has limits and faith is limitless; while knowledge, from the scientific perspective, asserts the controllability of phenomena, religion, at least for some matters, teaches the essential uncontrollability of phenomena.

Of course, as Yinger (1957) and others have well documented, a particular subject once regarded within the province of religion may become a scientific matter. For example, the question whether the earth rotated around the sun or the sun around the earth was once a religious matter. Even the most ardent believer now regards that question as a matter for the science of astronomy. Yinger concludes from reviewing the history of instances of conflict between science and religion that it has been religion that modifies its applications and interpretations to accommodate science, not the other way around (Yinger 1959, 37–40). Although we may have once burned as heretics scientists who studied the stars, now we pray for the successful landing of their space shuttle on the California desert.

Yinger further points out that religious accommodation to science has been to emphasize faith and its intuitive basis. Science, in contrast to religion, still creates a reality in which the role of intuition is relegated to beginning hunches and, perhaps, motivation for an inquiry into some topic of interest. In matters of knowing, it plays only a minor role.

Recently religionists have again begun to challenge conventional scientific knowledge. The emotional issue of the origins of life has highlighted the distinctions between religion and science we are introducing. It is as if history were repeating itself, only this time, the laws of the land seem to protect the right to ignorance of scientific facts. We mean that the success creationists have had in gaining equal time for their version of the origin of the universe symbolizes not so much a challenge to science but a retreat from it. What creationists often do is find some scientist who casts doubt on established knowledge. Nevertheless, while a few scientists may propose a creationist's scientific theory, most followers of creationism want to avoid science altogether and teach their children, for example, the literal biblical truth about the origins of life.

As social forces, then, science and religion are opposites: One asserts the potential of human mental capacity and the other defines the limitations of our minds. One regards expansive and cumulative progress as essential; the other is content to discover faith and then know about it according to its experience.

Topics of Religious Awareness

Religion assumes that the affairs of everyday life have special meaning. It transforms everyday life for the believer into signficant religious experiences within a religious interpretation of life, any of life's affairs become important, because such affairs are not mundane or trivial. Instead, they can be reinterpreted as manifestations of ultimate truths. In religion, no question goes without an answer. One can find reasons for the origin of life, its ending, and all the problems in between. Thus the untimely death of a loved one can be interpreted religiously.

> Mrs. McIntire was angry over the death of her husband, a good man - a good father, now he was gone. How can such a thing be God's will? Enraged, she expressed these sentiments to her pastor. His reply: "God has his reasons, and we may not understand them. God may be testing us, like He did Job. You must be strong and He will help you, and in time, you will see His reason. You must believe that it is His will that your husband died."

Simplicity

Another assumption of religion is simplicity, meaning that beliefs do not require eloquent knowledge or special training. To be sure, church membership may demand a study course or an indoctrination period. One may need to learn from preachers, and clergy. But rarely indeed is a person rejected who honestly and sincerely expresses a desire to become a member. It is assumed that everyone *can* understand. In short, there are no failures in matters of faith, only in the rational expression of it. A person may fail a course in New Testament theology, but this has nothing to do with his or her status as a Christian.

Ease of understanding and breadth of application characterize religious stocks of knowledge. Religious bits of information are simply organized, and in a fundamentalist's doctrine, minimal comprehension leads to membership in the "Kingdom of the Lord."

The Sacred Life

Another hallmark of the religious institution is that it presumes to offer its members an interpretation of the meanings of everyday affairs as sacred. This changes the mundane into the extraordinary, and, consequently, all of life can be interpreted as religious. Not only is death a part of God's plan, but so is doing the dishes and attending school. In short, this aspect of the institution of religion creates a sacred life. A mother or father, herding children from school to shopping center to dance lessons, is "really" doing God's work. She or he "actually" is charged with the ominous responsibility of rearing children in the ways of the Lord. What would be eschewed and even condemned by the nonbeliever as denigrating servitude becomes a lofty mission worthy of only the most upright, the strongest of Christians.

Thus religion requires of its believers that they see a "separate" reality. Although in appearance and routine their lives may vary little from those of nonbelievers, their views of life are rooted in a different mode of existence. The nonbeliever lives; the believer is merely present on earth. The nonbeliever earns a wage or salary for his or her work. The believer works to earn for his or her family and to give to the church so that the work of the Lord can continue on earth. The nonbeliever exercises to keep fit; the believer exercises to honor the body as the temple of the Lord. Religion gives its followers separate social semantics that transform the mundane into a special, meaningful kind of existence.

The Christian typically does not dread "another day, another dollar," for he or she does not live in the boring routine of the secular world. The secular world has become a place of testimony, a challenge in faith, a fertile soil in which one may toil. The meanings of everyday life come from the particular religious form, be it Presbyterian or Hare Krishna.

The Sacred and The Profane

A religious institution exists, in part, because it can coexist. We mean it can take any activity, like an accredited educational curriculum, and allow the ordinary meaning of a "sound education" to stand while superimposing a religious meaning over the ordinary. Thus, education, insofar as curriculum is concerned, at a major college like Church University, a Baptist college, looks very much the same as education at Biggest State University. This fact is recognized through accrediting agents. A graduate of Church University in secondary education has a teaching credential equally valid as that of Biggest State U graduates in a similar program. Nevertheless, whereas the secular institution imparts the meaning of "qualified" or "prepared" in the various senses that may apply, the church school curriculum does more. It adds another dimension—*Christian Education*. The subject matter taught does not really matter. The styles of teaching and other details or enactments may also be identical. The crucial point is that courses of study are thought of differently in the two settings—one is defined as sacred and the other as secular.

We can observe some differences in classroom activities at Church U and State U. In the former, one never hears religiously tabooed, profane words, used by a professor unless these are "quoted." At Biggest State U, these vocabulary items may be judiciously interjected in otherwise scholarly discourses. The styles of teaching may also vary, and a Church U student may expect to hear the Christian interpretation of the scientific theory of evolution. The religious institution does provide a set of potential meanings for everyday life "separate from" those readily available to ordinary members of society.

An entire society may be religious, and a single religious reality may dominate the organization of that society. The technical term for this is *ecclesia*.. Islam in Iran and Catholicism in Italy are both examples of ecclesia. Ecclesia is formally organized and has a highly trained corps of religious leaders and workers, and one leader usually dominates the entire structure. The authority of the leader of ecclesia is traditional and legal-rational, never strictly charismatic. The Ayatollah Khomeini, for example, had enormous power within Iran. He could go outside the legal system to punish criminals and set national policy. Of course, the pope in Italy is nowhere near as powerful as the Ayatollah was in his respective ecclesia. This is an interesting comparison because it helps us see the effects of modernization on religious organizations like ecclesia.

Sacred societies existed in medieval Western society, and the Italian ecclesia is a remnant of the most powerful one. Also, completely sacred societies have been discovered by anthropologists in their studies of "nonmodern people." Today, modernization trends stress the rational, scientific view of the everyday world. As a result, religious reality has been relegated to accommodating and complementary roles. Roof and McKinney (1987, 57), for example, cite survey data showing that, in America, there are no differences between "churched" and "unchurched" people in their overwhelming endorsement of basic values of individualism. This does not preclude the possibility of resurgent religious dominance, or even the possible impact that religious reality may have on the secular. A "good Christian," for example, may be elected to high office in hopes that his "separate reality" will translate into secular versions of just "plain honesty."

Religious Identity

Finally, religious institutions presume to organize the identity of believers. Conversions and switches of faith notwithstanding, the acquisition of the ability to live in the ordinary world and yet not be a part of it is usually the result of primary or childhood socialization. As Gordon's (1974) research shows, even what appears to be a dramatic shift in a person's identity, as was apparently the case with "Jesus People" in the 1970s, may actually be only a shift in styles of presenting identity. Gordon demonstrated that "Jesus Freaks" often simply accommodate "hip styles" of life to earlier acquired beliefs. What these people believed and espoused was not all that different from their religious upbringings. What differed, the ways in which they had changed, was the adopting of "hip life styles."

In the organization of the social self, the assumptions of a religious reality may play a central role. A Christian man thinks of himself as a Christian first (a believer), a father second, a U. S. senator third. A Christian woman decides on whether a career is right for her, if she should return to school and study for the law school entrance examinations when her children are of school age, according to her faith. This may work out to mean God wants her to use her talents at law to be a Christian lawyer, or He may desire that she continue her foreordained housewifery. Either way, her deep-rooted and central procedure for interpreting everyday life as a Christian generates the decision, and it does not affect the primary organization of selfhood.

As an institution, religion may provide tenets that are general and plastic enough to serve as primary socializers. In the modern world, it is rare that these tenets operate in isolation. The Osmonds are Christian showpersons. They are genuine Christians, startling in the contrast they provide with those who inhabit the secular world of big-money showbiz.

Tom Nolan's (1976) insightful report "The Family Plan of the Latter-Day Osmonds" relates the strong family, supportive environment that fosters a togetherness uncommon in the American society, let alone in the popular music industry. "Each Osmond seems to know precisely where any other Osmond is at any given moment and energies are pooled to a common task" (p. 48). Isolated from the "culture" of showbiz by their religious reality, the Osmonds use the new "sexy" moves of today's singers to advance their shared goal of an Osmond community. Their interest in things new "is limited to what will advance them or bring them closer together" (p. 49). Nolan characterizes them as "The Wizards who Live in the Land of Oz Worship their God and Obey the Laws Wear Ice Cream Suits without Bulges or Flaws And Smile with the Greatest Teeth since Jaws" (p. 46).

It is interesting to note that the Osmond kingdom fell on "bad times" during the 1980s. Their television program was canceled, and their studio in Utah is little used and in financial trouble. The only two Osmonds still successful are Donny and Marie, and we should note that to remain successes, they both have had to cultivate a more "worldly" image.

Although conversions, in the sense of radical change in the central tenets of selfhood, are infrequent and difficult to maintain, they do occur, and their occurrence exemplifies the function of religious institutions as problem-solving practices. Religion gives people a strong sense of identity, but in the modern, pluralistic social world, this vision may well be what Berger (1961) described as "precarious." We might add the precariousness of the vision increases with the lack of social support. A person may hear an evangelist present the word of the Lord, and may make a "decision for the Lord," marching down to the "stage" from which the evangelist preaches in the public affirmation of a change of faith. The authenticity of this person's religious experience may seem beyond reproach.

Nevertheless, as studies of Billy Graham's crusades indicate, people who experience conversion often revert to their old non-Christian ways, if they do not affiliate with a church or do not have the support of a network of other believers. Similarly, alcoholics who "convert" to Alcoholics Anonymous (AA) must depend on an elaborate supportive network of fellow believers to remain sober (Denzin1987), and, of course, a basic tenet of AA is belief in a "higher-order power." Any social view of the world, whether it be secular or sacred, depends on what Mehan and Wood (1975) call "constant interactional work." Without the constant application of the tenets of belief, the perspective or vision that religion offers fades. In the modern world, which is composed of pluralistic visions and many small social worlds, the religious vision is indeed precarious, fading in the more powerful light of "rational individualism."

Still, religious identity may remain quite strong and functional. The experiences of American Jews illustrate this point quite well. Historically, for Jewish people, the images of God and human relationships (Sklare 1971) derived directly from family, church, and residence; that is, the senses they had of who they were came from a nexus of information supplied to them, perhaps even by the same people, about who they were as family members, as religious believers, and as neighbors. In such a "little society" (Redfield 1960), the components of self are more or less consistently related. Hence religion provided guidelines and ways of knowing regarding marriage, life in the community, and moral decisions.

As Jews, like the rest of us, encountered modern society, however, the senses they had of who they were become variegated. Obviously, this means that as they moved from one aspect of institutional social life to another, they received what appear to them as confusing and inconsistent messages about who they are. In a religious context, for example, a woman may be required to play a passive and supportive role in worship, while in her secular life she may be rewarded for activity and leadership. Whenever such tensions of identity develop between religion and society, patterns of accommodation, conflict, and cooperation often appear. The history of Judaism in America follows such patterns.

Mass immigration to America, beginning in the 1880s and continuing into the 1920s, brought nearly 2 million Jews to the United States. These Jews, for the most part, had identities at odds with those of the Protestants already well established in the United States, and the resulting ethnic and religious bigotry is well documented (McNamara 1974; Sklare 1971). One adaptation for Jews was to retreat into their distinctive ethnic identity, marked by separate calendars, dress, and, perhaps most important, the Yiddish language. In this case, religious identity simply overpowered its competitors as a source for establishing senses of selfhood.

But this adaptation became more precarious as Jews, out of necessity, engaged the dominant Protestant population. Of course, some people of Jewish ancestry assimilated, either through conversion or more frequently, by secularizing their senses of who they were. But because of the strength of Judaism as a culture, the waves of immigration of people reinforcing this cultural system, and the reactions to them by the dominant population, American Jews rejected the idea of assimilation and accommodated their beliefs and practices to life in secular American society (Sklare 1971, 4). Hence the self-concepts of today's orthodox Jewish women may well contain ways of making sense out of supporting feminists causes, for example, while maintaining orthodox practices in the synagogue. On the face of it, this may appear contradictory, since women are not allowed full participation in worship (they may not enter parts of the synagogue or read from the Torah). But within the meaning system of the selves of these women, there are no contradictions. Some may interpret the apparent contradiction in terms of the benefits they believe they derive from membership in the Jewish community; others may make sharp distinctions in codes of conduct for religious and secular behavior.

Nevertheless, their identities illustrate how complex the relationship between secular and sacred identities may be. So, although religious institutions operate to give identity to those who espouse the faith, their ability to do so depends on the enactments of sacred assumptions into organizations, or, as we call them, group forms.

Religion as Organization

Articles of institutionalized faith become different kinds of concrete organizations depending on the emphasis and use people give each article. A *sect* may stress the supernatural aspects of faith, healing powers, snake handling, and, more recently the meditative occultism of the East. A *church* may rest firmly on a rational approach to faith, not denying the sacred assumptions of the unknown but circumscribing their application. A church leaves healing to medical sciences and visions to the margins and fringes of societal membership. The precise form institutional knowledge assumes results from complex and mutual influences, both secular and sacred. The way in which religious institutional knowledge interacts with the societal context in which it exists determines the form the religion assumes.

Any observable religious form may contain certain mixtures of all the assumptions of the religious institution, as well as those from other institutions of society. An Episcopalian church displays elements of traditional and modern trends. The battle for the right of women to become priests exemplifies these two forces. On the one hand, the interpretation of sacred knowledge, found mostly in biblical and other sacred literature, decrees one form of organization: a hierarchy of men ordered in terms of authority over church-related affairs. On the other hand, modern reinterpretation, influenced by a more general movement involving the equal application of the principles of rationalism, demands open admission to the traditional order and, in radical instances, reordering the hierarchy itself.

We cannot hope to describe every form that religious institutionalized knowledge can assume. We can, however, suggest that such forms may be placed on two continua that represent forces influencing the formation of religion: the sect-church continuum and the traditional–modern one.

From Sect to Church

The sect-church continuum has been widely used by sociologists of religion since Troeltsch (1931) first suggested it. It encompasses a vast range of religious groups—everything from a storefront church to the Roman Catholic hierarchy.

The dimensions of the continuum are three: (1) the degree of codification of beliefs; (2) the degree of formality in the organization of the religion itself; and (3) the legitimacy of both the beliefs and the organization of the religion.

At one extreme are sects, people banded together on the basis of similar beliefs, but who do not possess charters, doctrines, or recognition by other segments of society as legitimately established religion. Churches, by contrast, are marked by high degrees of formal organization, codified belief systems, and widely distributed recognition as established religious groups. Leaders of sects need not graduate from a seminary or even be ordained. They proclaim themselves leaders, and if followers can be found, a sect is born. Such persons are called *charismatic leaders*, and are people who are believed to possess certain distinctive qualities. They claim an endowment of special gifts of spiritual power. A sect, then, is a band of people who gather together because they share similar beliefs. Out of these beliefs emerges a social organizational form. It is usually ordered around a charismatic leader and may vary greatly in organizational detail from sect to sect according to the dictates of the leaders. A church, even if originated as a sect, has become an established form with definite requirements for membership and meeting places that are recognized as such by other persons in the society.

Sects do not stress continuity of practice from generation to generation, since they are concerned mostly with start-up problems, such as how to recruit members and raise necessary funds. Sects, therefore, rely on a kind of "rational motif" for the articulation of faith. We use the word "rational" here in its most general sense, meaning consistently reasonable according to the tenets of belief. Rationality, then, is a matter of how the individual demonstrates reasonably his or her beliefs. In sects, this is accomplished through testimony, not liturgy. In the sect, leaders do their own work, thinking up their own sermons or getting them directly through visions or other means of contacting God. In churches, sermon topics are often handed down by the "higher-ups" (e.g., bishops or commissions) in the form of outlines and suggested references.

Approaches to worship vary greatly from sect to sect, as do mannerisms and styles of interaction among the people involved. Often, these styles and mannerisms are derived from secular forms. Preachers wear business suits, not robes; meeting places are tents, not temples; and even permanent meeting places look like meeting halls or even sports pavilions.

To be sure, distinctions between sect and church are never completely clean, since many modern sects have adopted bureaucratic practices such as making announcements and collecting money during a service. But the sect has an impromptu character to it, while the church tends to ritualize all worship. In sects, rituals are used, but they are not beyond modification, as they may become in churches. What distinguishes the modern from the traditional church is ease of change. For change is a hallmark of individual rationalism, while it is a threat to tradition.

The differences between the traditional church and the modern one are very much like the differences between the positionally oriented families and the individually oriented ones we discussed earlier. The former are procedurally rooted in precedent and the latter operate on "goal-specific modes of thinking." The traditional church demonstrates its form in architecture from past eras, such as gothic arches and roofs. This kind of design is appropriate by precedent. The modern form uses edifices that resemble supermarkets or office buildings with a "tasteful, inconspicuous" ornamentation of small crosses or spirals. The modern choice of design is a matter of local churches and congregations to a much greater degree than in traditional church bodies.

A Typology of Religious Organizational Forms

With this preliminary discussion of organizational form, we present a typology of form for religious reality. There are many variations on the continua, and the following scheme, like any analytic device, gains its usefulness from how well it helps us portray religion as a social phenomenon. For each cell of the typology, we sketch a typical case illustrating a traditional sect, a traditional church, a modern sect, and a modern church (see Figure 5.1).

	Traditional	Modern
Sect	Reactionary movements	Rational individualizing movements
Church	The religious establishment	Religious progressivism

Figure 5.1
A typology of religious organizational forms

Reactionary Movements. Reactionary Movements combine the characteristics of the sect with those of the traditional form. This combination results in a following of a resurrected past, as Sid and Morton's experience illustrates.

Sid and Morton were seminary students at Southwestern Seminary, noted for its outstanding youth education program and dedicated to turning out well-prepared youth educators for Basic South churches across the land. Teaching at the seminary was excellent, and the buildings were quite modern. Sid, however, was depressed. He longed for the reverent, ascetic life, and could visualize himself clothed in collar and robe, leading chant after chant for a small number of obedient and meditative monks. He discovered that he was spending more time reading about the medieval era of church history. His regular studies lagged, but his knowledge of esoteric monasteries and orders grew. One especially appealed to him: the order of Florentine Monks.

Never more than 100 strong, historians have debated what actually took place within the walls of the monastery. Some believe that the monks daily enacted events from Christ's life. They were devoted to asceticism. They fasted, prayed for long hours, and their garb was drab. Only appointed messengers communicated with the monks. Their community was almost totally self-sufficient.

Sid shared his newfound fascination with Morton. Morton listened, sensing something extraordinary about Sid's enthusiasm. One day Sid said, "Why can't this be done today? My father left me some land in Montana that would be perfect for a monastery." Morton's interest sharpened as he and Sid planned to establish the place and seek recruits. The seminary was a bore. No one seemed to care about the crass, commercial, almost advertising-like quality of Basic South's evangelism. There was no respect for the past in this seminary, so Sid and Morton thought. The past was simply *Catholic* and irrelevant to the origins of the modern Basic South church. Sid began speaking publicly about his plans. He spoke of a neo-Florentine Order. After several unheeded warnings from the heads of the seminary, he was asked to resign. He did so. So did Morton and twelve others. This small band of believers moved to Montana, to the land on which stood the summer vacation cabin built by Sid's father. The men preached along the way, dressed in gray wool robes. They shaved their heads and fasted, preaching of the Second Coming of Jesus.

The townspeople of Chugwater have learned to tolerate these monks after two years of seeing them in the town's grocery and hardware stores. The monks come into town infrequently. When they do, they are quiet, speaking in low tones of second comings and requesting the necessities of life from store clerks.

Rational Individualized Movements. Rational, individualized movements combine the group characteristics of the sect with an emphasis on individual decision making found in the modern form. The recent popularity of religion among young people can illustrate this merger of forms.

Melisa is a Christian. People call her a "Jesus Freak." Her journey to Christ has been long and rough despite her young twenty-three years. Her story is simple. Born into a middle class family, her father is a junior high school teacher. Her mother owns and operates a fabric shop in a local shopping center. She has one younger sister. The family occasionally went to church—on Easter and Christmas Eve. For two summers Melisa went to a summer camp sponsored by the Presbyterians. Mostly, these early experiences with religion were pleasant. The pastor had a nice voice, and her parents respected his "intellectual" approach to religious matters. To Melisa, he seemed like a polished gentleman Sunday school teacher. The summer camps were great fun—lots of swimming and games, and the boys were cute. The evening devotionals generally dealt with abstract ideas like salvation, church heritage, and the Protestant movement. She remembers hearing a lot about Calvin, but she is vague on the details of the religious instruction of that summer.

By the time she entered high school, her contacts with organized religion decreased. Soon, Sunday mornings were used for "sleeping in," a time to recuperate from Saturday night's activities. Ah, Saturday night—the dances, the boys, the beer, and finally, the dope. Melisa at first really "had a good time." She learned to like the taste of beer and was becoming more and more "experienced" with the boys. By her junior year in high school, she was an organizer of "pot" parties. She felt a need to have "fun," "while I'm still young," as she would say. She often talked in a philosophical vein of her quest for "fun." She was frequently heard to say, "I just feel something inside me driving me to experience and experiment."

She graduated from high school without getting into serious trouble. She enrolled at Biggest State University. There she discovered the pursuit of pleasure offered even greater horizons. More and a wider variety of boys (men, now). There was "coke," M.J., and "harder stuff, if you wanted it"—the coed dorms made her feel mature, capable of handling almost anything. Sure, at first there were adjustments, but now she knew she was a woman—independent and living without fear. Still, a few hard break-ups with "live-in" men, some disappointments in classroom performance, and Melisa was "uptight," "hassled."

> I was in a turmoil inside—no inner peace. Then I met this woman from a dorm across campus. She was into "New Age"—Zen and yoga. I was intrigued, so I started visiting with her. Turns out she belonged to this commune. On weekends and during vacations, she would return there where she used to live for two years. She said to recharge and prepare for the "profane" world. Well, one weekend I went with her. It was not like a church camp. A guru led us in

meditation. We neatly kept schedules for work and discussion groups. We all cooked, cleaned, prepared meager meals, and cared for the goats we kept.

Melisa's interest in school waned, except for Professor Yernson's class on Eastern religions. Finally, she was on academic probation, then out altogether. She "vagabonded" for a while, hitchhiking across country. Exhausted, lost, with feelings of failure inside, she made her way back to the commune. There she "got it together" physically—off drugs, onto good food, and she was mentally "getting straight." Still, she never really believed like her friend apparently did. She spoke to the guru. He said, "There are many ways. Each must find his own to the rose garden of contentment."

After a few months, she left the guru's place, wandered a while longer, practicing her yoga and getting into and out of the drug scene, reading self-help paperbacks on TM, EST, and the like. One night, with some friends she happened to be living with for a few months, she went to hear the Reverend Mon Shine. In her words,

> Inside the glow burned brighter, more intense, until I felt tears in my eyes and something pulling at my heart. The music "softly and tenderly Jesus is calling, calling to you and to me—come home, come home. Ye who are weary, come home, come home." He was calling me and I went. The Reverend Shine welcomed me. When I told him how I felt God's presence, I knew I was home. Now I am complete.

Melisa lives with other converts now. They work for the Reverend Shine. They hit the shopping centers. In a southwestern city, they even did a ten-day jail sentence when the merchants at the shopping center had them arrested for trespassing. They sang and were really full of the Holy Spirit, content and complete in those jail cells. After their release, they moved on to a nearby town to seek new converts.

Melisa found her way, and now her only fear is her parents, who keep trying to get her to come home and get back into college. They once mentioned a reeducation program, but she replied that she would sue if they tried that. They seem to be reconciled to Melisa and her new religion now. At least, they do not worry about her involvement with drugs, as they did before. The Reverend Shine forbids their use.

The Religious Establishment The religious establishment derives from people utilizing the purest instance of the church form with a sense of preservation. The resultant organization is highly legitimate and seeks confirming links with tradition.

At the corner of fifth and Boulder in the downtown district of Midcity, USA, the spiral of the Church of Saint Mary's reaches up to the fifth storey of the bank building next to it. On the other side of the church's impressive buttressed walls begins the Latino ghetto. Father O'Neill has been the rector of the church for thirty years. He runs a tight church. He still offers a Latin Mass, the only church in town that does so. The old ladies come in chauffeur-driven, long black cars of ten-year vintage. Both cars and women show signs of aging. They offer charity through generous contributions made anonymously to the church for use by the shawl-covered Mexicans who kneel by their sides—juxtaposed to the old-rich Irish whose children are in corporate life away from the old neighbors in the suburban life they call "family"; and the newly arrived Spanish mother-tongued whose only tie with the familiar they find in the incomprehensible language of old-style worship.

Father O'Neill is kind. He puzzles at the surroundings of his church, the contrast between the decaying human habitat on its one side, the glitter of steel, white concrete, and plush carpets on its other. Yet, he knows that all is in God's hands and that his task is to serve in the only way he knows how. He tried once to reach the young Latinos on the streets. They were polite enough, and some did attend Mass and go to confession, but they never confided in him; they never seemed to communicate. Perhaps, if his Spanish were better. The young were too much influenced by a street existence of doubles, dozens, and rappin' and runnin'. It was hopeless, and Father O'Neill knew it. He retreated to the old and comfortable, awaiting the appointment of a younger, more energetic priest, who might have a better chance to reach the young people in the neighborhood. And he, in preservation and in the spirit of the old, resigned himself to an incomplete understanding of what was happening to him in the social surroundings of his church. "Things change but the sacred is constant, without change, forever and ever," he would mutter to himself on occasion.

Whenever Father O'Neill desires interfaith fellowship, he contacts Rabbi Sebran of the orthodox synagogue a few miles to the north, and they meet for coffee at a Denny's restaurant. They are good friends. Their backgrounds contrast, Irish and German, their congregations come from different cultures, but these matters of church modernization and the growing strength of reform Judaism seem to unite them in a common reverence for the past. In history, there is a bond between them even if their particular histories differ.

Neither the rabbi nor the priest knows what the future holds for their respective religions. Can they persevere and hold back a measure of heritage against the onslaught of the modern mind with its practicality, flexibility, and persistent tendency to calculate all things? The two men are united in opposition against a common enemy they do not fully understand.

Religious Progressivism. As our example illustrates, religious progressivism represents the modern church. The Church of the Ascension sits in the middle of what was once a wheat field. It is surrounded by a black asphalt parking lot with white painted lines marking off places for cars. On one side, an open field stretches into the hinterland; on the other, a few hundred yards from the parking spaces, houses line the street; houses with dark green yards of sodden grass and air conditioners whirring noisily up against the tightly closed windows of neighbor's residence. The brick facades of the houses blend nicely with the compact construction of the church. The church itself boasts wooden beams in its sanctuary that protrude outside, drawing attention away from the electrical boxes and conduit connections on the wall below. Gravel outlines the small bushes and groomed flowerbeds that nestle in front of the church. This church belongs to the suburbs. It contrasts with the stately edifices of its sister congregations in downtown Southville. But, here, it blends and complements. The billboard on the nearby freeway announces "Green Acre Estates—Family Living with Planned Churches and Schools."

The pastor of Ascension spends much of his energy raising money to maintain the church building. Electric bills alone run into the thousands of dollars monthly. During the first three years of his tenure in this newly opened church, the pastor struggled to keep his church open. One month there were so few donations and pledges and attendance was so low that he was barely able the pay the electric bill. Finally, he hit on an idea that seemed perfect for this pastorate: the *drive-in* church. After all, these people live on wheels—they commute to work, they drive the kids to school, drive a few blocks to the grocery store, and they often eat at drive-in restaurants. On Sunday morning, why not a *drive-in* church? The pastor remarked in an interview,

> These people like a casual way of life. They dress up all week to go to work and Sunday is a day to relax. When we required social gatherings on Sundays, our members just did not respond. This way [with the drive-in church] they can lounge around and do chores. All they need do is drive over to the church and plug into the speakers to receive the word of the Lord.

On Sundays, cars pack the lot. Drive-in movie speakers have been installed, and each car simply "plugs-in." The equivalent of "car hopping" altar boys pass among the cars and collect the offering at the appropriate time. There is still a service inside the church, and attendance for this inside service is up since the speakers were installed in the parking lot. While the church seems vital now, there can be little doubt that the drive-in service sustains the church.

At first there was some negative publicity about the drive-in concept of worship, but now all the "Green Acre people" simply take it for granted. The church is like a religious "Get and Go," a sacred convenience stop where you can get "the word of Lord and a whole lot more." To many members of the church, actually seeing one another regularly is not considered a necessary part of a religious experience. Their worlds of business, family, and religion have merged in a universal form. This form is mobile, dependent on a car, and private in the sense that the goal of every activity centers on "individual access to a service."

When we term this form "progressive," we mean that the form has assumed some characteristics of the secular world. We refer to the progressive step-by-step accommodation of the religious to the secular. The Church of the Ascension still preaches the word of the Lord in much the same language as the religious establishment, but the semantics of the expressions differ profoundly. The progressive form utilizes the forms of everyday life, not those of the past. It depends on a common set of life experiences already existing in its potential members. It taps these common experiences to realize religious intent.

In this form, the same "speaker" who conveys the breathy tones of a movie screen love scene may speak the words of Jesus. The commercial rationale for the use of the private automobile lends itself to the questions of the religious institution.

Of course, there are many variations in the degree of progressivism found in the modern church. Nevertheless, even in traditional strongholds, such as the Catholic church, there have been adaptations to the secular trends in society. Lay leadership and decollared priests and dehabited nuns reflect this adaptation. When we focus on organizational form, we can see clearly the influence of secular forms of the larger society. The supermarket architecture of the Southland Church, the absence or minimization of the objects of worship, and the increasing emphasis on the everyday character of religious experience, all illustrate how rational modes of modern thought have "infiltrated" religious organizations. In the progressive adaptation, we observe the members of the individually oriented family looking through the windshield of the family automobile, worshipping their image of God and answering ultimate questions.

Individaul Adaptations: Religious Awareness

Our guiding principle for description has been to look for inner connections among three main components of social existence: institutions, organizations, and individual awareness. Our descriptions themselves point to inextricable links among these considerations in any social scene. Hence, in detailing the aspects of one part, we allude to the other two. It should come as no surprise, therefore, that religious awareness among members of our society parallels their exposure to institutional knowledge through societal forms. This fact allows us to characterize the awareness an individual in society has of these social forces according to adaptations to organizational forms.

For purposes of illustration, we suggest the following ideal types: conventional believers, free thinkers, and hypocrites. Each of these individual means of organizing awareness may be found in each of the four organizational forms we have just depicted.

Conventional Believers

Essentially, conventional belief is an outcome of conformity, which may be defined as an alignment between forms, on the one hand, and individual thought patterns on the other. Even a sect has conformists. They adhere to the teaching of the reactionary leader or the rational accounts of the charismatic figure. Churches, too, have among their ranks conventional believers: A member of the Church of the Ascension who ascribes to the idea of a drive-in worship espouses the conventions of the progressive form. A member of St. Mary's who defends the traditional origins of practice is equally conventional for that form.

Conventional belief, then, must be understood as taking place within a system of relevancy. The question of the use of automobiles as vehicles of worship, as irreverent and profane as this might appear to traditional conventionalists, may be a matter of religious urgency to progressive conventionalists. Similarily, to the sect member, the question of the historical place of an item of belief, say the value of fasting, may be either crucial to the entire movement or may be completely dependent on the use to which individuals may put the knowledge. In the first case, we are discussing a matter of unity of belief, and in the second we are concerned with utility of belief.

In the case of sect movements, conventionalism transforms into a following, or retinue. The conventionalist is carefully attuned to shifts in the movement, adjusting his or her personal beliefs to these changes. In the church, however, conventionalism defines spheres of beliefs according to assumptions that are fundamental to the form itself. All the forms depend, for stability, on their members making a somewhat conventional adaptation. We must realize, though, that stability does not necessarily mean absence of change. In fact, sects and churches may depend on change and may foster a conventional outlook for their members that demands change, as long as this change can be interpreted as either sectlike or churchlike in character.

For example, within the progressive church, members expect a "good pastor" to come up with new and creative ideas for advertising the church, recruiting new members, and revising the actual practices of worship (jazz and rock music integrated into the service, for example). They, of course, impose boundaries on innovation: A preacher may go too far in doing spot commercials on radio; nevertheless, innovation in a rational mode is expected.

So the retinue of the guru expect new trips, new ways to meditate, and a plethora of the bizarre and esoteric. If these renewed beginnings are not forthcoming, the guru has been exhausted and a replacement may be sought. It is conventional, then, to seek the novel and strange within this adaptation. The judgment of "This is an ordinary thing we do" is to be avoided at all costs.

Free Thinkers

How much latitude a person has to "think for himself or herself" varies within each organizational form. For instance, the progressive's expectation of innovation allows greater freedom of thought than the established enactments of religious ritual. We would err, though, if we failed to acknowledge that opportunities for free thought exist within all the forms. Even the Latin or Hebrew chant can become an opportunity for individual expression.

But what we have in mind as "free thought" differs from these stylistic variations in enactment, as important as they may be in a full description of religious phenomena. We refer, instead, to new thought, and to the creation of ideas and practices that contrast with convention. The key lies in the juxtaposition of convention and free thought. Free thinkers use convention as a starting point. They expand, question, doubt, and, perhaps, innovate in a radical sense.

The established church, as well as the rational sect, must deal with this pattern of awareness. Religious institutions, especially in modern societies, rest on a "precarious vision." They function to offer alternative interpretations to the secular, mechanistic mentality of the modern person of reason and reasonable passion. The constant work required to sustain sacred assumptions may often become a burden too great even for the most devout. The problem of the "doubting Thomas" is a perennial threat to any religious version of reality. The believer may confront situations of life in which the religious reality is simply overwhelmed by interpretations from other institutionalized stocks of knowledge. The problems of poverty, illness and personal suffering may not fit with the tenets of faith.

These strains manifest themselves in what we are calling "free thought," which implies thought deriving from nonreligious sources or offering interpretations at odds with convention. Progressivists, such as Unitarians, may pride themselves on "free thinking," whereas established churches, such as Southern Baptists, insist on fewer degrees of freedom in belief regarding the "virgin birth" or, more generally, a literal interpretation of biblical materials.

Nevertheless, we contend that the "free thinker" is a proper category of individual consciousness for all forms. In cases of rationally dominated forms of religion, free thinking functions to motivate change. In cases of traditionally dominated forms, it operates slowly to instigate change that may be necessary for the overall survival of the form, like the accommodation of faith to specific scientific findings. Still another important function of "free thought" is to underscore and help believers understand what conventional belief is. We refer to the practice of portraying the doubts and secularism of heathens as negative illustrations for believers.

With Durkheim, we conclude that a little deviance within a form may be necessary for the survival of the form. An elementary social fact of religion may be that it needs free thinkers, both to relate to other aspects of society and to sustain a sense of its own separateness.

Hypocrites

A hypocrite is a person whose beliefs lack authenticity. This person feigns beliefs and pretends to be what he or she is not. The testimony of the hypocrite is hollow, without conviction. We write of the hypocrite with full awareness of the pejorative tone of the word. The word is frequently used as a negative term, and a hypocrite does indeed, from the standpoint of the social form, constitute a serious threat to the version of reality the form offers its members.

Hypocrisy undercuts the sacred assumption of religious versions of reality. A person pretending to be a good Baptist for the purposes of making business contacts, a women enjoying the accolades bestowed on her as a Christian wife and mother by her follow believers while secretly tasting the joys of an illicit love affair, represent a most serious danger to a "precarious vision." This is so because a hypocrite does not really believe. He or she only pretends to believe. Hypocrisy differs from chameleonism (Rosow 1966), an extreme adaptation in which a person changes social colors according to his or her environment. The chameleon is a naive conformist. The hypocrite is a "fake," and as such, cannot play a role in a religious mentality other than to manipulate it for instrumental purposes.

Of course, what counts as hypocrisy varies from organization to organization. A progressive hypocrite is the most difficult to identify, and a reactionary sect member the least difficult. In both the progressive form and the rationalized sect, pretense and inauthenticity are extremely difficult to describe. What may seem to be a clear case of unfaithfulness may be one person's version of faith. Or a contradiction between verbal statement and action may not necessarily be experienced as such by an individual. For example, a Unitarian minister's love affairs with several women may be an outward sign of his unbounding Christian capacity for warmth, whereas the youth minister's flirtations with the coeds in the choir at a conservative college might be seen as "the work of the devil." The question of hypocrisy, then, involves the authenticity of belief. The Unitarian may be authentic (of course, that does not assure concord with his congregation), whereas the youth minister could not behave as he does if he were really "born again."

We have outlined the descriptive difficulties hypocrisy presents for the observer, but we have not fully stated why such descriptions should be carried out. Simply, it is a matter of accurate characterization of the constructed reality. The presence of pretense in a belief system means that if we are not attuned to the ulterior motives of those we observe in an allegedly religious setting, we will fail to capture the essence of the reality itself.

When Max Weber described the relationship between the Protestant ethic and the spirit of capitalism, he was not concerned with hypocrisy. He focused on the affinity between the two authentically professed systems of knowledge. However, many of the examples he gave, like a person's credit references being associated with his being a deacon, may have been confounded by hypocrisy. In our descriptions of the versions of reality around us we must assess the authenticity of interactions within an organizational setting. Unfortunately, sociologists have rarely studied hypocrisy and the bearing it might have on the relationships between religion and the secular aspects of social life. You might keep this criticism in mind as you read through the next section of religiosity and behavior, and think about how hypocrisy might confound some of the relationships sociologists have studied.

Does Religion Make a Difference? Religiosity and Behavior

We have seen how religion reflects society, and how individuals draw on religion in a variety of ways to give meaning to their lives. We have also documented the twin processes of modernity and secularization that have clearly affected religion in modern society. Still, we recognized that religion remains a vital social force even in American society. Cults, social movements, and changing structures in the organization of religious experiences combine to give individuals resources for living.

Given the persistence of religion and religious experiences, it is not surprising that the question "Does religion make a difference in individual behavior?" still stimulates a great deal of sociological research. Of course, the classical sociologist Durkheim suggested that suicide was clearly related to the degree to which an individual is integrated into his or her society, and religion is major agent of social integration. Differences in suicide rates for groupings of people, therefore, will vary by the religious affiliation of individuals, with Protestants generally having higher rates than Catholics, married people lower rates than singles, and married with children even lower than married and childless. Not until the work of Gerhart Lenski (1961), however, did large-scale systematic research demonstrate the continued force of the *religious factor* in modern social life.

In 1958, while at the University of Michigan, Lenski directed the Detroit Area Study. Interviews were conducted with 656 persons with the special intent of gathering information about religious beliefs and backgrounds. Lenski was particularly interested in testing to see if the hypothesis of the classic sociologist Max Weber about the relationship between Protestant religious beliefs and secular capitalistic attitudes and behavior was relevant in modern society.

Weber had tried to show that the vigorous form of capitalism found in Germany, England, and the United States in the nineteenth century was at least partially the consequence of the Protestant Reformation. According to Weber's comparative studies of India, China, ancient Irasel, and the modern states of France, England, Germany, and the United States, the common factor present in nations with strong capitalistic tendencies and performance was that they were Protestant countries.

Lenski was not attempting to prove or disprove Weber's hypothesis because Weber himself had been very careful to state that his idea was about the origins of what he called the "spirit of capitalism." But Weber on a visit to the United States in 1904, noticed that membership in the Baptist church or similar sectarian groups served as a "credit reference" and proof of a man's business acumen and personal trustworthiness. So Lenski reasoned that in a city like Detroit, composed of people from many different racial, ethnic, and religious backgrounds, perhaps residuals of the affinity between religion and economics remained in the consciousness of the people. Specifically, Lenski wanted to see if religion made a difference in the attitudes and behaviors of people in the economic realm of everyday life. Lenski's sample was 41 percent white Protestants, 35 percent white Catholics, 15 percent black Protestants and 4 percent Jews; and on the basis of the analysis of the data collected, Lenski concluded that a white Protestant is more likely than a white Catholic.

> (1) to consider work important and to have a small family; (2) to avoid installment buying and save money for the future; (3) to vote Republican and question the welfare state; (4) to take a liberal view of freedom of speech, but hesitate to push for racial integration in the schools; (5) to migrate and leave close family ties in order to obtain more education, a better job, and a higher position in the class system; and (6) to develop a commitment to the principle of intellectual autonomy.

Lenski further probed the relationship between religion and values by asking people to rank things they considered important about work, for example, high income, no danger of being discharged, working short hours, chances for advancement, and the feelings of accomplishment one can gain from the job. He reasoned that closest to the Protestant ethic were feelings of accomplishment. Indeed, nearly half of all the people in the study ranked this attribute first, but the rank order by grouping was, as Weber's theory might suggest, White Protestants first, Jews second, white Catholics third, and black Protestants fourth.

In general, Lenski's research showed that the "religious factor" was still significant in American society. By simply knowing a person's religious affiliation and degree of involvement in the religion, we can know something about how he or she will act and think economically. Such a finding was welcome in sociology as a step in the direction of demonstrating a fundamental perspective of the social sciences: that the motivational basis for participation in one aspect of society may come from another, presumably unrelated, aspect.

So provocative was Lenski's research that it served as the basis for other research projects. Jackson, Fox, and Crockett (1970), for example, used a national sample, originally drawn in 1957, to test the relationship between religion and occupational achievement. They discovered that Protestants were more likely than Catholics of the same occupational origin to enter high-status occupations; that Catholics were more likely than Protestants of the same origin to enter low-status occupations; and, finally, that Protestants were more likely to move up rapidly in occupational status while Catholics were more likely to be sharply downwardly mobile. This study supported Lenski's view that the values one gains from religious experiences are relevant to occupational achievement.

When other sociologists attempted to verify these and other of Lenski's findings, however, the results were different. In his review of several of these studies, Gaede (1977) discovered that researchers uncovered different variables that accounted for mobility. His interpretation points to such "secular" variables as race and ethncity, gender, and community as more important than religious ones for predicting differences in values toward work, money, and the use of time. Of course, such findings suggest the diminished significance of the religious factor in modern social life.

Other studies have continued to illustrate that religion is an important variable for the explanation of different types of behaviors: general satisfaction with life; deviant behaviors such as drug use; juvenile delinquency, and alcoholism; and gender-related behaviors and attitudes. In order to appreciate this research, we need to introduce the concept of religiosity because this concept has become central in the assessment of the effects of religion on attitudes and behavior. Whenever we want to see if attitudes about abortion, war and peace, social justice, and the like, are linked to religion, we need to be as clear as possible about the scope of religion. Religiosity refers to the full range of meanings and behaviors associated with religion. Some people may consider themselves religious, but never go to church, others may frequently attend religious services but, for a variety of reasons, not consider themselves very devout. Because of this possibility and other problems with a singular definition of religion, a precise and complete definition of religiosity is needed

The one most often used is found in Glock and Stark's *Religion and Society in Tension* (1965). They suggest that religiosity has several dimensions and that to assess the influence of religion on attitudes and social behavior it is necessary to keep these separate, for they each may be related differently to "secular" aspects of social life. The dimensions are the experiential, the ideological, the intellectual, and the consequential.

The experiential dimension refers to the degree and intensity of a person's experience of God. People who "speak in tongues," for instance, have strong experiential religiosity, as do those who have visions and "close personal" encounters with saints or other figures of faith. The ideological dimension involves the individual's beliefs. Clearly, to some people the details, form, and history of what they believe about God is the most salient aspect of their religiosity. The ritualistic dimension refers to institutional or organized practices of religion, such as reading the Bible, carrying a religious charm, or observing religious holidays. The final, consequential dimension is somewhat different from the others, and is the one that concerns us. It refers to the consequences that religion has for the individual in a variety of areas.

A large body of research exists to assess the degree to which religious beliefs, practices, and experiences are associated with delinquency. Hirschi and Stark (1969) expected that the religious boys they studied would be less likely than the nonreligious to be involved in delinquent acts. But they discovered that lack of participation in religious activities was not correlated with delinquency. Nevertheless, this study, as you might guess, provoked a number of others that did demonstrate the expected link. Higgins and Albrecht (1977) studied teenagers in Atlanta, and Albrecht, Chadwick, and Alcorn (1977) analyzed a sample of members of the Mormon church. Both studies reported an inverse relationship between church attendance and rates of delinquent behavior. Stark (1984) returned to the issue with subsequent research and claims that the reason for the confusing results is that sociologists are looking at different things. In other words, different dimensions of religiosity may be involved. Stark reviewed the literature and, using his own work as a basis, writes, "It is not whether an individual kid goes to church or believes in hell that influences his or her delinquency. What is critical is whether a majority of the kid's friends are religious" (Stark 1984, 275). He goes on to note that social life is made up of daily interaction with friends and that these friends have more to do with our morality or values than does religion.

Such reasoning did not settle the argument. Peek, Curry, and Chalfant (1985) asked whether involvement in a religious subculture, where all or most of one's friends are religious, has a lasting effect on behavior and attitude. Following a cohort of students during their four years of high school, they found, in support of Stark's theory, that as long as the students remained within a religious subculture, they were deterred from delinquent behavior because their fear of divine punishment for deviance was supported by their group membership. But whenever these teenagers broke away from their religious peer groups, the deterrent effect of religion was lost. In fact, these students had higher rates of delinquency than those who were never members of a religious peer group (Chalfant, Beckley, and Palmer 1987). Religiosity, apparently, like all social reality, requires constant interactional work.

As the research we have discussed in this section begins to show, religiosity does play a role in contemporary society. Of course, with the development of the modern world, we have seen more and more concessions to the "secular" side of life. For example, stores that used to be closed on Sunday just two decades ago, now are routinely open, and perhaps are even open on Christmas. But in spite of the increased secularization of modern life, it is likely that society will always maintain some sense of religiosity and thus there will always be some structure and function for religious life.

Summary

Sociologists differ in the degree of importance they attribute to religion in society. Generally, in nonmodern societies, religion is a powerful force, and even in the history of Western society it was, indeed, a primary driving force for social change. Although the functions that religion performs have surely changed and religion has been challenged by secular and scientific forms of understanding, it remains significant and vital for many members of contemporary American society.

As social institutions, religious systems of knowledge manifest similar features. They all affirm the limits of human knowledge; they share topics of awareness; they are simple; and they define meanings for sacred life, typically making sharp distinctions between the sacred and the profane. They also give to their believers a strong sense of identity. Religious beliefs are carried in various social organizational forms. The distinction between sect and church involves codification of beliefs, formality of organizational structure, and legitimacy of beliefs. We drew a typology of religious organizational forms to illustrate this diversity. The forms are reactionary movements, rational movements, the establishment, and progressivism.

We characterized how individuals typically make sense out of the social forces that operate in their everyday lives. These interpretations we referred to as "religious awareness." There are conventional believers, free thinkers, and hypocrites. Each form of awareness stands for solutions to the problem of finding religious meanings in ordinary existence, and each functions differently within the individual's life.

Further, we explored the question of how powerful religion is in the everyday lives of members of society by examining the degree to which religiosity is associated with a variety of behaviors and attitudes. We found that religiosity, as measured by attendance at religious services, is not strongly related to the use of alcohol, but is negatively related to the use of drugs and attitudes toward drugs. Religiosity is related to deviance among teenagers, but this relationship is complicated by a youngster's involvement in peer groups. Apparently, as long as one is active in a religion and has friends in everyday life who are also religiously active, there is a strong negative relationship between delinquency and religiosity.

In the next chapter, we turn our attention to a discussion of the institutional meanings of economic inequality. We focus on what we call the "capitalism of everyday life."

Chapter	**6**	ECONOMICS AND THE MEANINGS OF INEQUALITY

Virtually all social institutions have something "economic" in them, and so technically they could be called economic institutions. Although their primary functions are not economic, schools, churches and even families must have ways of generating operating budgets and distributing goods, services and money to their members. Because of this, in this chapter, we speak as if society and economy were one, covering general economic issues that encompass the lives of everyone.

There is a great deal of irony in the economics of modern society, for while people believe that money is not *really* important to personal worth, most wish, for themselves, the highest placement possible in a system based on economic inequality. They desire the pleasures and power they believe are associated with success, yet they expect equal treatment from those who already have them. And while many members of society may wish it were not so, they must take the topic of money and its distribution seriously because their lives are affected in very profound ways by the things they must do to earn money and by the amount of money they have. In fact, a good predictor of a person's life expectancy and health is his or her economic resources. Beyond this, one way to tell about their educational backgrounds is to find out how much money people have; and, finally, we can learn a great deal about people if we know what they do to earn a living.

Inequality as a Feature of Society

One of the most striking features of modern society is the economic inequality in it, and the resulting differences in power that people have over one another. The topic of inequality is one that has challenged sociologists for accurate description and adequate explanation since the early days of empirical research. Since money is often a delicate subject, sociologists who study economic inequality must be particularly careful about not being influenced by their own values with respect to it. In the long run, sociologists are just like everyone else. Some are "elitist," and would like to use whatever resources they can to climb higher on the economic ladder. Others, like Marx, think we all should do everthing we can to reduce inequality to the point where we have a "classless" society. All sociologists must hold these values in check when studying economic issues.

Most studies of inequality begin, then, with a distinction between the awareness people have of their relative station in life and what their actual position is. In American society, for example, while approximately 80 percent of the adult population classify themselves as middle class, 70 percent of American families earned $35,000 or less in1983 (Commerce Department Figures). When you consider that the middle-class American dream includes a privately owned home and an automobile, the average cost of which, in1983, was $80,000 and $8500 respectively, it is fairly obvious that most Americans are not making the dream come true in their own lives. Further, when you discover that nearly two-thirds of the total income of the nation is concentrated in the top two-fifths of American families, one must conclude that what people say about their position in society does not always coincide with how they really compare to others.

Objective and Subjective Measures

Economic inequality generally refers to differences in social class, and we think of class in terms of the access people have to money, the amount they have, or can spend, and the consequences of possessing money in their everyday lives. Sociologists have measured social class in a variety of ways, but most seem to fall into two great categories: objective and subjective

In modern society, only one criterion works to discriminate among categories of people, and that is money. Hence, the U.S. Department of Commerce arranges people into categories of earnings, and we can tell about the distribution of this great resource in society by building tables showing the percentage of people who fall into each category. Table 6.1 illustrates indirectly what class structure looks like in American society.

Table 6.1
Yearly Family Income Percentage in the United States (1986)

Annual Income	Percentage of Population
Over $50,000	12
$35,000–50,000	14
$20,000–35,000	29
$10,000–20,000	23
Under $10,000	22

Source: NORC, General Social Survey (GSS) 1987.

Of course, once we have data like these, we can do a comparative analysis to show how the shape of inequality varies greatly from society to society. America and certain European societies tend to distribute wealth in ways that create middle classes. The class structure of "modern," or highly industrial, societies assumes a diamond shape. Relatively few people are at the top and the bottom of this structure, most people are at the middle.

We must be careful here to realize that while, in these societies, the majority of people are of middle income, this does not mean that most of the wealth of the society is controlled by most of the people. "Middle class" societies are often societies in which a relatively few people possess much of the wealth of society. Moreover, the relative size of the middle class can vary greatly. In Sweden, for example, the middle class is encompassing and the lower classes very small. Of course, Sweden has tax laws that promote the equal distribution of wealth. The very wealthy face a tax structure that can take upward of 90% of their income, while the poor live in a society that provides medical and social services free of charge.

So, the model of class can assume different shapes, from a low profile diamond to a tall-pyramid structure. Sweden represents the former, and Japan the latter. In Japan, for example, only about a third of the workforce is employed by large corporations like Nissan and Sony. While it is true that these corporations provide job security and a robust middle-class existence for most of their employees, most Japanese workers labor in small, family, or independently owned and operated shops whose fate is linked directly to the fate of the large corporations. Workers in these small shops manufacture goods for the corporations — small parts for automobiles or components for electric appliances. They do not have cradle-to-grave job security, nor do they enjoy the high wages of union representation. They make up a large working-class segment of Japan, and their numbers bulge the lower proportion of the diamond-shaped class structure of this industrial society.

An indirect measure of class variation among industrial societies is per capita income (what each person would receive if income were distributed evenly). In 1980, the per capita income of Sweden was about $16,000, $10,400 in the United States, and $8900 in Japan. We see that per capita income relates to the size of the middle class, for in societies like Sweden and Switzerland, the larger middle classes possess more wealth than, say, the smaller middle classes of Japan. Such objective facts about class structure are important for understanding the character of life in society. In Japan, for example, most people work very hard for small wages under conditions that many workers of Europe and American would find very difficult to endure. In a sense, these workers support the model of Japanese capitalism by doing the bidding of, and taking the risks for, large corporations. If business falters, small shop operators lay off workers or reduce their wages, while corporation employees continue to enjoy employment and high wages.

In Scandinavian societies, by contrast, the middle classes include some workers, and the burden of supporting these people has been shifted to the state. In the United States, the largest and most complicated of the modern societies, class structure is unique. We take up shortly the task of explaining how class structure influences, and even determines, the character and organization of society, but first we must complete our description of the class model of society.

Most societies of the world do not fit the diamond-shaped class structure. Instead they are hourglass shaped or more commonly, pyramidal. Of course, this means that most people are very poor, and only a very few people control the vast amount of the society's resources. Wealthy people can be found in virtually every nation of the world, but by the standards of industrial societies, most of the societies of the world are very poor. Using census data (1983) and the U.S. dollar as the standard, we see that per capita income in Egypt and China is $500 and $700, respectively, in Uganda, $200, in Zaire, India and Bangladesh, $100.

These figures are even more striking when we remember that per capita income is the amount of money each person would receive if income were distributed equally within countries. Under these conditions, each Indian would get $200 a year. Actually, many Indians live on far less. If income were distributed equally throughout the world within each country, the people of the wealthiest nations would receive more money each week than most of the world's inhabitants would receive each year.

Certainly, the name most often associated with linking the character and quality of life with class structure is Karl Marx, the nineteenth-century German political theorist. He first showed the link between class and politics, class and life chances, and class and mortality, suggesting that class conditions every aspect of social life. According to Marx, industrialization simplified and exasperated class structure and conflict. His theory suggests that class is ultimately determined by one's relationship to the fundamental way in which things get produced in society. This organization of work and the technologies of work, Marx referred to as the *mode of production*. If a person's labor is required for the production of goods, say he operates a machine or she expends energy assembling components of a computer, then that person is structurally a worker, or a member of the proletariat. Conversely, a business owner or manager, who profits from the production of goods or services but is only indirectly related to the actual productive processes, is a member of the bourgeoisie. These two terms, proletariat and bourgeoisie, were used by Marx to show what he thought was the tendency of capitalism to polarize people into two great classes.

His reasoning for this tendency was based on his understanding of capitalism. He believed that the value of a product was directly proportional to the labor required to produce it, that is, that the work of men and women determines the value of the things. But as capitalists invented different relations to the mode of production, labor-saving inventions such as the assembly line and mass production, it became possible for workers to produce more goods, without an increase in the cost of production. Then, by selling more goods but not paying laborers any more, it became possible to exploit labor. In capitalism, workers are paid less than the product value of their work. Finally, this created a surplus of value, called profit, which went to the owners. According to Marx, this way of organizing an economy was built on a contradiction: The people whose energy or work determine the value of things can never receive just or equal reward for their work. And, of course, workers have little or no control over the distribution of goods. They are therefore relatively powerless in capitalist society.

This contradiction would gradually widen the gap in material comfort between workers and owners, with owners always busy inventing ways to get more labor and more productivity out of employees while paying them relatively less and less. The owners, in turn, because they had surplus value, will use this for their own profit and comfort. Hence, in the long run, the capitalist economy will result in the two great classes and the eventual revolt of the proletariat against the bourgeoisie.

It is ironic that Marxist theory of a simplified class structure actually seems to describe best those societies that are not highly industrialized. The classic pyramid shape of the distribution of material rewards in Third World societies conforms closest to Marxist expectations and predictions, while highly industrial, high-technology societies have very complicated and even inconsistent class patterns.

The Theory of Status Inconsistency

Several sociologists have attempted to explain why the Marxist expectation about class polarization and the subsequent revolt of the workers has not taken place in highly industrial societies. One obvious reason is the persistence of the middle classes and their exercise of control over their own lives as well as their political power. Typically, people with middle-class life styles and chances identify with core cultural values and behave accordingly. For them, the expectation of upward mobility, if not for themselves at least for their children, seems reasonable and, in a very real sense, hard work and playing by the rules does have its rewards—new cars, fine homes, fashionable clothes, and travel.

While middle-class life in these societies is far from utopian, it does seem to offer, in world perspective, a high standard of living and a viable alternative to poverty and exploitation. Still, middle class people can be exploited by the stratification system of which they are a part. The meanings of the word exploitation must be modified and sharpened — some might say "distorted" — to account for the plight of the well-to-do.

Generally, the problems of the middle classes turn out to be psychic. This is exemplified in the award-winning movie *Ordinary People*. The middle-class family portrayed in this film is advantaged by world standards; their problems, the guilt the youngest son of the family feels over the sailboat accident that drowned his older brother, and his subsequent suicide attempt, can be understood as typical problems only against the background of material comfort and complicated peer and family emotional structures.

Perhaps the most powerful idea that explains why class structure seems to become more complicated in modern society, and why it becomes a less powerful factor in the exercise of power in society, is the theory of *status inconsistency*. According to this idea, the class structure of society has become so complex that most people, in their lifetimes, have experiences that reflect a wide range of class stations. A corporate executive may have worked as a common laborer in his youth, or a schoolteacher may paint houses during the summer months. But, more important, people can occupy different "classes" at the same time.

Norbert Wiley (1967) suggests that the class system of America consists of at least three major dimensions: (1) the labor market, which can be a source of conflict among occupational and property-owning groups, (2) the credit or money market, which is the basis for the conflict between creditors and debtors; and (3) the commodity market, which is the basis for conflict between buyers and sellers and landlords and tenants. A given individual participating in the class system may, of course, experience different ranks depending on his or her relationship to others in any and all of these dimensions. For example, a man may own a building, which puts him in conflict with tenants, but he may also owe a bank money which turns the tables and makes him a debtor. Since most of us experience all the conflicts of the three aspects of the class system, you can see how difficult it is to conceive of a system that pulls people together in common political and economic goals.

Wiley and others have used the theory of inconsistency to explain some of the history of political radicalism in American society. They suggest that people with inconsistent class attributes are especially prone to support extremist groups (Wiley 1967, 536). A small businessman, for example, may discover that the size of his debt and the struggle to get loans to stay in business, together with his relationships with customers and employees, highlights the inconsistencies of his place in the system. Although he has dominion over customers and employees, he is at the mercy of market forces that seem out of his control. His response, according to Wiley, is to stress the fundamental values of Americanism because they reinforce his relatively high status on the concrete level of business, while attributing his low status in the credit market to sinister forces that are essentially un-American. This theory helps us understand the right-wing tendencies of small business people, relatively high-income workers, and even retired people.

The picture of class and status in such highly developed societies as the United States, Sweden, and Japan is then a complicated one consisting of many dimensions, some of which reflect the unique historical development of the economic systems of the respective societies and others that relate to the structure of industrialism itself. The task of unraveling these forces and their effects on aspects of work and social life is ongoing and, at times, yields surprising findings.

Perhaps the most comprehensive effort to describe the full range of complexity of the American stratification system can be found in the volumes published as the Yankeetown studies. These studies were conducted, basically during the 1950s, under the direction of Lloyd Warner, an anthropologist by training, who published a summary volume for the series of investigations entitled *Social Class in America*. Over thirty years have passed since the data for these studies were collected, but the patterns first discovered are still valid today.

Warner proposed for his study the diamond-shaped model we introduced earlier, and he carefully devised a methodology for assessing the stratification system of communities, accounting for both subjective and objective dimensions of social class. In Warner's theory, the complete model for a given community consists of six strata: two levels for each of the basic strata. Hence he introduced the idea of upper-upper class and lower-upper class, upper-middle and lower-middle class, and upper-lower and lower-lower class.

This model is important for us because it shows the whole picture of social class. Objectively, one can determine a person's or family's place in the system by knowing a few things about their financial background. For example, Warner's research indicated that source of income is a very important indicator of status. One can rank sources accordingly: Welfare and money otherwise gained through some kind of "handout" indicate the lowest status, hourly wages and commissions for sales are lower than salaries, fees for services rendered move one up the system, and investments and money gained on the stock market or through other "money games" carry very high status. Highest of all, according to the Warner studies of actual eastern communities, is inherited wealth.

Of course, sources of income correlated well with occupation. Laborers receive wages, white collar workers are salaried, professionals receive fees, and the elite receive dividends and interest. There are ironies in this ranking system. The lowest and highest on the income scale are the most removed from the modes of production. Neither the welfare recipient nor the idle rich are required to work for their money.

Other objective indicators of class include educational level (which in Warner's research did not work as well to discriminate class as did source of income), place of residence, occupation, whether school-age children take college preparatory classes, the percentage of income spent for food and shelter, and type of housing.

By assigning numbers to his indicators, Warner was able to calculate numeric values that place a person or family within the model of social class. He discovered that, objectively, several of the middle sized eastern communities he studied that had a fully articulated six strata system broke down into the following composition of strata: 1.4 percent were upper-upper; 1.6 percent were lower-upper,10 percent were upper-middle, 28 percent were lower-middle, 34 percent were lower-upper, and 25 percent were lower-lower.

The composition of a community as measured by Warner's system, will of course vary from community to community, and some communities will not have a true upper-upper class, others will have a very small lower-lower class, and so forth. The following factors seem to be associated with the existence of what Warner called a truncated system (like a five-class pyramid): (1) Size. If a community is very small, it is not likely to have an aristocracy. (2) If a community depends on a simple or even one industry economic base, it is likely to have a truncated system. (3) If the community has experienced erratic population change and dramatic economic ups and downs (these two things often go together), the community will lack some strata.

Finally, ethnicity and race confound the class model. In some communities, there are systems within systems, sucg as a black community within the white in some southern locations, and, in large cities like New York, being Jewish can affect status regardless of other objective indicators.

Warner gave us a full view of social class in America. His work alerted us to the "hidden costs" of social class. He was among the first to show that all manner of life's circumstances — health, life expectancy, and quality of social life — are inextricably bound up with social class for social class functions to open and close opportunities for health care, education, life style and patterns of residence. Social class is, therefore, a major structural condition of economic institutions.

He went so far as to offer a list of conclusions about the significance of social class in American society. Economic factors alone are not sufficient to predict where a particular family or individual will be placed in a system, or to explain completely the phenomenon of social class. Money must be translated into socially approved behaviors and possessions according to the the values and norms of a particular community. The actions and possessions a family exhibits must be valued and accepted by the norms of the community, and to belong to a class, one must be accepted as equal by others who belong to it. Class affects a number of social functions: marriage, education, health, place of residence, friendship experiences, and life style. In America, at least, one may move up and down the scale by employing any number of the following methods: One can get money, change occupations, achieve skills, engage in philanthropy, and marry up or down. Class varies from community to community, but class-related actions, values, and life circumstances are patterned similarly within a given society.

Sexual Stratification

In recent years, the study of inequality has revealed that a major component of stratification systems is sexual, that is, based on gender identity. While anthropologists and sociologists have long analyzed the different roles that men and women play in the division of labor in society (Murdock 1935), when they focused on inequality, they did so without regard to gender. Hence, since most societies are male dominated in the sense of formal power and the control of financial resources, the role that gender played in stratification was overlooked.

Of course, as societies become modern, traditional sex roles break down in every institution. This is especially obvious in the realm of economics as increasing numbers of women enter the workforce, either delaying marriage and having children or working out accommodations in their personal lives that allow for joint participation in economic and family life. But simply entering the workforce and participating in economic institutional life has not resulted in equality between the sexes.

Women, especially in American society, have been entering the workforce in steadily increasing numbers since before the turn of the twentieth century. For example, according to U.S. Department of Commerce statistics, there has been a steady increase in females as a percentage of all workers of from 17 percent in 1890, to 28.8 percent in1950, and over 50 percent in the late1980s. Not only is this participation in economic institutional life historically strong for all women, it is pronounced for young women. U.S. Department of Labor figures show that for women between the ages of twenty and forty nearly 80 percent participate in the labor force. Of course, another way of appreciating this massive shift from family to economic institutions is to look at the percentage of married people whose spouses stay at home to "keep house." According to General Social Survey (GSS) data, in1987 only 6.8 percent of the people surveyed said that during the last week their spouse was "keeping house," and of those "keeping house," over 90 percent reported that they had worked for as long as one year. Since retired people and unemployed males may well be in the category "keeping house," it is obvious that married women no longer stay in the home full-time.

We might expect that as women's participation in the labor force equals that of men, their incomes should reflect this equality. But this is not the case. For example, the pay gap between men and women is easily documented. Again using GSS data, reported earnings for women and men in 1987 reflect a gap even when the educational level for women and men is equal.

While the differences in income for men and women in similar occupations may be decreasing, it is still quite true that women are concentrated in particular occupations. Elementary school teaching and nursing are the most notable examples. But as Glenn and Feldberg (1984, 317) put it, "Clerical work is . . . absolutely and proportionally, the largest single occupational for women."

Indeed, although there have been some changes in recent years, secretaries and typists are overwhelmingly female in the American workforce. What is significant for a discussion of economic inequality is the fact that "female occupations" are typically low-wage jobs. Therefore, while it true that women are participating in the labor force, they are not equally represented in the distribution of money in society because they are concentrated in low-paying occupations.

Table 6.2						
Percentage Distribution of Income: Males and Females by Education						
	Years of Education					
Yearly	0 to 11		12 (high school)		13-20 (college)	
Income	Male	Female	Male	Female	Male	Female
$12,000 and below	38.3	74.6	27.8	61.6	13.4	37.5
$12,500-22,500	36.7	20.6	40.0	30.1	29.2	44.6
$22,500 and above	25.0	4.8	32.2	8.3	57.4	17.9
Note: N = 1351.						
Source: NORC, GSS 1987.						

Of course, this matter of the distribution of income by gender is quite complex because of complex living arrangements between males and females. Since married couples are typically both working, there is a sense in which incomes are shared, as family income. And some researchers have attempted to demonstrate that discrimination against women in the workforce is confounded by discrimination against mothers. Since women are stereotypically understood as "going to have children," employers often are not willing to place them in positions that require uninterrupted career development. Discrimination so balant is, of course, illegal in American society. But the persistence of income and career differences between males and females suggests that some forms of subtle discrimination may be operating (see Wandersee 1988)

While the topic of discrimination against women and subsequent inequality between the sexes encompasses a vast and ever growing literature that we cannot possibly cover, we do want to offer one explanation of the sources of inequality in economic institutional life. This explanation deals specifically with the meanings of life in the context of the modernization process. We have seen repeatedly that scholars and researchers point to the development of rational, differentiated, and relatively manipulative modes of social life as a consequences of modernization. Perhaps nowhere is the process more clear than in the workplace where people deal routinely with one another as instruments, or means to ends, within the context of formal or bureucratic organizations.

Ferguson (1984) suggests that the bureaucratic form that much of economic life assumes disadvantages women. She carefully constructed a critique of rational-economic life from the point of view of feminism. Often women utilize ways to make sense of their jobs which contrast with the "official" view of a modern career. They may, for example, be concerned with problem solving in a diffuse sense; they may rely on relationships in ways that differ from their male co-employees; and they translate caring and nurturing approaches of private life into public life. Any and all of these "female" ways to work may either disadvantage a woman in the workplace as she attempts to gain more rewards for her efforts or result in a concentration of women in jobs within the workplace that require these skills. As we have seen, these jobs are often low paying and defined as "female" aspects of the workplace. Therefore, being a woman in the labor force may mean being subjected to pressures that are simply not present for males.

This presents a dilemma to the working woman. On the one hand, she can act like a man in the context of work, becoming assertive, aggressive, and competitive, or she may accommodate her understandings to work into a form of submission, resulting in occupational segregation, or acquiescence to various manifestations of discrimination (low pay, sexual harassment, and so on).

Ferguson (1984) adds a new twist to the dilemma. She places the sources of inequality for women in the context of the modern society itself. Hence, while she calls for social change favoring women, she does not favor fostering more participation. Instead, she suggests that bureaucracy itself must change.

> Women need power in order to change society, but power within bureaucracies is not change-making power. The organizational forms and discourse of bureaucratic capitalism institutionalize modes of domination that re-create the very patterns of oppression that feminism arose to combat. Feminist discourse offers both a critical vantage point from which to comprehend the inadequacies of the dominant language and structures a fresh direction. (Ferguson 1984, 203)

Social Mobility: What Kind and How Much?

In virtually all societies, people move up and down in the system that distributes social and material rewards. Of course, the degree of movement, or "mobility," as sociologists refer to it, varies from a great deal to very little.

Generally, for the purposes of discussing mobility, we can distinguish among three stratification systems: the caste, estate, and class systems. We have already discussed the class system and there is little reason to doubt that it is replacing the others worldwide. Still, examples, or at least remnants, of the other two exist.

In the caste system, strata are rigidly defined and are based on ascribed characteristics such as skin color or family identity. Here, people are born into a particular stratum, and contact between castes is often limited and governed by a set of rules. Perhaps the most notable caste system is the one that existed in India prior to the reform governments of the 1950s. In the old system, every aspect of life was affected by caste. For instance, intermarriage between a high-caste woman and a low-caste man was strictly prohibited, and a marriage between a high-caste man and low-caste women could be tolerated only under special conditions, say if the man's family was experiencing business hardships, or the man himself was "unattractive."

But perhaps most important, the religion of India and its tribes became part of the caste system. The Brahmins became officials and landlords occupying positions of power in the society, while the "untouchable" caste did society's labors. The Brahmin caste developed from subdivisions among the Hindi priests of Brahmin, and the lowly position of the "untouchables" was justified in terms of *karma*. And although mobility in the caste system is unlikely, the classical sociologist Max Weber, who studied the Indian caste system carefully, discovered there a complicated and fluid system that had changed over time, with one caste moving ahead of or behind another.

The estate system, which Weber also studied, existed during the Middle Ages in Europe, when there were three major estates: the nobility, the clergy, and the peasants. Each estate served a function in the social order. The nobility were warriors, defending territory and ruling the land; the clergy also helped rule and manage land, and they had dominion over spiritual matters, which were often also political. The peasants were legally tied to the land and labored there, and while people were born into an estate, there were some examples of movement. Sons of nobility might become clergy, or even a peasant might become a knight, a low-ranking noble.

Most change in both the caste and estate systems, however, takes place very slowly and can be appreciated only in historical relief. Class systems, in contrast, are much more open, allowing movement both within and between generations. The stories of men and women who rose from humble beginnings to great status, wealth, and power are legend in class societies. Among the most wealthy men in the world today are a number of Arabs and Hong Kong businessmen whose origins match in humility the log cabin of America's Abraham Lincoln.

Compared to the societal forms of old, class systems are mobile, but sociologists try to ask the difficult questions about historical trends and developments. One question is, "Just how much mobility really exists in class systems?" We know that revolutions can dramatically affect at least some portions of a system of inequality. For example, in the Cuban revolution of the late 1950s, the middle classes of Havana were forced to migrate to Miami; and during the Iranian revolution of the 1970s, the upper-class, modernists of that society were expelled. But, all things considered, do these political and historical forces actually change the experiences of inequality from generation to generation?

The answer to this question is far from straightforward. We must always judge rank, and the experience of inequality, within societal, community, and cultural contexts. This means that we must pay close attention to the way a system operated at the time we are investigating, the criteria of inequality that exist within the community in question and the general cultural meanings of equality. While we do not deny that major changes can take place in the stratification of a system, we must consider what these changes mean to individuals within the broadest possible perspective.

Let's look at a few cases. Since Fidel Castro came to power, the Cuban migration to America has taken place in three great waves. In the first wave, around 1960, it was basically businessmen and their families. They were shopowners, bakers, artisans, generally members of the bourgeoisie. These people established themselves in Miami, to a remarkable degree, in positions of business and power similar to the ones they left behind in Cuba. The second wave, in the mid-1980s, consisted of political prisoners freed by the Castro regime, some other prisoners, and many people who represented a variety of backgrounds. Finally, most recently, the third and well-publicized wave, consisted of criminals, mental patients, and other "misfits" of the people's society of Cuba.

These migrants have settled, as far as we can tell, according to their relative rank in Cuban society. The early migrants have become respected members of Miami's elite, and have preserved their native language, in some cases still doing business in Spanish. Some of the members of the second wave have become middle class, but most are primarily employed in service occupations and "lower" prestige occupations: the most recent migrants have simply been added to Miami's "underclass." Of course, it is too early to tell the fate of the emigrants in terms of their eventual place in American society, but we must point out what seems to be a pattern showing the relative stability of class from emigration to immigration.

Another way to appreciate the complexity of the question of social mobility is to look at movement from generation to generation within a class society. In America, for example, perhaps no stronger folk maxim exists than "I want my children to be better off than I am." Parents from any stratum want their children to surpass their accomplishments. For members of the upper-lower class, this may mean aspiring to an elite education for one's children; for lower-upper-class parents, it may mean the prospect of "passing on" family wealth that will, as inheritance, guarantee higher status. Indeed, for several generations, popular literature and common opinion seemed to support the idea that each generation could improve on its place in society. Higher education, for instance, became more accessible to large numbers of people after World War II because of the GI Bill. The1960s saw the ranks of colleges and universities swell with sons and daughters of parents who themselves had never even attended college. Education as the great device of upward mobility seemed to be working, as plumbers' sons became physicians and college professors.

But all this movement, all this apparent change in the system, cannot be fully understood in sociological relief until we submit it to three criteria. We must consider mobility within the contexts of society, community and culture.

Take the case of Professor Smith, forty-three years of age, who teaches at an elite liberal arts college. He is the son of man who worked for thirty-three years in an oil refinery, rising through the ranks from common laborer to a position of manager and operator of a computerized loading dock. His grandfather also worked at the same factory. When Professor Smith was a college student, he worked in the refinery during the summer, as the third generation of Smiths to be employed there.

On the surface, Professor Smith seems to have experienced quite a bit of upward mobility. His grandfather, at age forty-three, was a skilled sheet-metal worker, his father, at the same age, was a white collar worker, and he is a respected professional. Now, if we used a simple measurement of occupational status, like the ones widely used by survey researchers, we would conclude that the prestige of occupations these three generations of Smiths have achieved is steadily going up. But this would be a very misleading conclusion.

Beginning with grandfather Smith, we must apply our contextual criteria and first consider the full range of occupations available to grandfather Smith. During the 1920s and 1930s when he reached the pinnacle of his occupational status and material well-being, the job force was mostly male and the over-whelming portion of jobs dealt with either extracting raw materials from the earth or transforming them into goods for the marketplace (see Table 6.3). So there were relatively few white-collar jobs available. We must also note that most of the1930s was dominated by the Great Depression, which meant high unem-ployment rates and low wages.

Now, grandfather Smith never missed a day of work during the Great Depression. He held a job that was highly respected. He was a skilled craftsman who fashioned railroad cars and the great machinery of a massive oil refinery. Although he was a blue-collar worker, so were most of his contemporaries, and among them he was educated (a high school diploma). As a member of his community, grandfather Smith had high status. He was a member of the Free Masons; in fact, he was quite active in the lodge. And he was a gifted musician who performed regularly in the Baptist church where he was a deacon. In Oklahoma during this time, Baptists were the majority religion, and Free Masonry was highly respected by members of the community. By age forty-three, grandfather Smith had reach the exalted station of worshipful master for the entire state of Oklahoma, he had fathered six children, and he was generally considered to be a successful man in his community. We see that his occupation placed him in the upper middle of his contemporaries; his achievements in his community translate into a fine reputation as a moral leader; and the cultural values of his time and place in history locate him squarely in the mainstream for a white man, working in a white, male-dominated, industrial community. To be sure, grandfather Smith was not among the movers and shakers, the industrial magnates of his time, but his life was one of good reputation, a well-earned living, and the respect of his community.

Table 6.3.
Shifts in Employment, 1920–1980

Occupational Type	1920s	1950s	1980s
Extractive	30%	14.3%	4.4%
Transfomative	40	32.5	29.6
Service	20	53.2	66.0

Source: Nelson and Tsui, 1986, 3.

Father Smith lived in different era. He began his employment shortly after grandfather Smith died. Quitting college after only one year, he went to work full-time in the refinery. He started, as did all new employees, as a common laborer. World War II began soon after father Smith started working at the refinery. He enlisted in the navy, and his employers promised him another job after the war. He was at war in the South Pacific for three years. When he returned to his home and his job at the refinery, things had changed. The new technologies of the war had already begun to change the nature of work. More automation, more competition from other companies, and, most of all, more paperwork for a much larger workforce. Father Smith was bright and a fast learner. He was promoted to the job of timekeeper. In those days, just after the War, the refinery still maintained its own shops, as it had in grandfather's day. There was a carpenter's shop, machine shop, boilermaker's shop, sheet-metal shop, and so on. What father's job consisted of was traveling around the mammoth refinery on a bicycle, gathering up time cards, and taking them back to his office to tally hours so that men could receive their proper pay. This was a job for a responsible man, and father Smith did the job credit.

But the refinery was changing, and soon the various shops were closed as the refinery began to contract its work. Many of the high-status blue-collar workers lost their jobs in the refinery and went to work for the contractors. But father Smith had skills that the refinery management valued. He had the makings of being a white collar worker. So he was reassigned to the new accounting department where, by the 1950s, he spent his days punching numbers into mechanical calculators and preparing reports of the outputs and yields of various refinery processes.

By age forty-three, father Smith has followed his father into the Free Masonry. He become worshipful master of his local lodge, and he also attended church, but his church was a large downtown church, and while he and his family were regular attenders, he never became a deacon or held any lay office in the church. Compared to his father, he had risen to white collar status, but so had most of his contemporaries. (By the end of the 1950s more than half of all occupations in the United States were service occupations, that is, they had nothing to do with extraction or transformative work.) Father Smith's generation was the first to become mainly white collar. And father Smith, although he followed in the footsteps of his father, never became worshipful master of the state lodge, and this at a time when the status of Free Masonry had waned; and although quite talented musically, he never developed his singing talents in a way that compared to grandfather's accomplishments.

It seems that the occupational shift that took place between these two generations does not reflect upward mobility as much as it reflects the shifts that had taken place in society.

The third generation, father Smith's son, was the first Smith to graduate from college. He left the refinery and pursued a professional career. He married the daughter of a professional man, and he completed his Ph.D. His father was proud of him and regarded his son as a great success.

But by the time the last of the Smiths entered the job market, fully 66 percent of all occupations were service oriented, and the proportion of people in America who had completed college was roughly the same as the proportion of people who had completed high school in the 1920s, and the relative pay of his chosen "profession," college teaching, had declined to the point where blue-collar workers were earning as much as he. In the community where he taught, his college was know as a radical place, full of misfits and rabble-rousers. The last Smith was a professional of sorts, but he lived his life in isolation under a reputation as "one of those radicals at the college."

Although much more could be said about whether the Smith generations were upwardly mobile, our point should be clear. Society changes, and what was a high-status and powerful station in one distribution of jobs and wealth becomes commonplace and less influential in another. Communities change. They become urban, modern, impersonal, and fluid. In this setting, community work and even prestige do not mean the same thing as they did in a more homogeneous and stable setting. .

The Capitalism of Everyday Life

While many sociologists focus on the broad, structural questions, others want to understand the consequences of inequality in the daily lives of the people who make up society. In the class society, the meanings of inequality often revolve around the activities of "making a living." Different ways of earning money translate into different life styles, from the "rich and famous" to "ordinary men driving their ordinary vans." Distinctions between Porsche and Chevy, champagne and beer, and polo and bowling can be understood as the result of systematic interpretations people make about having or not having money, and the ways in which they pursue it.

Acts that we recognize as economic have an institutional meaning whenever their interpretation can be traced to any one or a combination of the following assumptions: (1) the ideal of equal exchange; (2) the ideal of profit; (3) the merger of ownership and self-identity; and (4) the extension of ownership to investment and acquisition of manipulative, monetary skills. We discuss each as if they were separate, but in actual interpretations of specific acts, they merge.

The Ideal of Equal Exchange

Economic acts rest on the assumption that, ideally, work performed will equal the reimbursement we receive for it (Schroyer1970, 213). This does not mean that we always receive what we regard as "just pay" for our work. Approaching the assumption from a different angle, people engaged in economic interaction assume that with the proper appreciation of the nature of their work, they should receive the right amount of pay, enjoyment, or reward.

Work refers not only to expending energy but to the general relationship between any given act of labor, that is, expending energy, and the total institutionalized stock of knowledge that is economic. Work, then, occurs whenever a person enters the economic institution. Work is the result of transforming action into economically relevant labor (Marx 1971, 74–76). A five-year-old boy may help his father mow the lawn by emptying the grass catcher when it is full. This activity is family-like since the motives for it come from either positional or individual control. Whenever the father offers to pay for such services, or the boy demands payment, the same act becomes "economic." Now the value of the act rests on the mutually sufficient assumption of father and son that, for instance, "grass catcher emptying" is worth about 50 cents. Of course, in this example, the services may bring more than this amount of reimbursement when performed by, say, a professional lawn-care company. The accomplishment of this father-son exchange depends on the son's ignorance of such matters. It is the ideal of equal exchange that allows for the construction of an economic meaning for the act.

When we speak of an ideal of exchange, we refer to ideas people have about work and rewards. The exchange occurs, therefore, between two minds, each mind having acquired the experience and knowledge necessary to recognize and use the idealization of work and reward for the purposes of social interaction. Consider a professor who is paid to teach economics. How will she decide if her salary is fair? She will take into account all the materials she thinks relevant to this exchange. She knows, for one thing, that her academic field commands higher wages nationally than some other fields, such as history. She knows she has the credentials of an experienced teacher and may actually believe her salary should be among the highest for persons her age and with her performance record. For the purposes of staying employed, that is, interacting economically, she tacitly accepts an equality between what she does as an employee of her university and what the university pays her both in actual salary and working conditions.

From these examples of the grass-cutting enterprise and teaching, we can see that exploitation can be arranged rather easily. We only need to control the assumption about work and reward. *Exploitation*, as we use it, refers to a situation in which one partner to the economic interaction allows the other person to think that the work-reward exchange is equal when he knows it is not. It is important to note that we are not necessarily talking about malicious intention. Exploitation is a widespread characteristic of the common-sense knowledge of economics. We have all heard the adage, "Let the buyer beware."

Exploitation in economic exchange is the consequence of a combination of assumptions. Perhaps we could imagine the absence of exploitation if the assumption of equivalency were the only grounds for economic social interactions. But there are others, and they do not necessarily relate in a consistent way to one another. A social reality may actually depend on contradictions among its assumptions. Perhaps nowhere is this observation more vividly illustrated than in the capitalism of everyday life, especially in meanings that derive from the assumptions of profit and exchange.

The Ideal of Profit

Each person in a class society approaches an economic interaction with the expectation of making a profit. We have learned to believe that an economic exchange should mean at least one and ideally both partners will receive rewards greater than the value of their work. This imbalance between what a thing is worth and what one gets for it is called *profit*. The goal of every economic transaction is the maximization of profit (Marx 1971, 103–105). Without profit, an exchange is a "break-even" affair. This assumption is so widely distributed among the members of society that we find it in the most "out-of-the-way places." In his study of flea markets, for instance, Maisel (1974) discovered that a good dealer searches out those with whom he can trade to "come out on top." "A good day, that is, a day of high profits, is the main source of their ambition and labor" (Maisel 1974, 505).

If we follow only the assumption of equal exchange, we would arrive at the description of a situation in which an employee of an automobile factory would receive pay in direct proportion to the amount of work he or she puts into the production of automobiles. But because of the ideal of profit, the matter is more complicated, and so work must be "managed." People not directly laboring in production have to earn a wage as well. Their pay comes from "surplus worth." It is these managers who speak the language of profit. Without the ideal of profit, there would still be workers and there would still be products, but there would be no management.

Although profit is generally thought of as a management concern, within modern class societies a similar expectation has emerged among workers. They expect that they should receive more reimbursement than is required to meet daily necessities. In short, regardless of the "true value" of their work, its relationship to the item of production, they want wages that will allow them to consume the things they want. They want better food, housing, and transportation. They want recreational vehicles, summer houses, vacation money, and just plain "fun money." To workers, profit is a "good wage." And wages are thought of in terms of consumption of wanted things. Both common-sense bits of economic knowledge rest on the assumption of ideal profit.

Ownership and the Self

In a class society, profit is often spent to extend the boundaries of selfhood. In the economic institution, this means money can purchase identity. For management, in a strict business sense, money put back into the company by way of buying new production equipment, investing in the stocks of the company, or even in purchasing new "assets" like a defunct competitor results in the merger of the ideas that managers have about who they are and what their worth is within the company. The manager speaks of *"my* company," *"our* new products," *"my* job," *"my* future with the company," and so forth. The identities of the person and the form become one and the same.

For the workers, such identity develops primarily through their consumption of goods and services in the larger society. Although workers talk of "my job" at the plant, it is the "boys at the top" who really run the show. The plant and the business it represents are really theirs, so to speak. The workers have jobs to do, which, as jobs, may be part of their identities (he is a carpenter; she a heavy equipment operator). But they rarely think of the corporate entity or the company as the real "me." A worker may speak of "my camper," "my new shotgun," or "my new motorcycle." His house, with the den he built, is part of his identity, as is his new car. The work done merges the outside world of objects with the inside world of feelings. He built that new bank building down on Seventh street, or she put the front fender on the 1988 Chevy she sees going past her home.

Perhaps the best illustration of self-identity is homeownership. People make contrasts in their thinking between "rent" and "payment," and to describe how they do this heightens our understanding of how economic participation becomes important to self-concept. When one rents, one's identity is not fully reflected in the place of residence. For instance, a person may rent an early American style house, when he really prefers ranch houses, because the house has a convenient location and a good price. It is a good rental.

A renter, then, lives in a house or apartment using a carefully contrived system of distinctions between "mine" and "that comes with the place." The interior of the apartment may reflect the resident's sense of self, but toilet fixtures, kitchen sinks, and other permanent features do not. A decorator attempts to cover up distasteful walls and corners of the living room with paint, shades, and screens. Such attempts are intended to convey to visitors the message "that this is not me, my distaste for that horrible wall is expressed through the screen you see in front of it."

The homeowner faces a different relationship between the house she lives in and her "self-identity." To buy something means that one finds, in that thing, qualities of one's own being. A positive attitude toward a modern style, flat-roofed, patioed house voiced by a person who has just "closed the deal" on a house sporting the pillar construction of a southern mansion motif evokes the obvious question, "Why did you buy that house?" Of course, there can be many reasons why a person might buy "out of taste." "It's a good investment, I intend to live there only a short time until I can find what I really like. Then I'll rent the house. It's got good location, you know." If the person has purchased the house for her own use, however, the contradictions between a definitive preference for style and occupancy of a house of another style does not make sense. After all, a house reflects a person's tastes, his or her very self, and the house is a proclamation to the abstract public of viewers about who lives there.

Hence even the person whose job requires that he move his family every several years will carefully shop for the right house in a new town. Attention will be given to appearance, room layout, and location (the neighborhood) as well as cost. In fact, the matter of cost typically becomes secondary to the potential merger of self and thing whenever the "right house" is spotted. Marge, after weekends of house hunting, proclaims to eye- and leg-weary Fred, "I know it's more than we can afford, but this house is just perfect — we just *have* to have it."

The idea of ownership is so paramount in the capitalism of everyday life that elaborate financing systems have developed to maintain it. Few people, even in very rich class societies, have $80,000 to $350,000 in ready assets. These amounts roughly represent the range of costs for modest, middle-class homes in the United States — the low figure for a home in small southern town and the high for a home in place like Palo Alto, California. All people must own something, ideally their own place of residence, yet few have experienced the "profit" required for purchasing even a modest house.

We have learned that institutions cope with such anomalies in ways that preserve the institutions themselves — contradictions and all. Since few people can buy a house outright and since the assumption of ownership is regarded as essential to basic economic meanings of everyday life, a way must be found to allow the ownership assumption to operate in the absence of sufficient individual capital. Credit is the answer. One can be seen as "potentially having money" if he or she can produce credentials showing that he or she is the kind of person who has, in the past, behaved in a way that illustrates a merger between things and self has taken place. A person who does not have and never has had large sums of money can be judged by representatives of loaning institutions as a person who ought to have money.

Having been so judged, that person may then act as if he or she has the money and "close the deal," entering into a long term debt with an organization that does have the money, or at least is likewise judged as having it.

So, with money never had and still not had, a person buys a house with "potential or symbolic profit." Now that the person has the house, he or she immediately experiences the merger of thing and self, and "pride in ownership" is the resulting feeling.

Impersonal Ownership

There is still another assumption of the economic institution we wish to describe. This one has to do with a kind of ownership that implicates selfhood in lesser degrees than the first types. Specifically, we are talking about investment that requires that "profit" be spent for things or agreements with no immediate use, either practical or symbolic.

We buy a savings certificate or shares of stock in a company, or we lend money to a friend with ideas for a new business venture. In a sense, we have foregone the usefulness of our profit in the hopes that our investment will "pay off." We hope it will return to us in a form that we can convert into items which can become part of our personal identities.

It is understood that investment contains risks. One must be willing to lose a great deal in the hope of gaining a great deal. Thus investments range from "sure things" (e.g., savings bonds) to "high risks" (e.g., loaning money to friends for the development of whistling, glow-in-the dark skateboard). Instead of using profit for personal identity, the person who invests has learned to use profit impersonally — absorbing losses and reinvesting gains. The task he or she must master is to separate his or her self from this money. Of course, in highly developed class societies, this type of thinking is the root of very important ways of spending money. Banks and corporations, any financial organization that depends on the stability of the value of money, are rooted in the ability of ordinary people to think of money in highly symbolic ways.

Forms of Everyday Economics

We know that institutionalized assumptions transform into organized action through repeated applications to actual situations of everyday life. The economic forms we discuss are those that derive in obvious fashion from the presumptive bases we have just outlined. Although there are many variations of each, two general forms dominate in the common sense world of economic reality: working for oneself and working for the other guy.

Working for Oneself

Working for oneself organizes the meanings of participating in the economic reality of society around the notion of individual responsibility. This form dictates that one must control the outcomes of economic interaction. Accountability resides directly in the person and his economically relevant activities. Virtually any activity can be transformed into an economic one. Likewise, any activity can be subsumed under the sole control of an individual. A "streetwalker" may be in business for herself. We say this of a prostitute whenever she decides on location for solicitation, determines the price for her "trick," and pockets or at least manages the money she earns herself. Of course, she has "overhead," such as new clothes and medical bills. But she does not work for a "pimp." She is not a part of an impersonal economic form to which she owes allegiance. Her fate as a prostitute depends on her own capabilities, hard work, and "cleverness."

A paperboy or girl and a hardware store owner work for themselves. Even though both depend on impersonal forms, a newspaper company to determine price and supply papers; a hardware supplier, tool manufacturer, an advertising agency, and so on, the performances of paperboy or girl and entrepreneur of nails and hammers lead to mergers of self and economics. If the paperboy fails to deliver dry papers on rainy days, of if she misses a house on her route, or if the store owner cannot sell enough hardware to profit and must declare bankruptcy, neither the *Daily Globe*, nor the Stanley Tool Factory can be held accountable. Of course, if the *Daily Globe* takes an unpopular editorial stand or the Stanley Tool Factory manufactures electric drills that do not work, the economic viability of the paper and hardware persons will be affected. But these considerations are the individual's business, to be coped with surely, but not apart from the form "working for oneself." To work for oneself, in essence, means to construct an economic reality over which the constructor believes he or she has dominion. The paper people speak of their routes and the hardware man of his store. Both have the convictions that they control transpiring activities within their respective "business" domains.

In the American version of class society, this form operates as a strong and widespread indicator of a person's general worth. An intriguing use of the form can be found among young people, who, in rejection of what they regard as the intolerable conformity of "working for the other guy," opt to go into business for themselves, The amazing number of "health food stores," "head shops," "bookstores," and other private, small businesses that sprang up during the 1970s attest to the modern uses of this form. Of course, during the 1980s many of these successful small businesses were sold to large corporations or formed business links that in effect transformed them into major, impersonal forms of working for the other guy.

Working for the Other Guy

To participate within this form, one must learn to think simultaneously of personal and impersonal economics. I have "my job," but it is with the company. My performances clearly relate to raises, promotions, and the general reputation I may acquire in my job. I know that what I do at work affects my fate, and I may give profound self-significance to my job. But to the company? That is a different matter.

There is a sense in which this form rests on a fatalistic mentality. A person comes to know that his or her fate depends on the company. No matter how well one has performed, a high-level corporate crisis can result in a transfer, a promotion, a demotion, or at worst, a "termination." The impact of some high-level policy is essentially outside the control of the worker and, perhaps most significantly, an employee knows this is so.

An employee can only await the decrees of the "new" boss or the new "company line." One can only complain about or praise the conclusion of the efficiency experts awarding a "job index" to the activities he has routinely and faithfully executed for over twenty years. "Job index," you are told, is an "objective measure" of your contribution to the productivity goals of the company. A 3 indicates "little" contribution to productivity, you learn, and your score is only 4. From the employee's point of view, there is no reason to give a low-priority job a high-level performance. All this boils down to the likelihood of a "layoff" on the horizon.

Negative aspects of working for the other guy demonstrate clearly the differences between the two forms of work. When working for the other guy, whether as a hip manager of a skateboard shop or the personnel manager of a multinational corporation, one does not presume to possess total control over one's economic fate. Such dominion resides outside the self, and hence the person is relieved, in measure, of responsibility for his or her participation in economic life.

This transfer of responsibility, naturally, can have positive functions for employees. In fact, we can say that this form specializes in managing responsibility. It even has executives in charge of making sure that the "form" survives. When serious errors are made, such as the explosion of the space shuttle *Challenger*, only people at the top of the organization are held accountable, and even they are not criminally responsible. None of the others involved in the tragic decision to go ahead with the launch in spite of cold temperatures that might affect the operational safety of the O-ring seals on the rocket booster were held responsible. Some employees without power who advised against the launch under cold-weather conditions were singled out for doing their job well, however, and a few were promoted to positions of greater responsibility. But in the event of another tragedy, these newly appointed heads of organizations will not be able to dissociate their work from that of the space agency any more than their predecessors could.

Some contemporary critics of large formal organizations, which are the epitome of the form "working for the other guy," argue that survival is the sole goal of the "other guys" we have come to think of as "the corporation" (Galbraith 1967). Thus, whenever people dissociate their self-worth from their participation in the large organization on the grounds that they do what they do "for a living," they establish a sharp distinction between their work and "what they are really about." It is no wonder that Americans, who in very large numbers work in impersonal economic settings, have difficulty conceiving of the common good or the collective whole whenever they must vote, strike, or otherwise make decisions which pit their own interests against those of the collective, social reality.

Within the form "working for oneself," distinctions between the company and oneself are meaningless. A person becomes the business. Self and collectivity merge into one energetic economic form, and people rarely rationalize their own work in terms of necessity or fate. In the "working for the other guy" form, a person tries to maintain as much of an identity as possible outside the job. He works for "Moon Oil," but he always wanted to be in construction — building houses. Now he has a good enough job, but his real pleasure in life comes from his "hobby." Almost any hour of the weekend, he can be found tinkering around in his home work shop. He talks about his hobby.

> I have finished some cabinets for the kitchen, built on a room to my house, finished it myself. When I stand back and look at what I have done, I can see my sweat, the mistakes I made, and the really skillful things I've done. Those cabinets are me, not the accounting work I do for Moon Oil. There I really never finish anything, and nothing bears my mark.

In comparison, both forms allow for self-job relationships. Working for oneself requires that work be transformed into self-expression, and self-expression into the chance for profit. Working for the other guy demands a diversity of self. It presupposes the cognitive ability to separate total self-worth and self-determination from the stricture of the job. It requires a fatalism about the total viability of the abstract economic reality of society, yet it allows the pursuit of idiosyncratic economic activities, whereas self employment requires the identity of self and business.

Social psychological indicators of how people feel about their jobs generally reflect these forms of working in modern society. For example, General Social Survey (GSS) data from 1972 through 1987, when grouped according to the forms, reveal that people who say they work for themselves are slightly happier than those who say they work for someone else, and they are slightly more optimistic about bringing children into the world (see Table 6.4).

The Meanings of Economic Participation

The two basic forms and the ways in which they are interrelated give rise to three patterns of meanings associated with an individual's participation in economic activities in a class society. These are (1) the self-made person; (2) the corporate person, and (3) the alienated individual. In this, the closing section of this chapter, we offer portrayals of each pattern of values and actions.

Individualism and the Self-Made Person

The form working for oneself and the individual adaptation of "self-madeness" are two aspects of the same phenomenon. Both are expressions of results of the tacit economic assumptions discussed earlier in this chapter.

Table 6.4
Percentage Reporting Degree of Happiness by Employment .

	Work for Self (N = 1837)	Work for Someone Else (N = 15,132)
Very Happy	37.78	32.78
Pretty Happy	52.26	54.30
Not too Happy	9.96	12.93

Chi Square = 24.97, df = 2, p < .001.

Percentage agreeing and disagreeing with statement, "It's hardly fair to bring a child into the world with the way things look for the future."

	Work for Self (N = 1210)	Work for Someone Else (N = 9821)
Agree	33.88	39.79
Disagree	66.12	60.92

Chi Square = 12.27, df = 1, p < .001.
Source: NORC, General Social Survey (GSS) 1972–1987.

To the self-made person, there is a direct relationship between one's perceived qualities of self and the cumulative consequences of economic life. What the person is, he or she did or is doing. In other words, a self-made person is master of his or her own economic destiny or soul. This adaptation, although it does not guarantee success, assures the person a clear-cut path to decide the meaning of his or her economic life. Success means self-accomplishment, and failure means individual inadequacy. Of course, the woman who operates her own brokerage firm only to see it fold a short time later can blame prejudice against women in the world of finance (i.e., social fate). But it is the decision to try and subsequent efforts toward success (try and try again) that best illustrates the adaptation we seek to understand.

The times might be right for women to enter "Wall Street society," but the women who make it, gaining the respect of their male peers, do so according to what they regard as their "qualities of self." For example, rarely will a successful woman claim that her success derives from her gender identity. Instead, such a person might typically remark that she became successful against great odds and, indeed, in spite of womanhood. She might say, "I am clever and an arduous applier of my skills and talents as a broker. I am a hard-working financier."

This is the hallmark of self-made interpretations of economic life, and such interpretations are individualistic. Even though one may acknowledge forces beyond one's control (e.g., prejudice), a limited education, and societal pressures, when all is said and done, a person is what she makes of herself. Destiny is created from the powers that reside within an individual, according to this configuration of values. Society and other people are either obstacles or aids in the course of building one's life. The "buck stops" at the individual. No other force, collective or individual, can potentially affect the total quality of a person's life.

As Max Weber pointed out in *The Protestant Ethic and the Spirit of Capitalism*, the self-made person's inclination is toward the acquisition of things, and things accumulate into a measure of self-worth. A course of study is worth it if it contributes to the development of qualities regarded as important to making something of oneself. Learning the skills and basics of accounting can come in handy. Following the techniques of mediation makes sense if such practices can aid in coping with the everyday frustrations of doing what is important, hard work and strains from competition. Self-improvement gets its meaning from within the adaptation. What one does is not "wasting time" if that something can be interpreted as part of self-improvement and the acquisition of more things.

"Wasting time," in contrast, refers to the superfluous expenditure of energy — having to deal with the emotional dishevelment of an affair gone wrong, visiting home to settle the details of the estate of a recently deceased relative, or living through the legal and personal hassles of a divorce settlement. To "waste time" is to engage in an activity not relevant to "progress toward success." A vacation in the Bahamas can be "productive" if it rejuvenates the pursuit of success.

Although such an adaptation fits with the form of working for oneself, it can be adapted by someone working for the other guy. The riverboat captain, the truck driver, the psychology major recently graduated from a liberal arts college who owns and operates a furniture refinishing shop — all of them embrace this adaptation. In like measure, the young professional who sets out to leave a mark on medical arts, dentistry, scientific research, or other "higher order" professional pursuits does so with faith in radical individualism. All self-made people test themselves against the world as they find it.

David Riesman (1950), as we have seen, observed that the rugged individualism of previous generations of Americans was being replaced by other-directed conformists. These conformists have different standards for determining what is appropriate action. They scan the actions, beliefs, and values of others to decide what they should do, think, and believe. Riesman offered an image of sheep without a herdsman and the death of herdsmen, but we have learned that his judgments were premature. Individualism is as alive in economic life as it is in religious, family, and political life. Even if only a myth, it is a truly important one to the ways in which members of class societies interpret their participation in economic activities.

Corporate Beings

Although the other-directed conformist Riesman envisioned may not have materialized, another closely related type did. This one exemplifies the pattern of values, beliefs, and actions that William Howton's (1969, 13–44) term, the "functionary," captures. Functionaries decide appropriate action not so much by looking at how others act but by taking on the identity of an organization as their own. The radical individualism of the self-made person is replaced by an individualized version of the organizational phenomenon itself. These people are not merely *in* an organization, they are *of* it. The synthesis between self and collectivity completes itself in functionaries. They are at the same time both persons and the corporation. They live for the corporation, and most important, they define their self-worth through association with a formal organization.

In many ways, the functionary is a person whose socialization experiences are tipped toward formal social settings. Now, according to socialization theorists, all people take on the attitudes and roles of others with whom they interact. For most people, however, the core attributes of self, the attitudes and roles taken on, are learned within the context of primary groups. The functionary, in contrast, has a kind of inverted self. He or she places identities and values acquired in the impersonal, efficient, and bureaucratic setting over those acquired in personal, informal, and intimate group settings.

Back in the 1950s, William H. Whyte identified this pattern in its infancy. He characterized the middle level of executive administration and clerical workers as "organization men." His description shows that such people model their life styles and, indeed, their very personalities after the requirements of organizational life. The wife of the organization man was either an asset or a liability to his existence within the corporation. So too were his children, their behavior, his home and its location, and virtually everything about his life. Whyte was close to describing the adaptation of the corporate being.

Nevertheless, he believed in the ultimate vulnerability of the organization. He even gave tips on how to cheat on personality tests so that one could fake the appearance of the "right kind of person," aggressive but cooperative and mindful of organizational imperatives. He then seemed to advocate a chameleon-like adaptation requiring from the individual at least two interpretations. One would be used for generating the action of the organization man and the other for the real person's affairs. But such a dual character, although it surely exists, does not capture the depth and extent of the synthesis between self and corporation that occurs in the corporate being.

The corporate being defines the worth of his or her self by treating two things as the same: personhood and organizational identity. As with all forms of social consciousness, when they are the basis for the meanings of everyday life, the details of this merger need not be formally expressed or fully understood by the individual. As with the self-made person, the job is everything for the corporate being. In the difference between the self-made person and the corporate being is found the roots for the meanings for actions. Such roots Whyte referred to as *ethics*.

For the self-made person, the ethic is individualistic. What makes sense as a life plan is a series of decisions and judgments, some *ad hoc*, others deliberate, that the individual can trace to internalized principles. Thus the risk of managing a gas station is outweighed by the loss of "self-dignity" that comes from being a cog in the corporate wheel, or better, a circuit in the computer's feedback loop. The self-made person will put in long hours of work, often for less pay than he can get from employment in a corporation, because "that's the way he is!" We know that this means hard work is relevant to the self, whereas the work one does for the other guy never can carry such self-significance.

Likewise, for the corporate being, work is self-relevant. It is just that a different way of interpreting self-other identities operates. Instead of an individualistic ethic, the corporate being lives by a social ethic, as Whyte chose to refer to it. The concept of socialization tells us that the configuration of meanings we call "individualism" is also social. To write of a social ethic, then, might seem redundant. Whyte, however, was careful in his depiction of the workings of the social ethic. The ethic, he suggested, operates not by relating events and judgments to principles presumed to be unique to the person, but by relating events and judgments to relationships themselves.

So a corporate being decides a course of action and defines a job as meaningful by believing that the worth of any particular practice comes from its relationship to an organizational phenomenon. The strength of one's "feelings of being the corporation" are proportionate to the numbers of ways a person relates to the corporation. The more involved a person is with his or her work, including recreational and "personal" senses of it, the more likely that person is to merge personal and corporate identities. For the self-made person, the relationship is inverse: The more ways one is involved with the a formal organization, the more one defines selfhood independently from organizational bases of meaning. The corporate being possesses a strong sense of other-awareness; the self-made person is inner-directed.

Alienation of Self in the Class Society

Probably no other word in the vocabulary of the social sciences carries more different meanings than *alienation*. For that reason, we convey a specific descriptive sense of the term: Alienation refers to a feeling of estrangement or an awareness of separateness from things and other persons (Israel 1971). An alienated person has no definitive way to place himself or herself in the world. He or she cannot belong to anything, believe in anything, or really think of himself or herself as part of anything.

The self-made person is not alienated. The job is everything. The corporate person also is not alienated. Personal and organizational identity have merged. Neither type feels separateness nor knows the confusion that comes from not being able to locate some unequivocal sense in the subjective world of feeling or emotions.

Both the person who works in the corporation and wants a self-job identity and the person who works for himself and desires the benefits of membership in a collectivity experience alienation. A clerk ritualistically identifies with his job, his desk, his mark on the forms he fills out and files. He decorates his desk with personal items, such as pictures of his family, and he has a comfortable chair. He lives with the stark possibility that something will happen to expose his fabricated illusions of ownership: a new manager who demands a strict following of company policy or a job transfer that will force him to remove, literally, the marks of his presence from the company.

Or consider the other extreme, the small business person who, given her precarious existence as a corner foodstore owner, believes she can demand protection from the "unfair" competition that food chains represent. Her political efforts at lobbying to pass a bill that limits the locations of supermarkets in established residential areas serve as a constant reminder that, on her own, she could not really survive. She despairs, longing for the ideals of free enterprise while negotiating a protected domain for her limited economic existence. This is also a portrait of alienation in class society.

Alienation, as we use the term, happens because forms are mixed. An alienated person experiences a conflict of form and awareness, a lack of fit between social and subjective reality. We are all aware that corporations have used the idea of ownership to increase allegiance among employees. They offer stocks at reduced rates and other profit-sharing programs to engender, among those who work for them, feelings of personal involvement with the corporation. But these policies can also result in alienation among employees because the employees do not interpret their investments as part of the self-made form. Consequently, the corporation, in catering to the individualistic ethic (they do this by allowing freedom to choose working hours, encouraging leisure walks in the company gardens, and promoting exercise programs) simply builds up conditions conducive to alienation. For example, no one doubts that the exercise programs some large corporations have made available to their employees are healthy and generally "good for" employees. But because of the nature of the relationship between employee and employer, such activities can be used to exploit employees and can increase feelings of alienation. Many corporations are now using computers to measure employees' use of exercise equipment and participation in exercise programs. To date, they have not used these data in a systematic way, but we can easily see how health insurance rates and others matters regarding what a company provides for their employees could be connected to their participation in "health promoting programs."

As the work of Studs Terkel (1974) indicates, alienation is a part of the economic reality of class society. We realize that it can occur in the mixed-family form, in reactionary sects, and in any instance of a clash between human awareness and institutional demands. In the economic sector, in class life, the essence of alienation derives from, on the one hand, an ideally envisioned individualism and, on the other, a growing trend in organizational life that merges person and collectivity. These two polar types clash and harmonize in patterns of awareness and form that, at best, lead to a genuine confusion about what one should do to "earn a buck!"

Summary

Inequality is a basic feature of society, and in modern societies many areas of life, including health, are affected by the amount of money a person has. Therefore, the meanings of inequality are often economic.

Sociologists approach the study of class objectively and subjectively. Objective measures usually begin with some assessment of monetary wealth — annual income per family, or per capita income. Subjective measures include reputation, tastes, life styles, and attitudes toward money.

Karl Marx left a legacy for building an entire sociology from the analysis of technologies of work and of the subsequent distribution of wealth. More modern objective class analysis distinguishes major dimensions of class: labor, credit, and commodity market. Class manifests itself differently in capitalistic and socialistic systems, as reflected in different attitudes toward and organizations for work.

The theory of status inconsistency is partially an attempt to include subjective factors in the analysis of social class. By examining inconsistency between, say, adherence to core cultural values and objective monetary ranking, the Marxist expectations about class polarization can be corrected.

The Yankeetown studies used both subjective and objective approaches to social class and resulted in the now familiar upper-upper, upper-middle, lower-middle, upper-lower, and lower-lower model of stratification. Warner correlated many aspects of social life to place them within a stratification scheme.

Movement within a stratification system is called *social mobility*. While all societies allow some form of mobility, it may vary from individual movement up and down the scale, as in modern society, to shifts for groupings of people, as in caste society.

Assessing the degree of individual social mobility is very difficult because society changes. This is particularly true in America where there have been major changes in the nature of work available to individuals and in the experience of community membership. To assess mobility, one needs to look at the cultural and historical context of status for each generation; the changes that have taken place in the relative availability and consequent prestige of occupations and the changes in the proportion of people within a given occupation.

Capitalism is more than a system for defining and distributing wealth. It also is an influence on the everyday lives of members of capitalistic societies. As a means for interpreting the meanings of everyday life, capitalism rests on assumptions of the ideal of equal exchange, of profit, of the relationship between ownership and self, and of impersonal ownership.

These assumptions are not necessarily consistent, and tension from relationships among them creates the forms "working for oneself" and "working for the other guy." Given the assumption of the capitalism of everyday life and its forms, people arrive at different meanings for their participation in the economic aspect of social life. Individualism and being self-made are very important themes in these meanings, but so is the opposite tendency toward conformity to the forms. This meaning we expressed in the "corporate being," or functionary.

Finally, a major consequence of the tensions among assumptions, forms, and consciousness is alienation. Alienation, or an individual's sense of separation from the economic system, is unevenly distributed among the forms, with self-made people experiencing it least and people who work in "mixed" forms experiencing it the most.

7 POLITICS: THE ORGANIZATION
OF POWER

Sociologists use the concept of power when referring to situations in which a person or a group of people can impose ideas of appropriate actions, thoughts, and feelings on another person or group. Power itself is a feature, not only of governments, but of relationships between people in their everyday lives. A father attempts to exercise power over his children, an employer over employees, and a preacher over a congregation. So even though we focus specifically on political power, there is also economic power, religious power, family power, educational power, and, of course, interpersonal power.

Although power is a fundamental fact of all social life and all social institutions, its experience is almost always indirect and subjective (Weber 1961). In family life, when a mother requests that her eight-year-old son "take out the garbage," she may not think she is exercising power, nor may her son think he is the subject of power. Instead, they both believe what they are doing is the usual way a particular problem is solved; in this case, how to get the garbage out of the house and to the street so the "garbage man" can take it away.

As this example suggests, power is typically experienced as "the way things are." It is usually framed as proper, right, and just; otherwise, it is experienced as coercion and manipulation. This idea of "framing" experiences (Goffman 1974) refers to the organization of how people think about what is happening to them and what they are doing to others. The process of learning to think about "normal" uses of power is a part of all institutionalized knowledge, but it is most vividly depicted in the arena of politics where the consequences of its exercise shape the organization and function of society.

Power as an Institution

The consequences of the exercise of power are referred to as *social order*, and such social order can vary from the tyranny of a dictatorship to the relative freedom in highly individualistic societies where people make their own decisions about what they want to do. While it is easy to see how a dictator attempts to regulate society, in modern, free societies, regulation is more complex, ranging from the functions of the marketplace, to such simple rules as traffic regulations.

When we ask, "How is social order possible?" as did the philosopher Machiavelli during the sixteenth century, we are asking about how people

157

influence each other's actions. Getting people to do what we want them to do, Machiavelli regarded as the most basic of all social processes. To his way of thinking, society stayed together by virtue of the exercise of power. Powerful people are either clever or threatening, he reasoned, tricking or intimidating others into accepting their lot. Machiavelli thought the life-and-death struggle of the "prince" was the manipulation of the wills of others into alignment with his own desires and aspirations.

While few contemporary sociologists share completely Machiavelli's emphasis on the role of a powerful elite in shaping society, many appreciate several of the points he made about social life as wielding power. In fact, Sanford Lyman and Marvin Scott (1989) suggest that all the ingredients necessary to understanding modern life can be found in Machiavelli's writings. They write that in his methodology, "we find all the elements of [modern] sociology in the perspective of optimum distance, the empathic identification with each person in an encounter in terms of their respective environments, a nonideological stance, and the game model of social interaction" (p. 15).

These sociologists have in mind a particular way of understanding the absurd nature of modern life. In everyday life, we maintain our distance from those with whom we interact, even "using" people to achieve our own goals. In order to do this, we, like Machiavelli's prince, must understand what they want and how they will deal with us. We must know our enemy; and in this brave new society, we play games with one another, each using the other as an instrument, a means to our own emotional and material ends. And we do this without regard for traditional loyalties or political alliances. According to Scott and Lyman, people become remarkably skilled at playing power games, and Machiavelli's theory of the function of power articulated, in his book *The Prince*, can be extended to most aspects of social life.

In previous chapters, we have seen that interaction often involves struggling for an advantage, of one person over another, of one way of thinking over another, and of one group of people over another group. Now we look more deeply for the fundamental features of social order that allow such struggles to occur, and we are concerned with how people think of, feel about, and practice both domination and submission.

The Problem of Power

All societies provide their members with ways to make judgments about particular instances of the exercise of power over them, and the members, through the use of these procedures, come to think of some instances of control over their lives as legitimate and others as illegitimate. A stable social order requires that the members of society think of influences over them as "right."

Such legitimate power we refer to as *authority* (Weber 1961, 4). The successful enactment of authority results in a stable consensus among those involved in willful action, which in turn functions as a basis of social order. Clashes among potential patterns of legitimacy, in contrast, result in crises, chaotic conditions, and possibly even revolutionary change.

Max Weber identified three very general patterns of legitimate power, or authority. Identifying these patterns, he believed, would help us understand changes in the established order of modern society. Through the methodology of the ideal type, Weber organized concrete observations about social order. As we have seen with other ideals, these types themselves are pure, or exaggerated, so that we can see clearly the process of legitimation and how authority serves as the basis for stable social organization.

Traditional Authority

On the evening of August 13, 1971, the president called me into the Oval Office. He told me that he believed a very real danger existed from the pro-Castro, Miami-based operation that his intelligence suggested might be contributing to democratic candidates' bids in the November elections. He said that we would have to find out more about this and he was authorizing "break-ins" of the Democratic headquarters. The matter was of utmost importance to national security, he said. Immediately, I began arranging the details of the break-in.

During the Nixon presidency, the nation was shocked at the revelation of the Watergate scandal. Television covered the House committee investigations of the break-in, and the nation heard the testimony of close aids to the president, and charges of illegal behavior in high places. Finally, we witnessed the resignation and subsequent pardon of the president. There is perhaps no clearer example of the attempted exercise of power and of the overextension of the legitimacy of traditional authority than in this instance (Woodward and Bernstein 1974).

According to Weber, traditional authority rests on an assumption that we can express explicitly: Historical precedent serves as the guide for the determination of legitimacy. Under traditional authority, the exercise of power is right if it has always been right. A person has authority by virtue of being a certain kind of person — a king, a prime minister, a president. Custom and tradition decree that the occupant of a position can do certain things. In the medieval notion of "divine right of royalty," custom had it that a monarch could do anything he or she wished, since this was a God-given privilege, even an obligation. In France during the 1700s, King Louis XIV declared that he was the state. He was not suffering from "delusions of grandeur," for according to his place in society, he was grandiose and his rule absolute.

Today the instances of traditional power are not as clear as they were in societies where traditions defined meanings in much greater detail than they do now. Nevertheless, an office like the presidency of the United States, after 200 years of precedent-establishing actions by those who have won the right of the office, picks up traditional prerogatives. A president thinks he can do things because he is president. And he can, since those around him and segments of the public concur in that decision. As president, he has use of a special airplane and helicopter, he has special security and entertainment services, and he may spend public money at his own discretion. These practices are not necessarily spelled out in a legal document; they are not, strictly speaking, part of the "law of the land." Instead, they are legitimate uses of power that are traditionally associated with the office of the presidency.

The origins of traditions are often very difficult to discover, but we can illustrate how a practice regarded as necessary at one time might become a traditional prerogative at another. Since John Wilkes Booth shot President Abraham Lincoln, American presidents have been in danger, especially in public places. Over the decades, sophisticated systems of security have been devised to protect presidents and other important officials, and these have built on traditional solutions to problems. For example, consider the motorcade where an official travels in an armor-plated automobile flanked front and rear by police cars with flashing red lights. Now the flashing red light is a symbol that something important is happening. It usually means there is an emergency in the community, a fire, a crime being committed, or that an accident has happened. Important people adopt the flashing red light to symbolize their importance, their immunity to ordinary rules.

If future society is less violent, if we can imagine a time when important people might feel less threatened in public, perhaps a symbol of their importance, a symbol powerful enough to allow them immunity from rules of traffic and conventional behavior will be a small, battery-powered flashing red light worn on the epaulets of their coat. If, in this future, we are standing in line waiting for tickets to a concert, and a person with flashing red epaulets approaches, we will stand aside and let her pass. Necessity can become tradition.

Charismatic Authority

Another way in which power is legitimated involves imputing authority to someone on the basis of the belief that the person possesses special, magical, or spiritual qualities. Whether one really can heal the sick, save the poor or reunite a fractured country is irrelevant to the ability to exercise power. As long as a following of people who believe he or she has this ability can be recruited, power can be wielded. Weber called this kind of power *charisma*. Charismatic leaders' ability to wield power comes from the psychological beliefs that followers have in them.

To the followers, the demonstration of the desired qualities of leadership is sufficient grounds "to obey." A presidential nominee mounts the speaker's platform and declares that he will set free the oppressed black people in America's inner-city slums, and his followers believe him. The leader's task, then, is to maintain the beliefs of the followers.

Whenever a charismatic leader is able to do so, he or she may lead a social movement aimed at bringing about fundamental changes in the social order, especially in the basic institutions of property and labor relationships. Power depends on a leader's being able to keep up a commotion, "a stirring among the people, an unrest, a collective attempt to reach a visualized goal" (Heberle 1951, 6). Social movements can instill in followers a sense of group identity and solidarity, attempting to cement a mass of people together with sentiments, attitudes, and goals.

Charismatic leaders come in many political persuasions, and charisma can be used in behalf of any policy, any grouping, or on either wing of the American Eagle. Hitler, the Kennedys, Martin Luther King, Jr., Joe McCarthy — all have been identified as charismatics. Charismatic authority is not a modern phenomenon. Naturally its style adapts to the organization and structure of society. From the soapbox orator to the polished appearance of the television spot commercial for a woman running for the Senate, all seek the magical quality. All try to "manage it," perhaps in careful mimicry of a past leader or boldly forging a novel approach in hopes of touching the right nerve on the body politic. What happens to candidates without charisma is perhaps best illustrated by the defeat of the 1984 Democratic presidential candidate, Walter Mondale, a man acknowledged to be well prepared and qualified for high office, is dynamic in person but presents a dull image on television. No one seems to know how to give charisma to a public figure. Apparently this is partially a matter of historical and situational chance. Some people embody, for a following, hopes, aspirations, and symbols of times past and future. These people can mold the beliefs people have in them into a formidable political force and can, under the right circumstances, change the entire course of a society.

Legal–Rational Authority

A "legal-rational" authority is one in which judgments of appropriateness and rightness derive from an ideal set of abstract rules. People create the rules; the rules then become an overriding reality. They are greater than the men and women who created them, and they are greater than the organizations they govern. They are the roots of social order in a modern society. This form of authority, Weber believed, fits the needs of a rapidly changing, modern society.

Legal-rational authority requires a special language so that rules can be stated in the most general terms and yet still be specifically applied. Their understanding cannot be trusted to tacitness, and their language is too complicated for word-of-mouth translation. The rules are so vast in volume and scope that no single person can memorize them.

The transformation of power into authority via abstract rules occurs through an interpersonal process. Only expert specialists of the law can exercise this authority because only they know how to use the specialized language of the law. This does not mean that the untrained have no recourse to law. Laypeople can share the order by referring to commonly understood bits of knowledge that are part of expert knowledge. For example, ordinary people can go to court, have a lawyer supplied by the court if they cannot afford one, or plead for themselves according to the provisions of an article of the abstract code, even if they do not fully understand it. A classic example of this is the prison inmate who spends all his time in the prison library studying law books and becomes a "jailhouse lawyer," usually filing appeals for himself and in behalf of his fellow convicts. While there are surely great risks, principally the likelihood of imprisonment, in going into court without a lawyer, such a practice is "legal," and, of course, the jailhouse lawyer and his clients have very little to lose.

Rational authority may be thought of as a legal interpretation of power. Hence a landowner has the right to post a No Trespassing sign because the law says a man has both a right to have private property and a right to protect it. Unlike traditional authority, here it is simply not enough that a practice has taken place for years for that practice to be "right." Fairness becomes a matter of a relationship between the practice and a set of abstract rules pertaining to it. Thus it is from the relationship between the practice and the law that legitimacy is accomplished.

In a rural region of northern Minnesota, a farmer received a long jail sentence for firing his rifle at trespassers on his property. Although farmers and landowners in the area assumed that firing guns at people not wanted on their land was a "legal" device for protecting their land, the court ruled otherwise. It seems that the men fired upon were city people, and they brought assault charges against the farmer claiming that they did not receive fair warning before the farmer opened fire. This case is interesting because it shows how the interpretation of the law stands or falls on rational grounds. In this instance, the right to protect property did not include the right to endanger the lives of people. The right to life took precedent over the rights of property. While the farmer involved became a sort of folk hero among other landholders in the area, a hero standing against the encroachment of city ways, he had to serve the major portion of a five-year prison sentence. Thus, law can suspend tradition.

Legal-rational authority requires that people have the cognitive ability to fit together an act with an abstract understanding of it. Thus a president may veto a bill even if he has never exercised a veto before, and even if the practice has been infrequently employed by his predecessors. Or, let us take the dramatic real-life example where, in 1972, Congress gave consent to the presidential appointment of a successor to Spiro Agnew who resigned as vice president under Richard Nixon. Although the practice of "appointing a vice-president" had never before taken place, it went smoothly and legitimately because the constitutional procedures, in their abstract form, were well understood. Thus, according to the law of the land, a committee was appointed, a recommendation offered and approved, and the country had its first nonelected vice-president ready to become president by virtue of another procedure of replacement when Nixon himself resigned. The practice acquired legitimacy by virtue of its link to a procedure articulated in an abstract document, the Constitution of the United States.

Social order as a consequence of the use of legal-rational authority depends on the wide distribution of a belief that legitimate interpretations and actions can be shown to relate to a body of abstract principles. Although the characteristics of Weber's legal-rational type of thinking are predominant in modern society, people may also think of authority as based on tradition and charisma, or some combination of meanings drawn from our ideal types. As we mentioned earlier, the types are derived from real systems of knowledge.

Power as an Organizational Form

The transformation of power into authority sorts out social action, resulting in arrangements of human activities we call *organizations*. These organizations are always, of course, within an institutional context. Organization may be thought of as the consequences of the ways people wield power, so to understand power in its social form is to look at types of organizations that derive from the three ways of legitimating it. Utilizing Weber's kinds of power and adding one new form, we distinguish four types of organizations, charismatic, traditional (or feudal administrative), legal-rational (or bureaucracy), and professional, each type embodying the processes and character of transformed power.

We have adapted materials from several sources into Table 7.1. By *elements*, we refer to the basic building blocks of organizations, for example, decision making or the ways resources are collected and managed. From left to right, the table shows the vast differences in the social reality of each organizational form. In the charismatic organization, a leader must be continuously involved in fund raising, which requires the continuous display of charisma. In bureaucracy, budgets are usually "given" to the organization. The actual money is typically derived from state or federal governments, or from endowments or others kinds of investments. While Weber identified only three forms of authority, following Stinchcombe we have added a fourth — the professional. Professional authority and its corresponding organization are becoming an increasingly common form in modern society. It is perhaps best understood as a composite of the other types with a few unique features of its own. We return to comparisons among forms after we describe more fully the character of each.

The Traditional Organization

Traditional organizations can be complicated and, to the modern mind, confounded with ritual. For example, the number of buttons on a king's cape could have significance in international affairs. The appointment of a favorite aide of proper royal blood could signal a new lineage of power. Matters of kinship and determining who is and who is not of royal blood are of utmost importance in traditional organizations.

Regardless of the degree of complexity, all traditional organizations can be identified by their unique characteristics. Max Weber captured the essence of these characteristics in the phrase "mirror image organization." By this he meant that whatever customary precedents ground a particular organization, these precedents (customs, rituals, etc.) are reflected in all the subsequent levels of organization. Each level of the organization is a mirror-image of the next. A prince is like, but less than, a king; a princess, like a queen; and a duke, like an earl. The legitimacy of authority shines through in each successive organizational position as if reflected in mirrors of ever decreasing size.

But what of modern examples of traditional organizations? No single organization is wholly traditional. Even within feudal society there were laws, courts for redress, and nascent forms of legal-rationalism. Hence, although we cannot find pure examples of traditional organizations of power in any society, we can highlight the features of a particular organization that are traditional. The overall character of an organization will be a function of the weight each feature receives in its overall operation. Arthur Stinchcombe (1973, 37) has suggested that the manner in which new automobiles are sold and distributed in America matches closely the traditional, mirror-image arrangement of power. Of course, power starts at the top with the automobile manufacturers. These giants of industry, which have a total budget greater than all but four nations in the world (Mintz and Cohen 1971), are managed by very powerful elites who make decisions about automobile design and type. They have biases. All seem committed to the internal combustion engine, and all favor a "free enterprise" approach to the operation of their industry. At least one company, Ford, has been run by a single family since its founding. Henry Ford was a folk hero to many people, and his ideas about how cars should be built and what they should be able to do still are reflected in the modern product.

Table 7.1

Types of Organizations

Elements	Charismatic Retinue	Feudal Administrative	Bureaucracy	Professional
How is truth of theory decided?	Inspired utterances of leader	Tradition	Rational procedure by management	Competence certified by peers
Who Controls resources?	Leader as person	Official holds permanent grant, income-producing property	Board of directors or legislature	Board of directors or body of professioanls
How are resources replenished?	Irregular contributions depend on leader	Land or franchise produces steady rents or profit	Varies, sales or investment	Sales, services, investment in future benefits
How are resources managed?	At disposition of leader	According to private interests of fief holder	Formal accounting	Formal accounting
How is responsibility divided?	Delegated by leader	Permanent delegation of inherited rights; little control	Limited delegation in jurisidictions of officials	Wide delegation based on peers' judgment
Who controls supervision?	Irregular supervision by leader	Virtually absent	Routine supervision	Rare, except at promotion or change in responsibility
What reward produces discipline?	Depends on belief in genius of leader and on leader's control of resources	Depends on sense of traditional obligation: "honor"	Organization controls promotions and pays salary	Career depends on reputation with peers and clients

Source: from Arthur L. Stinchcombe in Smelser 1973, 38-39.

Those at the top of the automobile industry live much like a royal elite. Weddings among their children are celebrated not unlike those of British royalty, and their life-styles are indeed regal. The lives of these industrial giants have fascinated scholars and laypeople for decades, for they constitute a powerful elite that can influence the lives of many people directly and indirectly.

Of course, as elites they may be unresponsive to democratic pressures. Although gadflies like Ralph Nader may challenge them, they make the final determination about what products roll off their assembly lines. They may even ignore significant segments of buyer preferences. In the 1950s and early 1960s, in spite of market research figures indicating one-third of the American public would purchase a small, economy car, the automakers decided to produce full-size cars exclusively.

These kings of cars do not sell their wares directly to the people who use them. Instead, like royalty of old, they have established a system of passing on merchandise. They, in effect, put out their work to lesser nobility — the new-car franchise holder. A would-be member of the automotive kingdom must qualify. He or she must prove worthiness. This can be done through bonding, collateral, and the use of persuasion. A man, perhaps successful in the sale of used cars, wins a new-car franchise. This means he is granted dominion over the sale of the cars he is allowed to buy from the corporation. Virtually all traditional power, of course, is now defined in terms of rational constraints such as contracts and laws. But a new-car franchiser can exercise considerable power. We also note here that the franchise is often passed on within a family through successive generations. Some dealers are now in the third generation of a franchise.

Stinchcombe refers to organizations that operate as franchises as "feudal administrative" ones. Many other examples from other arenas of power can be cited. Within government, an illustration of traditional organization can be found in the practice of a lower government body copying the form of a higher one. States pattern their governmental organization after that of the federal government. Although the bicameral division of the government into a House and Senate was familiar to the colonies before the Revolutionary War and became a part of the federal Constitution, it was not necessarily intended as a model for the states. The Constitution states, in Article IV, Section 4, "The United States shall guarantee to every state in this Union a Republican Form of Government" (Kelly and Harbison 1970, 1085–1086).

Even a casual perusal of state governments reveals that they often model their governance after the bicameral division. No doubt such mimicry of form was originally calculated to enhance entry into the Union. And we recognize that details of the organization of state governments vary (Nebraska, for example, has adopted a unicameral form in recent times). Our point is that the legal strictures of the Constitution cannot account, totally, for the strong tendency of the states to use the two-chamber division. Such a practice rests on a precedent traceable to tradition. Thus, an element of the traditional influences the composition of state governments. Tradition, in part, defines the relationships between lesser and greater powers. Consider, for instance, that urban areas in most states make up major proportions of the states' populations and that a city government may actually be larger than the state's. This does not mean that cities are more powerful in the realm of government than states, any more than the size of a duke's court reflected his dominion over the smaller staff of a king.

Within modern society, we discover many areas where precedent has resulted in a form or organization. We can find an entire support staff at the White House concerned with protocol, or unspoken or even contractualized agreements among market competitors that certain areas belong to one or the other company. The organization of government itself, like the system of committees and subcommittees, has no legal or constitutional basis, but is a predominant feature of life on Capitol Hill (cf. Weatherford 1981; Freudenburg 1986).

The traditional mode of stability survives in modern society as long as the practice of precedent goes unchallenged either by a charismatic person who redefines the meanings of the past or by legalists who reinterpret precedent as law.

The Charismatic Organization

Charismatic leaders spawn social movements, generally composed of ill-defined masses of believers clustered around an inner circle of associates close to the leader. Movements function to introduce new values, goals, or other culturally meaningful themes to society, and under some conditions they can be forceful agents for change. Movements can import new meanings to old forms or old meanings to new (Weber 1961, 10–14). A charismatic leader invariably surrounds himself or herself with members of the inner circle of true believers whose function is to buffer the leader from public scrutiny and interpret the messages of the leader to the masses.

A "charismatic" must be buffered from the masses in order to help maintain beliefs about his or her special qualities. A dynamic, forceful speaker exposed as a drab or opinionated conversationalist in real life can hardly maintain the image of a cool-headed, deliberate, and rational public figure. Charismatic leaders depend on a form of organization that makes it easy for believers to believe.

For the charismatic, the organization that best allows for appearance management is the small, well-defined center of power. After a person has risen to high office, he or she can carry along the inner circle. Since this is typically small in number, its members can accommodate themselves to virtually any preexisting organizational form. The cabinet of the president and the congress do not greatly affect the relationship between the leader and his or her aides, but the inner circle is an extension of the charismatic image of the leader. The identities of the aides derive from their contact and work with the "imagined leader." They carefully guard a publicly distributed image, and they must never betray the trust the leader has in them when he or she admits them to the inner group. If a member of the inner circle does not really believe and must constantly lie or adjust what he or she knows to be real, the leader will not last long. The tension between what one has to do to promote the leader's image and what one knows about him or her can be great, and the task of managing it is overwhelming.

A good example of this tension within the charismatic form occurred in 1968 in connection with the first presidential campaign of Eugene McCarthy. Because of his challenge to the legality and morality of the war in Vietnam, McCarthy excited many college students, but as a charismatic leader, he was unable to sustain a movement. The aides he enlisted joined him basically to support his opposition to the incumbent president, Lyndon Johnson. While many of his aides were very competent and even scholarly types, they were not true believers — their faith was in the cause, not the man. One economics professor who served both McCarthy and Jimmy Carter compared the two men. About Carter he remarked, "He is quick to synthesize, and he has a wide range of gut feelings about good and bad economic policies." About his affiliation with McCarthy, however, he said, "McCarthy did with my work what he did with all his papers: stuck them in his back pocket and said whatever he thought" (*People* 1976, 39–40).

This adviser was not a true believer in either candidate's charisma. He reportedly tested Carter by having him read papers on technical economic matters, and he was not happy about what McCarthy did with his advice. A true follower would have accepted that Carter was a genius and would have used McCarthy's extemporaneous flights as evidence of his insightfulness, his ability to assimilate materials rapidly and, most important, his "decisive judgment." In fact, had the organization been truly charismatic, the precise details of the relationships between "leader" and "aides" would be carefully guarded and not likely to turn up in *People* magazine.

In addition to the buffering circle of true believers, another device frequently employed by charismatic leaders to heighten and sustain belief in their special powers is *mystification*. Mystification refers to a manner of speaking in which two things are accomplished: (1) The leader expresses a uniqueness of style; and (2) meanings are communicated through innuendo, analogy, parable, or other ways that avoid direct and open statements. Mystification is a rhetorical device. Through its use, an impression is conveyed that only the leader really understands the significance of what is said and that the followers, although they do not fully comprehend, sense the profundity and urgency of the message (cf. Scott and Lyman 1968).

Mystification is integral to charismatic movements. Since the leader's messages and the thrust of the movement are often ambiguous, they require interpretation, and the only people capable of interpreting are inner-circle members. Thus, the organization of a charismatic movement includes a well-defined elite situated strategically throughout the movement. For instance, a local campaign headquarters in Iowa may be staffed by volunteers, but it is advised by a state manager who is close to the top. Workers may even be visited periodically, not by the actual candidate, but by one of his or her close associates.

In sum, a charismatic organization has a core that is personally created by the leader and that is flexible enough to use whatever strictures other organizations may impose on it. The core is surrounded by an ill-defined mass of believers whose faith is sustained through the use of mystification as well as the interpretation that inner-circle members make of the mystifying messages coming from the top.

Max Weber pointed out that such an organizational arrangement is difficult to sustain over long periods of time. Usually a movement will merge with existing forms and lose its charismatic character. But residuals of the movement's charismatic basis can linger within another form, coloring a presidency with a special quality, for instance. In modern society, with its bias toward functional rationalism, charismatic movements often evolve toward rational forms. A political campaign becomes well organized; it has levels of responsibility, a hierarchy, authority that rests on expertise, and so on. Except perhaps at the top, the charismatic movement becomes very much like the dominant organization of modern society — the bureaucracy.

The Legal–Rational Form: Bureaucracy

In modern politics, it is not enough to be well-liked, dynamic, and patriotic; a person must "know what he or she is doing." In other words, a judgment must be made about qualifications. By studying common-sense ideas that people have of what a qualified person is and by examining how people present themselves as qualified, we can see the essence of legal-rational procedures that transform power into bureaucratic authority. This form displays the following properties: (1) It requires education; (2) it depends on expertise: (3) it is principled; and (4) it thrives on change, which it anticipates and, on occasion, creates.

To enter and belong to the legal–rational, one must be *eligible*. At the center of power in America, Washington, D.C., the most mundane job carries detailed requirements of eligibility. A Senate aide must have letters of recommendation and high standing in his or her school class, and a secretary in any office of a government organization must be carefully screened for background and credentials.

A candidate must be welleducated but not *over*educated (there seems to be a strong bias against "intellectuals" in public life). His or her education must meet the needs of exercising power. He or she must be able to recall facts and figures rapidly and accurately, know how to interpret expert knowledge about scientific matters ranging from nuclear physics to supply-side economics, and, above all, to create the impression of a well-informed leader.

In the organization of power, the theme of education reflects itself in specific eligibility requirements. No staff can be considered complete without a legal division, an advisory staff on domestic affairs, a public relations office, and the like. Many analysts have noted that "educational prerequisites" for power, both at individual and organization levels, have become synonymous with "legal education" (Auerbach 1976). Although not constitutionally stipulated, a law degree is almost a prerequisite for access to political power.

Expertise. The requirement of education in its specific legal rendition intermingles with the assumption of expertise. Legitimate power often derives from the capability to match a problem with its potential solution. Thus an organization divides itself according to problems — energy allocation and development, welfare, conservation — and these divisions are staffed by experts. The "solution" to a problem raised by an extended threat, such as an embargo on oil, amounts to the assignment of it to the appropriate "expert." The rank and file clearly do not understand the details of solutions. But such understanding is not necessary within the legal-rational form. What is essential is an understanding that the problem is in "good hands."

Consider an event that is probably forgotten now but once occupied space in the national news media: the swine flu immunization program of 1976. Then President Gerald Ford, as leader of the federal government, declared that the country should be immunized against the possibly deadly flu virus. This declaration of intent then set into movement complex organizational mechanisms. First, legislative legitimation was necessary. A bill was introduced in the House, passed, moved to the Senate, approved and sent to the president's desk, where it was signed into law. But our glossing over these complicated procedures does not conclude the story of the swine flu immunization. Before the actual shots could be administered, the vaccine had to be proven safe. This means that the "testing" methodology of medical science ranks higher in the capability to legitimate a decision concerning the health of the population than does the law itself. Hence, although President Ford wished for total inoculation of the American populace, tests indicated that children might experience unacceptable side effects from the vaccine. To be sure, the risks were not considered great, but according to the predefined notions of "safety" for programs of this type (rates of complications and serious side effects must be below 1 instance in 100,000 cases), the decision was made to vaccinate the adult population first. Medical people explained that they were now after what they called "herd immunization." They hoped that by vaccinating the majority of the population, the rest would not be significantly affected by the disease. Of course, this theory must have been effective, since you probably have never even heard of swine flu, or at least were never vaccinated for it.

From our sociological perspective, the example of "swine flu shots" shows that a political decision can be modified by a "rational decision." In this case, the rationality of science superseded the political process, at least in the capacity to modify and legitimate a politically motivated decision. Hence, although "herd immunization" had nothing to do with the form of decision making in its beginning stage, it became a vital part of the "rationale" for action by a large bureaucracy charged with the task of distributing a vaccine to the population of America.

The ill-fated swine flu program also illustrates a second meaning of expertise. Expertise is specialized. Physicians, not engineers, legitimated the immunization program. Within the rational form, the task of legitimating power is partially accomplished by building the expertise of specialists into the organization itself. This is typically accomplished through the proliferation of "divisions" within the organization.

Principled Action. The legal–rational form is principled. In the management and presentation of its appearance, the people in this type of organization try to act in principle on behalf of the organization. Such an organization polices itself and applies its own rules of orderliness.

One way the legal–rational organization manages the appearance of "principledness" is through periodic purges. These purges are not ideological, like those of charismatic organizations, in which "faithfulness" to a leader's position is assured by a process of elimination. Instead, these are purges of lawfulness, rituals in which the organization allows itself to be judged by its own standards. For example, laws enacted against income tax evasion may be used to prosecute members of Congress. Or standards for "fairness" and "unbiased" decision making embodied in the strictures against conflict of interest may be used to disqualify a particular legislator from membership on a committee.

Perhaps, the best example of "principledness" comes from legislative prohibitions governing the financing of political campaigns. These laws pertain to no one else but members, aspirants and supporters of members of the organization. The laws function ideally to assure the rational basis of selection to the government. They guard against the undue influence of a wealthy supporter on a powerful political figure. As in our discussion of bureaucracy, we discover again that legal documents and their interpretation are socially constructed realities greater than either the parts or the individual members of the organization.

Rational Change. Although we are often led to believe that legal-rational organizations resist change, this belief is only partially validated in research literature. Actually, such forms thrive on change. The change, however, must be interpreted within the form. As the sign on a tenement wall stated, "If voting changed things, voting would be outlawed."

Some people, especially in modern society, believe that the vote has become a meaningless gesture. According to NORC data, in 1984, 21 percent of the American people responded that voting is only somewhat important as part of a citizen's responsibility to society. While a majority of Americans still say voting is important, a full 20 percent of them admitting that they did not regard the act as important, coupled with the fact that rarely do half of the eligible voters actually vote, is strong evidence that a cynical attitude about "representative government" has become prevalent among the people. Some of these cynics regard voting as simply endorsing personality and policy. As one remarked, "I never vote. I discovered it simply encourages politicians."

As these people are questioned further, we see that they are not merely rambling irresponsibly. In fact, a majority regard reporting crimes, keeping informed on public issues, and serving in the military (both for men and women) during times of war as important. So people still have ideas about what responsible citizenship is. But an apparently growing number of them want some kind of change that results in dramatic, forceful leadership. At the least, we can say that they do not believe that Congress represents them very well. In the 1987 NORC data, for example, 18 percent expressed "hardly any" confidence in Congress, and another 62 percent have "only some" confidence in these elected leaders.

With historical hindsight, we can note that the issues of guns and butter, education, health care for the elderly, government spending and its impact on the value of the dollar, were issues debated more than twenty years ago by candidates Richard Nixon and John F. Kennedy. Both men served as president, having the opportunity to solve the problems. Yet these same issues, discussed very much in similar terms, made up the topics of the televisions debates between Jimmy Carter and Gerald Ford, and later between Walter Mondale and Ronald Reagan and Michael Dukakis and George Bush. And, we can expect them to continue to be important in future presidential campaign debates.

Our sociological vantage point seems to confirm cynical sentiments about the power of elected officials. But we must recognize that cynics, calling for a change of form, are correct in their understanding of how legal-rational forms gloss organizational matters with policy talk. One political scientist, Murray Edelman, aptly put it in the title of his book, *Political Language: Words That Succeed and Policies That Fail* (1977). These same cynics are incorrect, on the other hand, in failing to appreciate the role that change plays within the form.

Stability depends on the organization's ability to adapt to pressures placed on it by other organizations and by changes in its environment. A new development in the policy of a foreign country must be swiftly and convincingly countered. A shift in basic resources, be this a matter of fossil to nuclear fuel or a change in the ethnic, cultural, and linguistic background of voters, must be dealt with in a way that is flexible enough both to preserve the character of the form and, at the same time utilize the new resources. It is this capacity of *co-optation* that allows the forms to change and yet remain essentially the same.

Philip Selznick's (1949) classic study of the organization responsible for transforming the Tennessee river into a massive complex of dams, power plants, and navigable waterways, the Tennessee Valley Authority (TVA), demonstrated that government projects do not always function according to the policy that justified them in the first place. He was able to show that a liberal New Deal policy that advocated the use of grass-roots, local leadership resulted in the establishment of a conservative administration for the TVA. This administration, composed mostly of local businessmen, operated according to the vested interests of the leaders rather than to the benefit of the poor and underprivileged.

In this example, we see that conservative bias in the functionally rational organization seems to appear regardless of stated intent of policy. The ability to persevere is the hallmark of this form. And perseverance means the accommodation of change in ways that can be interpreted as "making sense" from the perspective of the form.

Selznick's study serves to remind us that rational organizations often function in nonrational ways. In fact, his study is but one of many conducted by sociologists to show nonrational aspects of bureaucratic organizations. Perhaps our favorite among these is the study of the use of a tool called a "tap" in the construction of airplanes. In the early days of modern commercial airplane construction, after World War II, a design was used that required that rivets be inserted in holes perfectly lined up to hold together the metal parts of the plane. Now the regulations handed down by the Federal Aviation Agency to govern construction strictly forbade the use of a "tap," a small tool which could be used to drill out holes that did not match so that a rivet could be inserted. Joseph Bensman, a sociologist, worked at the time in a factory constructing airplanes. He learned that the rational prohibition on the use of the tap was not fully obeyed. In fact, he believed that airplane production would have been significantly slowed and perhaps even stopped if the tap was not used. Workers, if caught with a tap, would be fired. So foremen and workers alike developed ways not to look for and carry the tap so that it could be used, on necessary occasions, to assemble components (Bensman and Gerver 1963).

After several decades of studies such as these, sociologists began to doubt whether the bureaucratic structure was truly rational. Of course, Weber's depiction of the ideal type of the form stood, but actual work in organizations seemed to tell a story of humanizing and working around the rational feature of particular organizations. In many ways, these sociological studies serve as correctives for the tendency, in such fields as economics and administrative science, to adopt uncritically the rational model of decision making. The role of emotion and other nonrational elements in the exercise of power must be appreciated, and our discussion of tradition and charisma suggests that the range of legitimate power is vast. Nonetheless, we must not overlook the degree to which power has become rational in modern society. Recently, several social scientists (Weatherford 1983; Kinsey 1985; and Freudenburg 1986) have had rare opportunities to observe the inner-workings of the capital of the United States.

From these studies, we once again learn of the nonrational nature of life and work within a form that is supposed to be rational. To be sure, life on "the Hill" is a little like life in a small town, where reputations and interpersonal relationships are very important to wielding power. But at least one of these researchers, Freudenburg, came away from his tenure on the Hill with new understanding of the dominance of rationality in the organization of power. He reported that while he too had learned to debunk the idea of rational decision making after observing the exercise of power among congressional staffers, members of government agencies, and members of Congress, he gained a new appreciation of the role of information and its presentation.

> There is no question that Congressional decision making is anything but dispassionate, being profoundly affected by power and parochialism, but it also becomes quite clear, quite quickly, that information is often the most important single weapon in the battles that take place. Members and their staffs have very little patience for the kinds of detailed technical analyses that are found in most academic journals, but accurate capsule summaries take on a nearly phenomenal importance. Perhaps the most important single task of staffers — and of lobbyists — is to obtain information that is accurate, timely and convincing. If the information will lead to unexpected embarrassment for one's opponents, so much the better. (Freudenburg 1986, 313–326)

Professionalism

Perhaps because of disenchantment with the rational organizational form, or perhaps reflecting the unique requirements of scientific and technical knowledge in modern society, a new composite form has emerged: the professional organization. In this form, competency is the key to the transformation of power into authority. Presumably, the person who is "best" has authority. While this criterion of competency is closely related to bureaucratic forms, it differs in that professional competency is understood more in terms of core cultural values and less abstractly or procedurally. Hence, on television, we see depictions of physicians as caring people, breaking rules on behalf of the proper practice of their profession. Think of how many times you have seen a television doctor go up against a hospital administrator on behalf of a patient's needs. Similarly, lawyers pursue justice and defeat the clumsy, unfair bureaucracy of city hall. Of course, television programs are not intended to be sociological descriptions, so we must not take their version literally. But they do give us a characterization of the relationship between cultural values and professional life, and by pitting the professional against the bureaucrat, they help us see the distinction.

Bureaucracy levels social values and diversity. As a form, it treats all clients equally, and by implication, it does not respect values. It is, after all, an instrumental form. But a profession justifies itself with historical links to rich human values — justice, health, and knowledge, for example. It is when a profession can legitimately control money that it becomes a powerful social force. As Talcott Parsons (1959) wrote,

> I conceive of profession to be a category of occupational role which is organized about the mastery of and fiduciary responsibility for any important segment of a society's cultural tradition, including responsibility for its perpetuation and for its future development. In addition, a profession may have responsibility for application of its knowledge in practical situations. (P. 547)

One of the reasons people hold politicians in such low regard is that they have come to expect professionalism in all walks of life. A profession, however, enacts rather than creates values. Hence, except in rare cases, such as those involved with issues of "living wills," people do not question the values upon which a profession rests. Politicians, in contrast, create laws and perhaps values. They are in the powerful but not necessarily legitimate position of passing laws that might not correspond with the values of all their constituents. Think of the major issues of today: abortion, gun control, arms reduction, environmental issues. For each, we can identify strong values and sentiments associated with both sides. Abortion is legal, but a strong and vocal minority of people oppose the law on religious and ethical grounds. And while a clear majority (72 percent) of the American people favor strong gun control laws (NORC, GSS, 1987), the sentiments and values of a few (notably members of the National Rifle Association) dictate the limits and enforceability of the laws that do pass.

The persona of the politician embodies the value conflicts of society. Therefore, we expect perhaps higher ethical and behavioral standards for politicians than we do for professionals. Professionals can be idiosyncratic, and we seem forgiving of their character flaws. Indeed, we might even expect them. Politicians, however, are subject to what can often be relentless scrutiny of their character, as when a judge is appointed to a high bench or a president makes an appointment to a high-level cabinet position, which requires Senate confirmation.

Obviously, any particular organization might have elements of any of the four types of organizations. And, often, the conflicts people experience within a given organization derive from a mixing of forms. For instance, a professional may find himself or herself with opportunities to "misuse" funds, since the professional form lacks routine accountability checks. Or, in a bureaucratic organization, promotions based on informal or traditional considerations, such as membership in a family, can fuel great conflict.

Nevertheless, each form can be said to have certain affinity for others. That is, one form seems to go better with one than another. Professionals who gain positions of prestige may discover they have perks and privileges very much like the person who occupies a high position in a traditional organization. Or the professional who deals routinely with similar problems may develop rational solutions to these problems (physicians' waiting rooms, insurance forms, for example). But other aspects of the exercise of power conflict within and across forms. It is difficult to envision how to account for charisma, or how to justify keeping a family business within the family and still maintain professional standards. Hence we see typical structures within a structure for organizations. We refer to this concept as *embeddedness* and we can visualize it.

Imagine the professional organization as composed of overlapping layers, each representing a level of competency and practice; bureaucracies are, of course, hierarchical; charismatic retinue forms are circular, and feudal administrative pyramidal. We can graph these forms with their embedded structures. The professional type consists of layers of competent people, each layer ranked hierarchically (see Figure 7.1). Within each layer, however, a charismatic professional may have a retinue, and acquire rights and privileges. In a bureaucracy, forceful and creative people can likewise subjugate co-workers, and, as we have noted, top-level functionaries can enjoy perks and special treatment (see Figure 7.2). In a feudal organization, such as a family-owned and operated business, hired professional staff may acquire a great deal of power, especially if they are charismatic (see Figure 7.3). And, finally, within the charismatic structure, there can be smaller circles of power based on charisma, legal-rational, or traditional power (see Figure 7.4).

Political Characters

In everyday life, we experience power in all its various forms. Our parents give us advice. A boss rebukes us for being late to work, or for using a tap to make

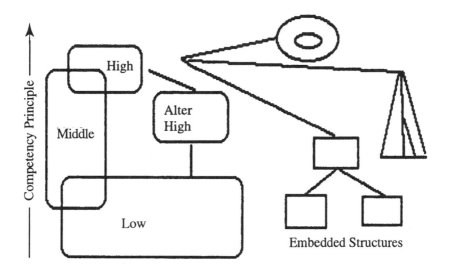

Figure 7.1
Professional organizational structure.

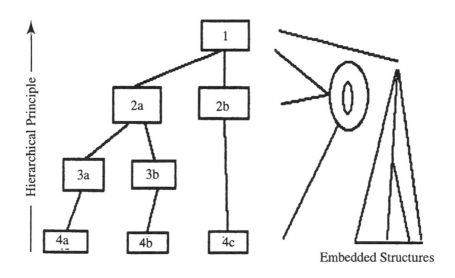

Figure 7.2.
Bureaucratic organizational structure.

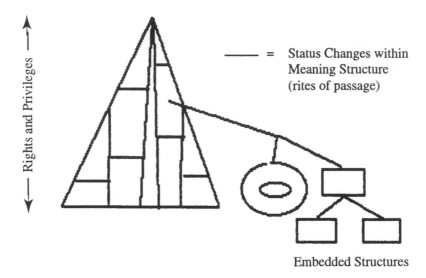

Figure 7.3.
Feudal organizational structure.

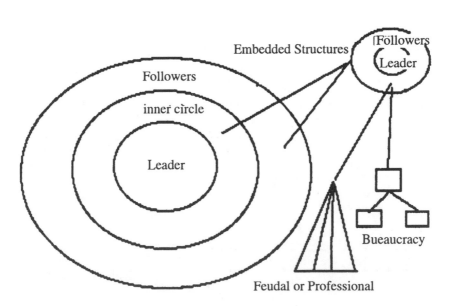

Figure 7.4
Charismatic organizational structure

a rivet fit. We seek the counsel of a minister or a teacher. We also deal with the organization of power. We fill out tax forms, complain about a defective product we have purchased, vote for the candidate of our choice, or face a judge for some violation of the law.

We organize our experiences with power into patterns of awareness that in varying degrees and combinations reflect the meanings we give to authority and its forms. By describing some instances of the enactment of power, we can see how people experience and react to politics in their everyday lives. Each of the examples points up features of the types of authority that Weber identified. Nevertheless, in modern life, power organized as rational authority seems to pervade all aspects of social life.

Rule Followers

Some people seem to be quite ritualistic about the exercise of power; they simply follow rules. An unusual conflict between farmers and the electric company in rural Minnesota illustrates rule following characteristics. A crowd of some sixty angry farmers caught up with a surveying team at Meeker County Road 3 and Highway 4. The team, doing the preliminary work for a planned 400–kilovolt transmission line through the farmers' land was stopped from continuing their work. A spokesman for the farmers remarked, "They want violence. They're goin' to continue this thing till they get it!" The farmers formed an organization, Counties United for Rural Environment (CURE). They believe the power line will adversely affect their livestock and crops, and intend to stop its construction at all costs. A general manager for United Power Association asks the Meeker County sheriff to remove the farmers from the rear of the surveyor's truck. He declines, saying he is there only to prevent violence.

In this confrontation between locals protecting their land under the law and a large corporation exercising its legitimate right to expand its services, we can spot the rule-following consciousness. For example, the general manager can only implement policy. His order is to survey the land. He cannot be expected to use his discretionary talents to rule on the "justice" of the order. The land will be surveyed regardless of the farmers' opposition. He may privately sympathize with CURE, but as a representative of the power company, he can only obey. His role performance does not allow for discretion on matters of policy. He ritualistically orders the trucks out to the same location each day knowing they will be confronted by the farmers. The standoff results from two different types of obedience. The farmers obey their concept of ownership, which entails the synthesis of self and land, and the general manager obeys a "rule." Likewise, the surveyors themselves, sitting by the roadside observing the heated discussion between farmers, sheriff, and corporate spokesman, are obeying the rules of the organization. The nonproductive and even destructive consequences of the rule obedience are irrelevant to the tasks of doing "work."

The truly nonpartisan drive to register voters also demonstrates rule following of the rational-ritualistic type. We know that voter registration drives are generally supported by whichever side stands to profit from a larger-than-average voter participation in an election. However, some organizations, among them the League of Women Voters, involve themselves in the process without regard to goals (i.e., the outcome of a particular election). They believe that voting, in and of itself, is a desired accomplishment. Such a participatory mandate has been carried to its extreme in countries where the entire electorate is ordered or otherwise compelled to vote for a single candidate or party policy. The vote is a procedure hollowed of any goal-related significance and enacted for the sole purpose of reaffirming membership in organization, community, and country. Voting, under these conditions, becomes something people do simply because they have membership in a social collectivity, and participation for its own sake becomes the basis for determining the meaning of political acts.

In short, in varying degrees, political social meanings depend on fostering a mentality of conformity for its own sake and membership *qua* membership. In high places, this adaptation manifests itself in a rhetoric calling for respect, honor, and responsibility without specification of the objects for such virtues.

True Believers

> For men to plunge headlong into an undertaking of vast change, they must be intensely discontented yet not destitute, and they must have the feeling that the possession of some potent doctrine, infallible leader, or some new technique they have access to is a source of irresistible power. They must also have an extravagant conception of the prospects and potentialities of the future. Finally, they must be wholly ignorant of the difficulties involved in their vast undertaking. Experience is a handicap. (Hoffer 1951)

We have learned that charismatic leaders must have followers, and we can see that rule following, fostered in the rational-legal type of social organization, does not produce the type of follower the charismatic requires. Although Eric Hoffer was not a professional sociologist, his concept of the true believer goes a long way toward depicting the character of the follower of the charismatic leader. According to Hoffer's idea, a true believer must (1) assimilate the qualities of charisma seen in the leader, making them his or her own; (2) recognize that he or she will never actually live up to these standards; and (3) cope with doubts about the efficacy of the leader and the given doctrine.

As Hoffer (1951) points out , true believers search for something missing in their lives. They may long for honesty in government, justice in the legal system, and integrity of the individual. They begin their longing with a judgment that such conditions do not exist in the present political system. A strong sense of discontent motivates the true believer to seek something or someone to emulate. In many ways, the advent of membership in a social movement can be understood as a response to social pressures.

In a society that upholds standards of equality, justice and freedom for all and yet operates on the basis of a legal system that offers differential treatment depending on a person's ability to pay legal fees (Spradley 1988; and Auerbach 1976), a strong and conflicting set of pressures exert themselves on some members. For instance, a poor person, say a tramp arrested for public drunkenness, knows that if he can raise bail money, he may avoid spending time in jail. Spradley (1988) describes how tramps "jump bail" and travel on the tramp's circuit, moving from city to city. All the while these men keep track of how many "days hanging" they have in the various cities where they have been arrested and have posted bail. They know that after a certain number of days, the warrant for arrest is usually dropped for such offenses, and they can start all over again with a fresh arrest and new bail money. As Spradley concludes, the system of justice operates to free a man if he can afford the crime and imprison him if he cannot.

At another extreme, the very rich multinational corporations depend on the expertise of lawyers to plead their cases in court and read the tax codes to their advantage. The average person, then, can become caught between the ideals of his culture and the realization of the necessity of money to achieve these ideals. Such a mentality fosters the longing and discontent that spawn the true believer, who latches on to a fiery political figure promising reform, rejecting the system of "justice for those who can pay for it," and holding out the promise of a new day.

The believers must also know their leader. In matters of reform, the believers need not be specific regarding plans of action, but must be consistent in doctrine. They must say what the leader would say. At the same time, true believers must know their place. They must recognize that the lofty ideals of reform and decency are not truly theirs. The ideals are embodied, instead, in leader or myth. They must be so because the true believer must be able to cope daily with discontent stemming from the ordinary nature of life. The believer still works as a clerk at Gasco Oil, he still relies on the same legal system that benefits the rich and imprisons the poor. Because true believers live in the world as it is given to them and because they cannot accept it as it is, they must be able to separate things longed for from what actually is.

How can true believers maintain the balance between what should be done and what they can do? The answer lies in their association with other members of the movement. A worker for a political candidate once confided that all her friends seemed to be other political workers. Her life was centered in the definition and redefinition of ordinary life as politically relevant. She discussed strategy and policy, hopes and aspirations in every conversational topic. In the true believer, the presence of other true believers is necessary for any long-term continuation of faith in doctrine or leader.

For example, to true believers of the right wing, détente between the Soviet Union and the United States is a sign of weakness on America's part. It is further evidence that "we are experiencing the decay of the moral fiber that made the nation great." In spite of popular opinion, they maintain their own version of the meanings of all affairs. They seek the company of one another because those of their kind are the only ones who understand them. To preserve and nurture their own way of making sense of their lives, they cluster together often as "ostracized splinter groups." They devote energy to such activities as purifying their world views and policing their own membership.

Professional Politicians

Jane Jones is eminently qualified for her freshman seat in the House of Representatives. A political science major in college and a lawyer, her attractiveness on camera, her command of the issues, and her convincing exhibits of genuine concern for women's rights won her the November election. Now she is ready for the upcoming session of Congress. She contacts some of her old college professors and begins to cluster experts around her. Jones is briefed on international relationships by the outstanding professor at State University. She has been brushing up on her decision-making skills by pouring over law books. Although she admits to some apprehension about being a freshman lawmaker (the first woman to serve in this office from her district), she is self-assured and at ease at the prospect of the move to Capitol Hill.

"Her background will serve her well," remarks her lawyer mentor from the Regency Academy of Law. "She has been a long time getting to where she is now. There was her first marriage, the children and the divorce; the long years of schooling and, then, the building of support necessary to aspire to high political office," he continues. The congresswoman held several minor offices, the state senate for two terms, and an appointed position as a legal adviser for the governor. She acquired the reputation of a hard worker, one who "does her homework" and "plays to win." Also, she has no skeletons in her closets. Her past is clean, a real political asset, no corporate involvements, no sex scandals. In fact, her divorce shows her "human side," and her children her maternal side. Here we see the embodiment of the modern politician — a person of power.

Although she won the support of feminist organizations in the state, she prides herself on her ability to appreciate all sides of an issue. She will vote what she calls her "studied conscience." She has pledged not to be swayed by special-interest groups of any kind. She put it this way in her remarks at the victory celebration on election night.

> We went to the people with a professional campaign and they bought it. We explained the issues and they listened. We have passed the time of prejudice based on sex. People want the best-qualified person in office. The person with the background and experience to govern. We offered ourselves as this kind of candidate and they endorsed us with their votes. Now it is time to get to work and serve the people.

The modern politician talks the language of power. Yet the language she uses is "rational." She need not harangue and she need not promise. She must analyze, but in a way that means something to her constituency. She must show that as a person she reflects the ideas of the legal–rational form. In the present-day political world, this means she presents an image of maturity, levelheadedness, legal practicality, and, above all, belief in the essentials of modern organizational technology. The entry of women into the political world shows us these attributes in strategic vividness.

One scene in recent politics illustrates what we mean. Barbara Jordan, a black women from Texas, displayed her linguistic verbosity to the 1976 Democratic National Convention. Her talk signified that she knew the rules of modern politics. Even if overplayed, the display illustrated that sets of rules for becoming powerful exist and that important among them is the requirement of being the "right kind of person." The right kind of person can think and talk like the organization—efficient in style, thought, and wit, compact in purpose, flexible in operation.

Women, as late-comers to the political scene, have the opportunity to acquire and utilize these characteristics in untainted fashion. Men of power may have risen by means other than their merit; women of power must be of merit, and where merit can be as explicitly defined, as it can in modern politics, the woman politician becomes the typification of the individual adaptation to form-generated pressures. It is interesting to note in this connection that the "problems" that plagued Geraldine Ferraro during her 1984 bid for the office of vice-president of the United State were not matters of her personal achievements but questions about the means employed by her husband to become powerful.

Summary

Sociologists conceive of politics as the exercise of power, which they define broadly to include any instance of dominion. Power is organized differently in various situations of social life.

Power is institutionally transformed into authority. This happens whenever social circumstances operate so that people exercising power and those influenced by it think of it as "right and just." The classical sociologist Max Weber identified the means by which power is transformed into authority: tradition, charisma, and rationality. Each type of authority can be characterized according to the ways in which all those involved must think and act. Traditional authority is essentially based on looking backward for some precedent for social action. Charismatic authority rests on a sometimes fragile belief in the special qualities of a leader; legal-rational authority derives from abstract, impersonal, and situationally free rules. Contemporary sociologists have added the professional type to complete the description of ways in which power is transformed into authority. Professional authority is based on competency, as assessed and controlled by those who have it. Professional authority is a composite of traditional, rational, and charismatic.

Each means of processing power into authority produces a distinctive organizational form. Traditional organizations are stable and well ordered. Charismatic organizations are transitional and dynamic; legal-rational ones are plastic, able to accommodate change and maintain order. Professional organizations usually depend on other forms for their existence, but have distinctive forms within the others.

We can also depict the ways that people experience power in their everyday lives. We did this by characterizing rule followers who are ritualistic about the exercise of power, true believers who are fanatical, and professional politicians who are coolly rational and formal.

Having reviewed the five basic institutions of society, we may now move to a general discussion of institutional change within the context of modernization. While our treatment of modern society is surely incomplete, in order to outline more fully the effects of modernization, we turn to a discussion of new forms of institutional social life, sometimes referred to as postmodernism.

8 INSTITUTIONAL CHANGE AND
POSTMODERNISM

Although social institutions can act as stabilizing forces, as society undergoes the process of modernization, its institutions also undergo profound change. While people in society might not see their institutions changing, they sense it when their children behave in ways virtually unthought of in their own childhoods, when the values they thought they passed on to their children are distorted by practical necessity, and when they feel frustrated by prospects of a future only dimly resembling the present, a future that seems unamenable to conventional solution.

Perhaps nowhere is the extent of institutional change more clear than in attempts to cope with technological change. Sociologists began examining the relationship among inventions and their consequences on the practical affairs of human life as early as the 1920s. Perhaps the most famous hypothesis about this relationship is encompassed by William Ogburn's idea of "cultural lag." Writing in 1927, he suggested that the culture of society is composed to two somewhat independent components: "material culture," which includes technology; and "adaptive" culture, which includes social institutions. A social problem, in Ogburn's theory, is created by a lack of fit between these two components. Moreover, whenever a society innovates, that is, puts new technology into practice, a lack of fit is virtually assured, since a change in material culture "forces changes in other parts of culture such as social organization and customs, but these latter parts of culture do not change as quickly. They lag behind the material-culture changes, hence we are living in a period of maladjustment" (Ogburn 1927, 196).

Ogburn's theory has been the basis not only of many empirical studies of the effects of technology on society but of the way change itself is conceived. A tinkerer who comes up with a gadget of some kind to help do the routine work of society better hardly ever imagines the possible implications of his or her invention on society. We can see a better way to open a can, record an image, or make a car ride smoother. It is another matter to see the relationship between the organization of kitchen work and can openers, libraries archives and video images, and jobs in automobile repair and suspension systems. It is the task of sociologists to be alert to these kinds of consequences. Even though Ogburn's theory has been criticized as too conservative and as underestimating institutional forces, he nevertheless should be credited with underlining the conceptual task at hand. As modernization has developed since his era, we see the increasing role that technological innovation plays in society. Hence we suspect that cars, telephones, computers, and mass media technologies (radio, television, and communication networks) not only change how we accomplish things in society but also have an impact on social institutions. The legacy of Ogburn's theory is sensitivity about the unintended effects of modernization on society. Generally, we suspect these effects to create new problems, which we try to solve by using old institutional, and often inadequate, solutions. While institutions continue to function under the pressures of modern life, they embody the tension of trying to solve new problems with old solutions.

By taking a broad view the processes of modernization, we see that not only do institutions adapt to technological innovation, but the very character of society is transformed. About the global transformations of society he calls civilization, Norbert Elias (1982) writes

> Nothing in history indicated that this change was brought about "rationally," through any purposive education of individual people or groups. It happened by and large unplanned; but it did not happen, nevertheless, without a specific type of order. . . This basic issue resulting from many single plans and actions of men can give rise to changes and patterns that no individual person has planned or created. From this interdependence of people arises an order *sui generis*, an order more compelling and stronger than the will and reason of the individual people composing it. (P. 230).

Therefore, the plans and actions of modern people have changed the institutional structure of society, created a new order that is neither what is left of the old nor completely new. The impetus of change, moreover, has been in the form of things and the uses to which people put them. The list of technologies of modern society, a society that in essence depends on technological intervention in and control over nature, is too long to catalog, but some things stand out for the profundity of their impact on social organization.

In this concluding chapter, we suggest some of the profound and unintended changes technology has had on institutions and introduce the novel idea that new, partial, or quasi institutions may be evolving out of the tension between doing things in new ways while thinking about these things in old forms.

Cars and Society

The idea of the automobile was simple: Figure out how to make the carriage self-propelled. In Europe and the settled regions of America, horsedrawn transportation had been adapted to institutional needs during the nineteenth century. Horses pulled families in carriages to church and to the countryside for picnics. With more sturdy wagons, the horse did the work of transporting families and their possessions west across the plains. They also hauled loads too heavy for men, solving the commercial problem of getting goods to factories and raw materials to processing plants. But the horse was a part of nature, weak compared to the "iron horse," the steam locomotive, which supplanted it as the principal vehicle of transportation in the nineteenth century.

The successful solution to problems of mobility made possible by the domestication of the horse and the invention of trains afforded some Europeans the luxuries of time and resources to tinker with the carriage mentality of transportation. At first, the idea of a "car" was simply the preoccupation of inventors. It consisted of putting together already existing technologies—the internal combustion engine and the carriage. The result was the "horseless carriage."

It is inconceivable that the early inventors of the automobile could have anticipated the institutional changes their invention would foster. Who, for instance, could have foreseen the extent and depth of the relationship Americans, Europeans, and Japanese would develop between affairs of the heart and "wheels"?

The Car and Romantic Love

The courting practices of early Americans were completely alien to those of contemporary Americans, yet they were well institutionalized until about the 1920s. Old-fashioned, pre-automobile courting began with a young man's gaining permission from a young woman's father to visit. He would arrive at his date's home, visit with her family, and court in the family parlor. In rural areas of America, where a young man might have traveled great distances on horseback to visit, he would be invited to stay the night. Of course, the connotations of staying the night have greatly changed. The courting beau was expected to make no sexual advances. The practice of sleeping together in the same bed (a partition separated the young man and woman) was condoned. This elaborate practice of courting, with its origins in European society, varied from region to region in eighteenth and nineteenth century America, and assumed a stable family structure. The young man was always within earshot of some family member. A younger sister would giggle at the sight of the beau trying to hold her sister's hand, and mother and father were close by.

Henry Ford is a controversial figure in American history. He had opinions about everything from politics to diet, but he was no moral libertine (cf. Lacey 1986). Nowhere in the vast literature historians have created about the great automobile manufacturer do we read that Henry Ford was antifamily, that he intended to weaken the authority of fathers in the family, that he desired to empower children with the means to escape from parental supervision, that he wished to foster trends that atomize society, that he wanted to further conditions leading to the spread of the ideology of individualism.

Yet we find among the list of social consequences brought on by the wide availability of the automobile many of these things. Ford wanted to make available to the common man a machine that would help him with his work. Indeed, the Ford models T and A did this. They were used by farmers to plow fields; they were converted into pumps and sawmills by using their drive wheels as a power source. In short, they became an integral part of the institutionalized lives of many Americans. But as Berger, Berger, and Kellner (1974) have demonstrated, when we speak of technology and society, we must distinguish between the intrinsic and extrinsic characteristics of each.

With regard to technology, this means that we must be aware not only of the legitimate reasons for the use of technology, that is, what the technology is supposed to do according to institutionalized meanings that frame its introduction, but also of the ways the technology is organized itself—its intrinsic structure.

The automobile is built to be responsive to the decisions and reactions of an operator. It does not have the ability to monitor the wisdom of turning right instead of left, braking instead of accelerating. Yet there is something about the design of it, its feel, its appearance, that appeals to us. Of course, as artifact, the car reflects the values and aspirations of designer and customer, and there is much to be said about the ways that cars have been designed to please and even manipulate customers. What we focus on here is structural design, the tendencies of movement and operation that are intrinsic to the machine. These are mobility, speed, and control. A car enhances these human attributes, these aspects of human vitality. Like all technologies, cars are basically an extension of what humans can already do. We move where we want, when we want, and according to our individual vitality.

The car enhances each of these capabilities and, in the process, equalizes us. The immobile person moves in the automobile, the indecisive driver must decide while driving, and the weak become strong with revolutions of the crankshaft. As the institution of the family began to change with the forces of modernization, the role of the father changed. Since he was employed in the factory or outside the home, and not as a self-sustaining farmer, he was absent from the family for long periods each day. When he was home, he would act in authoritarian ways to regain the power he sensed he had lost. Fathers could be quite restrictive of their daughters and place many obstacles in the path of a courting beau.

As tensions in the organization of family life play themselves out, a new potential becomes available. The prospect of mobility and power, the freedom of movement, was injected into the courtship relationship. Fathers now approved of a date, but could not supervise what happened in the back seat of the Ford.

They might control the use of the family car, but they could not stem the tide of assembly-line production. As cars became more available, it was inevitable that they would enhance the social forces already at work transforming institutions.

Today we still advise our children not to get into cars with strangers, yet we often entrust their lives and safety to drivers whom we barely and sometimes even do not know at all, for example, school bus drivers. The car enhances freedom, but it also decreases the effectiveness of family restraint. The corollary of this is that as an institutional presence becomes further removed from the regulation of individual action, the institution must become a more efficient socialization agent. We mean that if the father is not there directly to remind his daughter about the proper way to act, she must be trusted to act as if she knows the proper way. She must have internalized the institutional values. The principal impact of the automobile on the family in general, and on expressions of romantic love in particular, has been to increase the importance of the internal regulation of social action. Of course, given the changes we outlined earlier, it should be no surprise that a consequence of introducing the automobile into the dynamic of courtship has been increased departure from traditional norms of moral behavior.

Elias (1988) evokes the metaphor of traffic to help us understand this aspect of modernization, and we can extend it to assessing the impact of the car on intimate relationships outside of the institution of marriage. To appreciate differing modes of integration for societies fully, Elias suggests thinking of road systems.

> One should think of the country roads of a simple warrior society with a barter economy, uneven, unmetalled, exposed to damage from wind and rain. With few exceptions, there is very little traffic; the main danger which man here represents for other men is an attack by soldiers or thieves. When people look around them, scanning the trees and hills or the road itself, they do so primarily because they must always be prepared for armed attack, and only secondarily because they have to avoid collision. Life on the main roads of this society demands a constant readiness to fight and free play of the emotions in defense of one's life or possessions from physical attack. Traffic on the main roads of a big city in the complex society of our time demands a quite different moulding of the psychological apparatus. Here the danger of physical attack is minimal. Cars are rushing in all directions; pedestrians and cyclists are trying to thread their way through the melee of cars; policemen stand at the main crossroads to regulate the traffic with varying success. But this external control is founded on the assumption that every individual is himself regulating his behavior with the utmost exactitude in accordance with the necessities of this network. The chief danger

that people here represent for others results from someone in this bustle losing his self-control. (Elias 1988, 233–34)

What Elias says for the operation of the automobile can be readily extended to the highly personal behavior of courting. What cars did when they made courting mobile was to shift the focus of social control from the structure of the family to the internalization of norms; that is, they hastened modernization of the family, a process that was already well under way by the time the Model T and Model A Fords became part of the family. It is, therefore, no surprise to learn that changes in morals about such things as premarital sexual behavior changed most dramatically at the same time that automobiles became widely available—in the 1920s, with its flappers and Fords, and again in the 1950s and 1960s when the merger of cars and "love" became so commonplace that the popular music of the era acknowledged the car as a symbol of sex itself: "She'll have fun, fun, fun 'til her daddy takes the T-bird away."

Parking Lots and High School Days

Cars have had a similar impact on educational institutions of society. The high school education, once a major goal for the modernizing society, meant that a community was preparing its citizens for participation in the institutions of society. What a person learned in school was supposed to be linked with practical and symbolic concerns of community based society.

While the car's effect on the idea of education as a great moralizing force for democracy has been indirect, nevertheless, it finally changed education in the direction of actualizing goals and norms, first by allowing the school to move from a neighborhood to locations farther removed from the home and community and, then, with the availability of cars extended to almost every licensed driver, to the high school parking lot. The high school car, the car owned or at least operated by a teenager, empowers that operator with means to further escape the supervising and constraining norms of education as a socialization agent.

Specialized education and curricula that proliferate choice (some major cities now allow students and their parents to select any school within their district to attend) have separated sense of place and learning. Today's students think of schools as places in and of themselves, not as extensions of community. Of course, part of the allure of private schools is that they often are designed to impart senses of community—uniforms, distinctive curricula, rituals, and traditions associated with and, in some instances, created for the image of the school function to define the place, set it apart from the specialized and functionally equal opportunity structures of the public school.

Cars allow students to spend less time with friends and school associates in school-related enterprises and more time with them in social activities. Cars interact with the forces of change we have identified as strengthening peer culture and the youth microsociety. Given the tension built into the educational institution itself, the dynamics between instrumental values and actualization, authoritative and libertarian forms, there is room for freed children to construct their own version of the meanings of "going to school." A catalyst in this process is the automobile. Imagine the conversations that go on in the car as high school students discuss the meanings of "going to school."

Cars and God

Obviously the increased freedom afforded the operator of an automobile further individualizes the religious experience. Cars, as we mentioned in our chapter on religion, can adapt the worship ritual to a mobile society, as in the case of drive-in church services, but they can also, in an inadvertent way, transform the organizational basis of religious life. Consider the parish in an established neighborhood of a large eastern city. On a Sunday morning, at time for Mass, one can observe people walking to church. They do so in all kinds of weather. The mere act of walking in one's neighborhood affirms a sense of place, integrating the motive of worship with those of residence.

But the modern parish, church, and synagogue depend on the commuter in the same way that many businesses do. Downtown churches are composed almost exclusively of members who do not themselves live downtown. The downtown church may minister to those who live there—the homeless, gays, and members of youth cultures, but the resources on which they depend—pledges, tithes, contributions of time and money—come from people living outside the "place" of worship. Certainly the most spectacular symbols of worship remaining in modern society are often located downtown. The Methodist church in downtown Chicago, the oldest in the city and built to be a towering monument to God, is nestled between giant edifices of corporate power, the skyscrapers. The church stands as a quaint symbol of history, its walls lined with documents of its past greatness and vision. Today its congregation struggles to cope with the incongruity their presence creates in the commercial center of the city.

Without the car to move members swiftly in and out of the city, without the means to locate one's sense of self and participation in multiple locations, the experience of religion would be much more segmental and less functional, to use Elias's terms. Again, religion has modified and adjusted to the changes that mobile people require of it. A consequence of this adaptation is a transformed meaning of the relationships between being in society and being religious. The nature of society is problematic in this formula, since its very location moves literally with turns of wheels.

Governmental Cars

The relationship between the increased use of cars and governmental structures is subtle and latent. No constitution of nation or state explicitly guarantees the right of automobile ownership. Certainly the bulk of laws dealing with the car are designed to constrain and limit its use (Crandall 1986). Licenses, inspections, and laws governing the proper operation of the car control and govern. Yet the car remains a symbol of individual freedom and power. Its use is required by the very infrastructures of modern cities. The cop walking the beat is just a nostalgic memory—replaced with the patrol car. The verbal warning and glance as devices to communicate with those about to break a law have been replaced with the flashing lights and siren of an approaching police car.

Cars are symbols of authority and exclusivity. VIP motorcades mark the arrival of people of power. It is only because of the breakdown and, ironically, the democracy of the American road that some of the very rich and powerful have taken to the sky, a frontier of increasing regulatory problems.

Cars and Money

Clearly it is in the economic realm that the car has had its most direct impact on society. Since the invasion of Japanese cars in the 1970s, the American economy has rebounded somewhat by co-opting the competition, either by joint manufacturing ventures or by buying components for American automobiles. And we might not be accurate in saying that Detroit controls the economic fortunes of the nation, but the automobile industry is still vital and integral to the modern consumer economy. Cars are sold with sex and symbols. They impart meanings to their owners that are both resonant with and influential upon the meanings of life itself. The sensible Volkswagen bug of the 1960s and 1970s challenged the image that Detroit car makers had of the American driver. Recently, a folk hero emerged from the rubble of a collapsing automobile giant. Lee Iacocca did not single handedly save Chrysler, he was aided by government loans and public opinion, to name only of a few of the complexities of that economic miracle, but his amazing rise to public prominence and esteem can be explained only in terms of the importance of the car in American life (Iacocca 1988).

The economic dragons of the Far East, Japan and more recently Korea, measure their successes, in part, in terms of the numbers of automobiles they sell.

Modernity measured in terms of per capita income, percent of population living in urban areas, levels of education, life expectancies, and other indicators is correlated with automobiles per capita. For example, using data from the United Nation's *Demographic Yearbook* and *Statistical Yearbook*, one can calculate the numbers of cars per 100 people from selected nations to get an idea about the car and modernity.

Tabie 8.1
Cars per people, Selected Nations

Nation	Cars per l00 people	Nation	Cars per l00 people
Kenya	16	Egypt	2
Zimbabwi	3	India	1
Canada	44	Turkey	16
U.S.	56	West Germany	41
Argentina	13	Sweden	38
Peru	3	United Kingdom	29
Japan	22	Italy	36

In fact, the economics of modern nations of the world are heavily indebted to the automobile industry. In the United States, in 1986, nearly 5 percent of the gross national product (GNP) was accounted for in the sales of new and used cars alone. In current dollar values, that amounted to $320 billion. (Statistical Abstracts of the United States 1988) Americans spent another $85 billion at service stations. A household with a motor vehicle in this country had an average expenditure of $1274 on fuel . And it is was further estimated that the average cost of owning and operating an automobile in 1985 was $2441.85 per year. Couple these statistics with the fact that there were about 136 million registered automobiles in 1986 (about 563 for every 1000 people) and you get an idea of the degree to which the automobile is involved in the lives of the American people.

While we can measure the economic magnitude of the automobile industry, this is only a partial gauge of the role the car plays in the economy of modern society. In addition to new- and used-car sales, and the people employed directly in the manufacture of cars, there are auxiliary enterprises woven into the fabric of society. Insurance, road construction, police departments, shopping centers, and automobile parts stores make up a section of the car economy—and this does not even include the oil and gas or energy industries.

But the impact of the automobile on peoples' participation in the economic aspects of social life goes far beyond the exchange of money for cars. It includes values and life styles as well. First Detroit and later Tokyo and Seoul learned that style sells cars. As Paul Simon sings, "Cars and cars, all over the world, engine in the front, jack in the back." In a fundamental sense, this is so. An inventory of the improvements and changes made in the design and functions of the modern car shows that virtually everything about the 1989 car includes technology that goes back to the 1920s and earlier. Fuel injection, turbochargers, disk brakes, independent suspension, and air suspension systems were all invented and in use by 1930. What distinguishes the modern car from the older vintage (save the addition of computers, which we discuss below) is style.

People buy an image when they buy a car. Cars are symbols of power, independence, and are part of the way we make statements about who we are and what we want others to think about us. It is interesting to note, in this context, that today nearly 50 percent of all new- and used-car sales are trucks. This is astounding given that the processes of modernization have moved all but a fraction of us into urban living conditions and into jobs that are far removed from the farm or a construction site. If we are less and less involved in farming, construction, and heavy labor, why is the truck so popular a consumption item?

The answer, and an intriguing way to see the effects of the car as a symbol of modernization in economic relief, is that a new product has been developed to satisfy an emotional need in the modern consumer: the symbolic truck. These are small truck-shaped vehicles that usually carry only two passengers in comfort; cannot carry a heavy load; might well be equipped with high-technology sound systems, fancy trim, fog lights, a roll bar, and other extras, which are often quite fragile. Consumer reports further indicate that most four-wheel-drive vehicles are rarely, if ever, driven off the road. In other words, what the symbolic truck is, is a small car, not much different from the standard car, if there is such a thing. But it is configured to give the impression of outdoorsmanship, or rough individualism and the spirit of adventure.

In similar symbolic significance, upscale automobiles are capable of traveling nearly three times the speed limit, and have the power to accelerate faster than legally allowed. All these trucks and high-powered, racing-design sedans are, of course, locked bumper to bumper on the congested freeway system with older cars of all shapes and styles in a steady flow of regulated traffic (cf. Stinchcombe 1974). In modern society, we consume style and experiences, and our economy reflects this.

Hello, Is That You?

When Alexander Graham Bell invented the telephone, he made possible many social changes he might not have anticipated, nor personally approved of.

In fact, Bell, whose wife was hearing impaired, was developing a system to amplify sound so that he could help hearing-impaired people deal with daily life when he invented the telephone. Of course, his discovery of how to transmit sound through a wire created conditions that would place great importance on skills of communication with voice only.

The telephone has become an ubiquitous and central mode of communication in today's world, and those of us who live in societies where phones abound take for granted their availability and usefulness. What we do not often think about is how phones have changed the social organization of daily life. In perhaps the first attempt to uncover the sociological implications of communication by phone, Donald Ball (1968) offers a overview of the significance of telephones in society. He points out how people create the reality of their society through conversations, using the full range of verbal and nonverbal skills they possess, and how telephones create a version of reality that reflects the features of the phone.

Some of the features of telephone talk are profound in their impact on everyday life: (1) the phone is pervasive; (2) it has a decentralizing effect on relationships; (3) there is an insistency to communication over it; (4) it functions like an "irresistible intruder" in time and place; (5) communications over it have an "equalitarian intensity" to them; and (6) the very act of communicating over the phone imparts a social identity to its users.

As you would expect, the number of telephones per capita varies among nations of the world in a pattern similar to automobiles. Generally the more modern the nation, the more equal the ratio of phones to people. According to the United Nations *Statistical Yearbook, 1984/85,* for example, Kenya had 1.3 phones per 100 inhabitants, Zimbabwe 3.2, Egypt 1.5, while Finland had 59.2, Israel, 36.9, Italy, 42.6, Japan, 53.5, France 60, and the United States nearly as many telephones as people (the 1984 ratio was 80, but with the recent deregulation of the manufacture of phones and the flood of designer and speciality phones on the market, one might well guess that now there are more phones than people in the United States).

When we refer to the phone as pervasive, we mean not only that it is an ever-present aspect of life in modern society but that its role in the daily lives of members of society is fully integrated with virtually all their social activities. Business deals, dates, chats, and serious intellectual discussions take place on the phone.

But the phone is more than a convenient device that has become widely available and extensively put to use. The fact that it pervades all aspects of social existence in modern society suggests that something about the phone allows its to be all things in all places to all people.

Primarily, of course, the phone focuses communicative skills on spoken language alone. It allows one to manage to sound a certain way without necessarily being that way. Think of the many times when you have met someone you had previously communicated with only on the phone. Rarely does a person's appearance match the image we have of them from voice-only communication. In fact, it is the focus on the skill of using the voice that allows the phone to be pervasive—allows it to sit unobtrusively and even decoratively in the most private location of the home: the bedroom. Even here, the management of voice belies the "actual" activities taking place.

It is because one can make faces and use other devices to express true emotions and meanings while sounding a certain way on the phone that makes the phone an addition to otherwise private spaces of daily life. The mobile phone represents the ultimate pervasiveness of the phone. To include a phone as equipment in an automobile means that the phone fits with the design and demands of different technologies. People in modern societies even have answering machines in their cars, an ultimate affirmation of dynamic communication.

But the phone also carries a tendency toward decentralized social relationships. As Ball (1968) pointed out, whenever the phone is everywhere and everyone has access to a phone, anyone can call anyone else. This design feature of the phone decentralizes social relationships, and, in the process, may well change the character of a society.

The implications of everyone in a society having access to everyone else are profound. First, structures of power always limit access to the powerful. In both modern and nonmodern societies, powerful people are buffered from contact with those over whom they have power. Open-door policies rarely are truly so, even in highly democratic societies. Obviously, since the flow of requests to a powerful person will overwhelm the resources of any person to respond individually to each request, every organization has methods for screening and selecting the messages their elites receive. These typically involve using such mediating devices as secretaries, receptionists and lower-level communication structures.

Second, the style and modes of communication among members of specific organizations and even societies depend on a full array of communicative skills, verbal and nonverbal. In fact, a great deal of research in contemporary social science is directed at uncovering the role that language and speech play in establishing social identity. The telephone masks many of the important signals of status and power, among them dress, comportment, and using a high variety of language. So not only may a powerful person be called by a person of lowly power and influence, but such a person may sound "powerful and influential" on the phone.

Third, the way information is spread on the phone makes knowing something (fact or falsehood, rumor or truth) simply a matter of contacting or being contacted by someone else who knows. While we do not suggest that simply wiring everyone to everyone else will bring about radical challenges to hierarchical power structures, whenever the phone becomes widely accessible to all members of society, new means of controlling access to information must be developed.

In American society, we can trace the development of these devices for telecommunication from the "old" pyramid arrangement in which lines are strung from the individuals to supervisory stations at the top level without "feedback" options to the "newer" PBX or networked arrangements where phones are interconnected. The juxtaposition of hierarchy and network symbolizes the decentralizing tendencies of phone communication.

As if the phone's pervasiveness and decentralization of information were not enough, several scholars have noted that the character of communication over the phone has a insistent quality to it (see Singer 1981 for one of few empirical studies of uses of the telephone). Since all calls are equal, one never knows, from the ring itself, whether the call or caller is a trivial nuisance or bears an important message. If you have ever awaited an important call, perhaps news about the health or safety of a relative, you have experienced this insistent character of the phone summons. Not only is the summons insistent, but much study has been devoted to the organization of phone conversations themselves, and these inquiries suggest that, for competent conversationalists, there are rules for hurrying along the conversation. The person who calls, for example, is obligated to finish the exchange, and requests are often made indirectly in the form of questions ("Is Jimmy home?" rather than "I would like to speak to Jimmy").

Summarizing some experiments to determine whether people bargain and negotiate differently over the phone, Muson (1982) writes

> If a person wants to leave a certain impression with a potential employer, but has something to hide, he may be better off arranging a face-to-face meeting than talking on the phone. On the other hand, if he wants to coldly assess another's intentions, he might have a better chance on the phone. Getting together enables people to schmooze, to become more intimate, and also to be taken in. (P. 49)

Telephones transform the quality of interaction, and this has the effect of enhancing venerability and emphasizing the factual or informative character of the exchange. It is the insistency of communication over the phone that creates these tendencies. This insistency is part and parcel of the irresistible nature of the phone. Without it, one might somehow be out of control, not in touch with others. Clearly, in the modern society, with the increased importance of dealing instrumentally with one another, the phone has emerged as a major device for sales, emergency communication, and the exchange of factual information.

But the phone, perhaps ironically, also functions to impart to its user an identity. In a humorous scene from Steve Martin's film *The Jerk*, the principal character in the film, a person without identity (a white man raised by a poor black family) claims with joy that he has become somebody when he finds his name printed in the phone book. Similarly, when a teenager persuades her parents that she needs her own phone and phone number, she is seeking an individual identity symbolized by a separate listing. But this identity, a source of initial pride and accomplishment, also carries with it obligations and consequences of participation in phone communication and, hence, presses each phone user toward an equalitarian status. All phones and phoners are equal.

The technology of the phone furthers the dilemma of modern existence. It opens communication vistas and increases individual vulnerability. It takes away some communicative skills and forces new ones. It underscores individualistic thinking and links people by interpersonal networks of impulses and tones.

But what impact does all this have on the institutions of society? Not surprisingly, much institutionally meaningful activity revolves around who can use the telephone and for what purposes? In the typical American family, for instance, who is audacious enough to guess the number of arguments that take place daily about who is spending too much time on the phone, who may call whom at what hours during the day? While such matters might seem trivial compared to more newsworthy problems, we suggest that understanding how telephones are part of the complex of events and circumstances we refer to as modern society actually reveals the essential structure of society, an organization of meaning that imparts significance to all acts, large and small, mundane or noteworthy.

Telephone communication in the context of family life further illustrates trends and tendencies we documented in our chapter on the modern family. Individually oriented families, hence, often allow a wide latitude of choice about telephone usage. In middle-class families, youngsters might even be encouraged to learn proper phone etiquette at a very early age, and the telephone becomes a primary link in their peer group by the time they reach adolescence. Likewise, mothers and fathers compete with their children for use of the phone, and the phone can be a productive and informative link to society. For example, families with computers can access networks of information that school-age children can put to good use in their education. In short, as Bernstein (1970) concluded about the elaborate code, individual-oriented family, the same general values on choice, self-management, and manipulative styles that compose the character of modern society are played out in the context of family life.

In contrast, the positional, restrictive-code-using family may well see the telephone as an intruder, a link to the undesirable aspects of contact with society. Hence, phone use among children may be regulated by the number of calls allowed, and especially close supervision may be given to make sure that children do not participate in the new networked communication such as dating lines, joke numbers, and the like. For the more traditionally defined family, the telephone is a potential problem, since the very authority of the family is challenged by the intruding, decentralizing qualities of phone communication. Little wonder that the Amish realized this threat of technology and in parts of the United States remain without phone service.

But in less extreme examples, even typical middle-class families must cope with the flow of information into the home from the phone. Parents cannot possibly monitor calls in a systematic way, and there are ample opportunities for teenagers to use the phone to deal drugs, make dates, and engage in youth cultural activities without their parents knowing about it. Over and above it all, the phone may become a symbolic link to worlds outside the family. The search for self-fulfillment, as Yankelovich (1981) put it, might lead outside the family, and the telephone could be the route.

The other four major institutions of society—education, religion, government, and economics—also have been transformed by the telephone, but perhaps less profoundly than the family. Still, education is wired to other institutions of society, and conference phoning may play an increasing role in classrooms of the future. But the major impact on education reflects the general transformation that phones have had on interpersonal relationships. Since phone communication connects administration, faculty, and student to other sources of information in society, educational institutions must deal with changes in society in a more comprehensive way than in the past. Education, however, remains a text-oriented activity. Books and the textbook in particular are at the center of the function of the institution, and we still place greater emphasis on reading than on hearing or seeing.

Similarly, religion as an institution is only indirectly affected by telephones. To the degree that its members rely on phones to communicate, modern religion is "wired." But the basic activities of religion (worship, indoctrination, and socialization) take place face-to-face, or at least in more personal interactive settings. One can, of course, "dial a prayer," but there seems little prospect for the teleconferenced Sunday morning service. In short, to the degree that religion deals with other institutions of society, and with the characters that society creates, it is affected by the tendencies of phones to transform social interaction, but these effects have not had a direct impact on the religious experience.

Phones are big business, and everyone seems to want to get into the act. It is in how routine business is conducted that the phone has had a major effect on the institution of economics. No one is safe from the intruding call of the telemarketer; few of us have not conducted business over the phone. Banks and their customers transfer funds, make deals, and establish credit lines by phone. It is no exaggeration to say that modern economics depends on fast and efficient phone communication. It is less obvious just how the phone interacts with the transaction of business, and there are very few sociological studies of this question. We believe it is safe to say that one consequence has been increased emphasis on the ability to control the impression given in interactive encounters.

As Goffman would have said, the phone affords another set of opportunities for people to manage their self-presentation. The enhanced manipulative character of the phone conversation has opened vistas of marketing and deal making, Muson's (1982) account of the research pertains. Perhaps reliance on phone-based business transactions will enhance rational, logical persuasion. This might be why car salespeople insist that customers come into the showroom to "cut a deal."

In government, we could hardly venture a guess about what role the phone plays. It has been important enough to give us the "wiretap," and we know that in Washington and Moscow only the most naive functionary would discuss "sensitive" matters over the phone. So while the intrinsic structure of phone conversation may overly democratize information, it also symbolizes the hopes of the world in a very empathic way. During the cold war, and even today, with lessening tension between the United States and the USSR, the red "hotline" phone stands as the final guard against world destruction.

Biting the Byte: Computers in the Modern Age

Although computers were invented nearly forty years ago, only when the micro-computer was introduced in the late 1970s did computers become affordable and available for general use. The rate of their dissemination and use in modern society is truly phenomenal. Virtually every month, new and more powerful models are introduced. And the software to use computers for writing, drawing, composing music, playing games, and doing routine computations is becoming cheaper and more accessible to the ordinary citizen. Today nearly one-third of all American households have a computer of some kind.

Of all the technological innovations we might discuss, the computer, along with the communication revolution it is unleashing, is the most astounding in terms of the speed with which it has become adopted and, arguably, the profundity of its impact on the basic institutions of society. In fact, computers are simply little machines that route circuits of electricity in small "off and on" impulses. They are perfect symbols of modernity because they are a composite of many inventions—telephone technology, microcircuits, television, and logical gridworks of information. They are impersonal objects which take on a full range of emotive meanings in everyday life, and they embody tendencies to both simplify and accelerate human knowledge. So, how can a small, electronic, plastic object change society? In a word, by altering our relationships with the physical environment and one another. All tools alter the way we deal with our environment, natural and social, in unique and often unanticipated ways; the same principle applies for the wheel, the knife, the lever, the car, and the computer. With the expanded capabilities of tools, people can establish new relationships. We saw how intimate relationships changed because of cars, and we have traced the effects of telephones on the distribution of power in society.

Computers differ from these earlier inventions because they are information tools. They do not move people directly around like cars, nor is their significance found solely in extending the human senses, as is true with the telephone, radio, and television. Instead, the computer extends what people know and allows information, in a pure and abstract form, to become the basis of relationships. When we work on a computer, we are working with logical solutions to problems invented by other people. Popularly, computers are thought of as isolating and even as separating people from one another. Workers often complain that working on a computer is a lonely task and that they require more human contact to be happy and productive.

While we appreciate this way to understand the computer as a machine like any other, it is really not a machine at all in the classical sense of the term. It is a memory of work that can be applied over and over again in the solution of unique problems. Writing on a computer is creative and individualistic, but the word-processing program on which the creative enterprise takes place is a highly logical system for the routine arranging of bits of information. How these bits of information are arranged varies with word-processing programs. When we write on a computer, hence, we are using what someone else thinks of how to organize information. We, of course, select from these ready-made solutions to accomplish our tasks, but still, we are dependent on others and, in a fundamental way, we interact with them each time we use the computer.

Certainly, this is true of all human inventions, but the computer is unique because it is extensively a relational instrument. By providing us with the power to build relationships, it can transform all our relationships. First, consider our relationship with nature.

Computerizing Nature

The Florida Everglades have been irrevocably changed by the growing pressures on its ecology from population, urbanization, and industrialization. The natural balance of flooding, drought, and brush fires has been upset by the use of underground water sources by nearby cities. Today, such species as the Snowy Egret have diminished in number or are on the verge of extinction.

We can relate many instances of the effects of human tools on the natural environment. We mention them here not to sound another alarm, for there have been many, but to make a case for the uniqueness of the potential of computers to redefine not only social systems but the very nature of the world we live in.

While we think of the Everglades as natural, they are becoming more and more the creation of society. Not only are they sanctuaries by virtue of the exercise of political power (the laws of the federal government define them as a "natural" park), they are now entering a new computer era in which the flow of water into and out of the park is regulated by a complex system of computer-controlled monitors on the old-fashioned gates and sloughs. The water flow is determined by a continuous reading that a very fast and powerful computer makes of weather forecasts, current water conditions, and the complex interplay of canals and rivers. No single individual, committee of scholars or naturalists, or branch of government could make these decisions.

Of course, the computer operates according to a program that models the natural conditions of the Everglades, conditions that have been reconstructed from the natural history of the area. The system is new and not completely in control. If conditions warrant it, for example, the program can be overridden so that a city receives water even at the expense of the swamp. We are not suggesting that political and environmental issues will be solved by computers. Instead, we underscore the potential of computers to alter relationships between humans and their built, symbolic, and natural environments. It is not far-fetched to imagine a time when the ozone layer, which protects the earth and has been the cause for much popular concern because of its depletion, will be monitored by computers and adjusted like the water flow of the Everglades.

Computers and Learning

An example of social change intrinsic to computers is the role they could play in education. Our analysis of education as an institution has uncovered solutions to the problems of organizing learning and knowledge that reflect centuries of ways to educate. It is obvious that the primary way to educate has been to write down whatever constitutes education, or to codify what is know so that it can be passed on, improved, or otherwise modified.

Not by coincidence, the symbol of education is the library. For the library houses the things of education, namely, texts. The tensions that drive education, instrumentalism and actualization, are captured in texts. The spoken word is still an important part of educational experience, but the final arbiter is the book. We read, cite, quote, and critique books. And, as Goffman (1981) demonstrates, even the lecture as a form of talk is predicated on the text. As he suggests, when we hear a lecture, we assume that it is based on texts, or could even become one. Further, the skilled lecturer makes the text "come alive" by organizing it through anecdotal renditions, by memorizing it, or by personalizing it.

Over the centuries, education has become a reflexive system of books about books, of ways of thinking and expressing ourselves in terms of books. Indeed, the modern educational institution would not exist without the printing press. There are many provocative analyses of the role of print media on social change, and we are not suggesting that printing caused the organization of education. We do, however, note that many features of what education is, and of what being an educated person means, derive from relationships with the permanent and tangible products of education: books.

But now comes the age of ROMs, REMs, bytes, and bits, and with this new age come new ways to code, retrieve, and process information. One of the new forms the computer has taken has vast implications for education: the read-only disk. It is possible now to convert all the books of a huge library to the densely packed memory of a disk. Rows of shelves, and the smell of dusty books, can be replaced by small plastic machines wired to monitors. A student, or reader, can access everything that is on the disk, with the aid of a well-organized program. She can recall everything said about theories of social change in the year 1987 by people who write sociology, for example. Or he can scan the literature of any subject catalogued into the program. You may well have already contacted a prototype of this system if your school's library has some kind of electronic card catalog.

But we are not talking about supplements to books. We refer, instead, to substitutes for books. Computers have the potential radically to transform the institution of education by changing the form of information, which is the foundation of it. We can imagine an educational experience that consists of sitting in front of a high-resolution color monitor and viewing great art of the world; but more, actually doing visual analysis of that art by deconstructing it on the screen, modifying it according to different techniques and theories. For sociologists, a course on social institutions and modern society could be programmed into a databank of resources so that when a student comes to a section of text, and wishes to see the evidence for a statement (for instance, the original research an author cites), all that will be required is to tap into the read-only storage devices and call up the information.

The ideas we refer to here are germane to the burgeoning interest in networked worked stations. What is usually envisioned in the work station is a computer linked to other computers and information storage devices in way that allows a worker, a person sitting at the computer, to use all the sources and capabilities that his or her station is linked to. Since the communication revolution (Williams 1982) increasingly links together all the world via satellites, sources of information that a student can be linked into are global. Hence the computer breaks down the association we customarily make between scholarly activities and locations, especially libraries. In the computer age, a scholar does not necessarily have to travel to a library that specializes in a particular area. She can access it through a computer wherever in the world it is.

In his discussion of how global scholarship can be supported, Langenberg (1989) distinguishes between libraries and what he calls the "inforum." The library is a place of books; the inforum is not necessarily a place at all. It is a concept referring to a synthesis of information and forum. It could consist of resources and expertise on using them, providing not only information but the means by which scholars can communicate with one another over space. It would help scholars manipulate information, assisting in their efforts to create new information, new insights, and new knowledge; and it could provide both human and nonhuman assistance to those using it As Langenberg (1989) points out, "a fully developed inforum will bear less resemblance to today's library than a modern automobile bears to a Nineteenth Century carriage". (P. 14)

The inforum would encompass the full range of human learning from music to mathematics, from art to architecture, from philosophy to poetry. In short, it would contain whatever the scholars of the world wanted it to contain. Would such a technological breakthrough be welcomed by all, and would it radically change the social institution of education? Not necessarily, because, as Langenberg clearly indicates, the library is a part of one institutional setting, or infrastructure, and the inforum would be part of another.

The library's institutional infrastructure derives from the assumptions we enumerated in Chapter 4. Chief among these are ideas of expertise and teachers, teachers in this context being real, expert people. The concept of the inforum would strain organization in fundamental ways because it would call into question these assumptions. The text model of education operates on the assumption that authorship can be located in a person who masters knowledge and imparts to it unique interpretations. Goffman (1981) shows one reason that the lecture is an essential ingredient in education is that it allows the lecturer to be located in a textually relevant way. This means that when we attend a lecture, we are hearing text relevant talk. A lecturer cites other authors, building a world of conversation that, while punctuated with ancedotal materials (jokes, personal stories and the like), is actually an occasion for the celebration of text. Lecturers are authors, or potential authors, and their authority resides in books. To check out the truth of what they say requires documentation—returning to the text. In the great tradition of Western education, learned people are referred to as members of the literati, people of letters. While scientists are less text oriented than, say, a professor of English, and while the history of the inclusion of science in a curriculum itself is an interesting story of the legitimation of observation by translating it into text form (the research report), still, scientists have taken their place in the institution of education by producing a textualized version of their work.

The inforum might change all this in the following ways. Whereas rewards for and place in the educational institution are defined in terms of authorship as a measure of expertise, how might the collective character of information clash with the traditional text/author relationship? When a global scholar scans information, the notion of authorship would become much less clear, and the collective nature of science, in particular, would be obvious. No longer could careers be built on finding and explicating obscure sources. All sources would be equally accessible to all scholars. No longer could authors be located in text, since the very idea of coding information in words might not apply to visual, auditory, or spatial reasoning and understanding. Likewise, the matter of who can use the inforum would change our understanding of education.

In the present institutional scheme, only credentialed people have access to textual materials. We do not mean that actual access to books is limited, although this is one meaning of the library card. We mean that only certain people, those trained in the context of the current structure, can interpret text; only the scholar can demand an audience for his or her reading of text. This is so because they have knowledge that allows them to see what is present in the library. They can arrange the materials to generate insights and new ways of interpreting things.

In the inforum, the very logic of interpretation could be made available to anyone on the system, and the speed with which information could be transmitted might allow new people, even those who do not have the status deriving from having studied at places of great learning, to provide alternative readings of information. In short, like the telephone, computers decentralize information, and ironically, individualize the interpretative process itself.

Who is to say whose version of information (knowledge) is to be honored? In essence, the inforum calls into question the control of information, and in the process, the essential character of institutions of education. Imagine being able to consult with the authors we draw on in writing this text. You could check our citations with a click of the keyboard, or interact with a program that would generate Weberian interpretations of materials on religion, or ask a program to extrapolate what Ogburn might have said about the computer's effects on the organization of education. If you could do this, why would you need this book?

Perhaps the radical implications of decentralizing knowledge and individualizing its applications are not yet fully appreciated. Or perhaps, they are at the root of resistance to transforming the educational experience itself by way of computer-assisted learning and access to global information. Either way, that the potential for radical change exists in the computer is no assurance that change will come about.

Our computerized simulation of Ogburn's analysis might tell us that education will lag behind the potentials of the computer technology in its organization. Or Berger might warn that the extrinsic forces of existing educational institutions will block the change of its structures by gaining control over the technology.

Certainly this is the way that bureaucratic organizations attempted to control the effects of telephones on their structures. Is it coincidence that the most rapidly growing subdivision of academe today is computer science?

That change *can* take place does not mean that it *will*. People can reject what a technology can do. They can bring back the past in the form of nostalgia. And they can attempt to halt the forces of modernization by acts of political power, as is the case with the Iranian heads of state. But the image of social change we have developed in this book suggests that there is an inevitability to the consequences of modernization. Whatever their manifestations, modern society seems to exhibit the characteristics we enumerated in Chapter 1. Ideas about the fatefulness of change give way to the belief that individuals control their own destiny; with the diminished impact of religion, the search for God is replaced with the search for self; with the search for self comes the fragmentation of the meanings of everyday life and the many voices of those meanings; with the rationalization of meaning itself comes a longing for transcendence and the irony that individual pursuit of that transcedence produces.

As always, however, the sociological eye focuses on the consequences of change at the juncture of the individual and society, of biography and history, and we can now characterize the nature of modern institutional life with a discussion of the nature of the individual located squarely in modern social experience.

The Postmodern Self: The Individual in the Modern World

Our portrait of the modern world underscores the way prominent features of modernity permeate all aspects of institutional social life. Family, church, school, government, and economy exhibit, in varying degrees and combinations, increased individualism, rationalizing, and fragmentation. This creates a nexus of alternative meanings, corresponding social forms, and modes of adaptation. The context of modern society, then, becomes the background against which individuals negotiate the ways they act, feel, and think about themselves and others.

While classical sociologists, Marx, Durkheim, Weber, and Mead identified the structure, form, and meaning of modern experiences, their observations were, of course, limited to what they could see in their time, and what they envisioned for the future was based on their ways of interpreting the present. We have drawn on their insights and augmented them with materials available to us, including the insight from symbolic interactionist thought about the reflexive relationship between institutions and self. According to this insight, institutions and the self-concepts of people living and acting within them change together. While the institutions provide the raw materials for attributing meaning to social life, people enact these meanings, experiencing their consequences in personal ways. In experience, they are both influenced by social forces and gain a degree of control over them. Hence we expect that the dramatic and powerful changes we have documented in previous chapters, together with the interactional work to which people put these forces, might well result in changes in the fundamental senses people have about who they are.

In this concluding section of the text, we introduce contemporary attempts to summarize what is happening to the character of individuals, in the face of modernization and perhaps even in reaction to it.

Some scholars (Daniel Bell 1973, most notably) refer to society as having moved through the modern stage into a postmodern or postindustrial form. We have used the word *modernity* to refer to features of the interaction between institutional meanings, forms, and adaptations as they manifest themselves largely in the lives of people. We have resisted introducing the term postmodernism for several reasons. The term is itself awkward. If modern means contemporary—the current state of affairs—postmodern can mean only "after now," or the future. And the sociological task we undertake is to trace consequences of social change through the current context of institutional meanings, forms, and adaptations. We do not predict the future, for we heed the advice of Schutz (1971), who, when discussing the question of the predictability of the future, reminds us of the Greek myth of Tiresias. Tiresias, as a mortal child, saw the naked body of the goddess Athena, and was blinded as punishment. The gods, however, gave him the power to foresee the future. He could foresee what was going to happen in every encounter, yet was blind to the present. He could never participate in the here and now with his fellow mortals, so he could never tell them of the beauty of Athena. Yet he was "blessed" with foresight. Tiresias could know the future, but not the present. Being preoccupied with the future may well be as much of a curse for sociology as it was for Tiresias.

While the term postmodern may seem awkward and its meanings elusive, it does suggest something beyond the effects of the great transformation of society from rural to urban, from folk to modern. It contains an idea that has grounded our analysis: The idea of postmodernity is not so much that society has moved through being modern but that it is continuing to change in response to the factors we have outlined for each of the major institutions. The shifts and tendencies are so profound some authors believe that this new term, postmodernism, is necessary to capture the essence of living in a society of impression management, style manipulation, engrossment in self, consumption, and the deconstruction of myths and cultural beliefs. We have identified all of these as features of modernity, but some authors argue that they have become significant enough forces in themselves to have produced effects on individuals. These authors refer to the resulting postmodern self.

In their ingenious study of diary writers, Wood and Zurcher (1988) recast the theory of the postmodern self so that we can appreciate the way in which social forces shape character. The weakening and transformation of institutions as agents of socialization does not mean that people are freed from the influence of society. It might mean, however, that the forces of institutions will clash and compete in the individual. We used the concept of oppositional meanings to refer to this consequence of modernity, the idea being that within an individual, self-development reflects the dominant influences of society. Hence, people socialized during the early phase of industrialization will exhibit characteristics consistent with that form of society. Those living in later stages will likewise have an appropriate character. As we have seen, however, whenever society embodies oppositional meanings, varied and even contradictory interpretations of social life, the character of members of society will mirror these clashes of meanings in their own concepts of who they are and how they relate to others.

In an effort to understand these forces of change, Wood and Zurcher (1988) isolate two oppositional continua. First, they suggest that early modern or industrial society stressed the significance of institutional arrangements for conducting the affairs of society. By this they refer to the continuity of form underlying factory models of production.

Capital growth depended, of course, on a cheap and reliable labor force, and forms of investment were predicated on a stable social order. Hence the typical socialization experience of members of early modern society reinforced values, which in turn contributed to stable institutional order. For example, what we have called positional orientation in families adapted nicely the hierarchical nature of industrial society. A father became boss of his home, and his wife and children were his property (cf. Zaretsky 1976). Similarly, religion underwrote the idea of stability and order in all things, including selfhood. This was particularly true with such mainline Protestant churches as the Presbyterians, whose manual of government is, incidentally, still called *The Book of Order*. Education, not surprisingly, also became a significant agent of socialization, inculcating the values of punctuality, thrift, and a work ethic. In short, the major institutions of everyday life could be seen as creating a context for socialization that fostered a self ready for the demands of participation in industry.

Using a computer program to identify words used in the personal dairies of persons chosen to be representative of three distinctive phases of society—premodern (1818–1860), modern (1911–1939), and postmodern (1949–1972)—Wood and Zurcher counted words representing various themes used by the writers in their dairies. Two critical but opposing themes are institution-impulse and product-process. Institutional themes are those referring to authority, conformity, law, and duty; impulse themes are found in words connoting emotion, experiences, irrationality, and nonconformity. Product themes refer to words such as *accomplishment, completion, task,* and *establishment;* process themes to *becoming, chaos, discovery, movement* and *succession.*

In the early development of modern society, stress on institutional stability was typically pared with a task- or product-oriented approach to life. Contemporary feminist scholars have argued that this characterization is male biased, and indeed it probably does best describe the participation of males in industry, since primarily males were involved, and their relationships with females were defined in terms of institutions. Given this, Wood and Zurcher's characterization still seems apt.

When they analyzed diaries, they coded themes that seemed to view the self as a product or task. For example, whenever writers referred to themselves in terms of form, structure, constancy and duration, finishing and outcomes, completion, achievements, attainment and future time, they were said to have product-oriented selves.

The opposite of product, Wood and Zurcher conceived as process, which they used to refer to themes of multiplicity, movement and succession, alternation and transience, discovery, spontaneity, and present time (Wood and Zurcher 1988, 19). What they noticed was that diary writers who depicted themselves in terms of their continuing development and who were focused on the present were more concentrated in the later historical periods. They found that diary writers in the early dates used more words having institutional and product meanings than they used words having impulse and process meanings. The authors theorized that people writing personal accounts of their lives would use the dominant meanings of their time, and hence their diaries could be taken as evidence for the quality of selfhood for that particular epoch.

The dairy writers of the first period, then, saw themselves in terms of their relationship to institutions, and they measured their development in terms of what they had accomplished, the things that they were doing. And their selves were seen as accomplishments or things. As society became more modern, the themes used for self-expression moved toward accounts that emphasize the importance of spur-of-the-moment occurrences (impulses), and of the continual development of personal experiences. While the statistical regularity of these trends was not entirely convincing, it was suggestive enough to Wood and Zurcher that they offered a theory of the postmodern self, a theory that captures the dynamics of the oppositional meanings of selfhood. Figure 8.1 is our rendition of their chart.

Current states of self can be understood as the result of the clashes of meanings among product-process and institution-impulse interpretations. People may well understand themselves as rooted in family or religion (institution) and be about the enterprise of doing things in society (product); but as institutions change, weaken, and combine with one another, other forms of self are possible, and in these alternative forms we see the idea of the postmodern self.emerging

If people derive the sense of who they are from product or doing in society, but these senses of self are rooted in impulse and not institution, then we may be seeing a new ethic, which we might call the *therapeutic ethic*. Here people would be motivated to participate in society and interpret the meaning of their participation in terms of self-exploration. For these postmoderns, life is largely a matter of coping with possible meanings in the context of a fractured and segmentalized society. They give less importance to stability and more to change and are interested in remedial approaches to self and other relationships. These people are the new helpers, and we are familiar with their message. It underlies the popularity of self-help movements, and in terms of our view of societal changes, the object of their participation is the self. We can understand efforts to lose weight, shape bodies, and become "fashionable," as motivated by the therapeutic ethic. The product becomes the self in a form that can be supported by a loosely arranged, rapidly changing social organization.

	Institution	Impulse
Product	Modern ethic	Therapeutic ethic
Process	Organizational ethic	Postmodern ethic

Table 8.1
Dimensions of meaning for the postmodern self.
Adapted from Wood and Zurcker 1987, 139

For example, as Faberman (1980) has shown, the pursuit of excitement through fantasy has vast economic implications in the fashion world, entertainment, and the growing human services component of the labor force. This sense of being modern, then, is rooted in the never-ending task of dealing with the impulses stimulated and exploited by consumerism and materialism. For the therapeutic self, life is a continuous patching up of the consequences of the clashes of values in society, these clashes resolving themselves, if only for the moment, in the latest activity that makes sense.

The coupling of process and institution has produced a new form of organizational beings. These moderns are not the mere functionaries we discussed in Chapter 7, they are motivated by the creation of new forms of stability.

For them, institutions as product are passe, and organizations themselves become the process. Hence the meanings of self are derived not from simply being in an institution, but from creating one. These are people who are actively restructuring the dominant forms of society which are, of course, increasingly bureaucratic. They define their self-worth in terms of efforts to humanize the formal organization. They are the new managers who do not see themselves as managers, but more as organizational guerrillas, fighting to replace the bureaucracy of the modern society with postmodern bureaucratic policy, which is processual and impulsive. Perhaps the most eloquent spokesperson for this movement, Ralph Hummel, writes,

> There is no way back to a premodern picture of the universe . . . . The citizens and politicians who help design a postmodern bureaucratic policy. . . start doing so by viewing the world in terms entirely different from those of traditional science. They also set aside compensating approaches that merely seek to repair what science has ripped asunder. Among the new assumptions about the world, these are already clear: 1. Socially. The unit of analysis is not the lone individual, but the dyad and combination of dyads: teams in the field. 2. Culturally. Values are derived from what a thing is (quality) not from how much there is of a thing (quantity). 3. Psychologically. Our emotional being is shaped by the fact that we are born into the world already in the company of others and that our first experiences are those of mother/child unity, not of separateness, 4. Linguistically/ thoughtfully. We come to knowledge in unity with reality, including the work we encounter and those we work with; we communicate, as against inform, when we construct language in the company of others. 5. Politically. We are at our political best not when struggling for power over deciding who gets what, when, how of those goods and services that have already been valued and created, but when we convoke the political community to formulate values that do not exist. (Hummel 1987, 269)

Hummel's proposals for how to live within and transform bureaucracy embody both the notions of institutions and process, and he calls for a new world of institutions defined in more human terms. He calls for a caring and understanding reorganization of the consequences of modernization. Perhaps he is suggesting that the ways in which everyday life have changed as the result of the forces we have traced can be the basis for new forms of society.

Finally, the coupling of impulse and process creates the postmodern self, a person for whom actions are driven by impulses, but impulsive action is itself interpreted as process. As we have indicated, the postmodern surge, fueled by rapid technological change, is impossible to keep up with. It is youthful and energetic. It is stylish and calculated, and it is even self-destructive. The postmodern self is a celebration of senselessness, and it can be found in its purest expression in music and art, which specialize in antimony. The postmodern self probably is not possible to maintain, since it grows out of the oppositional and ironic nature of modern society itself. Yet it is real in its manifestations; we know it when we see it. It seeks danger in the midst of the safe society. It shapes chaos by establishing forms that it destroys, and it merges the strains of conflicting meanings into expressive styles—a blue jeans jacket with slogans of reform written on it, with a price tag of $100.

Conclusion

We have begun a task we cannot finish, for the character of self is a continuous reflection of change. A society driven by technological change will create contexts for socialization that contain residuals of old institutional meanings and elements of the new. In this book, we have taken a focused view of social change, choosing to look at the five basic institutions of society. There are, of course, many other aspects to institutional life in modern society— military and welfare institutions, for example, could well be subjects of another book. We took the narrower approach because we think the essentials of modernity are more clearly understood through familiar experiences, and we all have experiences in the basic institutions of society.

Further, the elemental features of modernity clash most profoundly with the established conventions of society within the basic institutions, for the underlying assumptions we use to interpret our social experiences often have their roots in meanings of fundamental institutions. As we tried to document in this chapter, technologically induced change (cars, phones, and computers) plays itself in the dynamics of institutional life from dating to the management of earth's resources.

As we move into the twenty-first century, barring major ecological/political disasters, we can expect more elaboration of social structure as the result of technological change. It is difficult to imagine people giving up the mobility they have come to take for granted, withdrawing from the video screen, or returning to less self-reflective ways of making sense out of their participation in society. We suspect that change has become the only constancy in the modern world.

Yet is there some stability in how we understand change? A radio commercial for new houses lists modern options. "Today the average family is a man and woman and two children, or a woman and two children, or a man and one child, or even just you! Regardless of your needs, we have the house for your family." One might wonder how "just you" can be a family, but the commercial makes sense. We know what they mean. Everyone must have a home, everyone must have some kind of family, even if it's "just you." Our modern God bears little resemblance to the patriarch of the past, yet most of us say we still need God. The educational experiences children have are remote from those of their parents, yet parents affirm the importance of an education they really do not understand. The new economy is fast paced, highly complex and innovative, with family business a quaint image. Politics seems a public relations game, and people still devote their lives to public service.

We suggest that the extent of change in the basic institutions of society is so great that what we count as experiences in institutions probably would not even be recognizable to members of other societies and even past members of our own. What counts as family life, parents coordinating their children's play and microwaving supper while watching television, is essentially remote from the family dinner where father says the blessing and sits as head of the family dinner table. But we still call the "nuked" dinner, the constant glow of the television and the "parent conference" at the local junior high school affairs of the family. We still accord great popularity to television programs that present versions of what family life is supposed be. What is constant is that we use a language similar to what other generations used to talk about institutions. It is the language and not much else that creates continuity.

In our talk about the basic institutions of society, we create and re-create them in form and substance. The recurring patterns of talk in everyday life are the social structure, and the resources that we must identify and understand if we are to understand the effects of change on organization and individual (Molotch and Boden 1985). Particulars of the language we use may well change as new terms for the participants in institutional life are introduced, but the syntax of institutional language will change more slowly. Father and mother, daughter and son; boss and worker, employer and employee; preacher, priest, and rabbi; teacher-student; and elected official—these are the words of institutions, and they anchor our sense of everyday life.

While rates of change will vary (can we still used the word congressman?) for different domains of institutional life, discourse about the meanings of social life will continue to take place. In effect, we understand nothing outside the meaning systems provided to us by social institutions. Still, we uniquely apply these meanings, and other applications have varying implications and consequences for daily lives. The impetus for modern society is technology, but the sense we make of technology is institutional. Hence we have family-work-pleasure cars, personal-business-family computers, religious-educational-commercial television networks. We amend and modify the meanings of institutions with each application to the next technology.

The study of changing institutions is truly the study of the creation and maintenance of society. From the perspective of everyday life, technologies seem to come on us. While actually they are complex inventions taking place within the context of communication and institution, they are more or less a drop in the flow of institutional life. A grandmother gives her daughter a microwave oven for Christmas. A vendor introduces a new computer to school administrators, who in turn present it to teachers and students. We know that the relationship between technology and institutions is complicated, and sometimes quite indirect. But whatever the consequences and however they are enacted, they travel on the language of institutions. By talking about our social world in terms we get from institutions, we create, change, and maintain society. Let the talk continue.

REFERENCES

Albrecht, S.L., B.A. Chadwick, and D.S. Alcron. 1977. "Religiosity and Deviance: Application of an Attitude–Behavior Consistency Model." *Journal for the Scientific Study of Religion* 16:263–274.

Atwater, Lynn. 1987. "Women and Marriage: Adding an Extramarital Role." Pp. 556–567 in Candace Clark and Howard Robboy, eds., *Social Interaction: Readings in Sociology*. 3rd ed. New York: St. Martin's Press.

Auerbach, Jerold S. 1976. *Unequal Justice: Lawyers and Social Change in Modern America.* New York: Academic Press.

Ball, Donald W. 1968. "Toward a Sociology of Telephones and Telephoners." Pp. 59–75 in Marcello Truzzi, ed., *Sociology and Everyday Life*. Englewood Cliffs, N.J.: Prentice-Hall.

Bell, Daniel. 1973. *The Coming of the Post-Industrial Society: A Venture in Social Forecasting.* New York: Basic Books.

———. 1978. *The Cultural Contradictions of Capitalism.* New York: Basic Books.

Bennett, William J. 1988. *Our Children and Our Country: Improving America's Schools and Affirming the Common Culture.* New York: Simon and Schuster.

Bensman, Joseph, and Israel Gerver. 1963. "Crime and Punishment in the Factory." Pp. 589–596 in Alvin W. Gouldner and Helen P. Gouldner, eds., *Modern Sociology.* New York: Harcourt, Brace and World.

Berger, Peter. 1961. *The Precarious Vision.* Garden City, N.Y.: Doubleday.

———. 1967. *The Sacred Canopy: Elements of a Sociological Theory of Religion.* New York: Doubleday.

Berger, Brigitte, and Peter Berger. 1983. *The War Over the Family.* Garden City, N.Y.: Doubleday Anchor.

Berger, Peter, Brigitte Berger, and Hansfried Kellner. 1974. *The Homeless Mind: Modernization and Consciousness.* New York: Vintage.

Berger, Peter, and Hansfreid Kellner. 1964. "Marriage and the Construction of Social Reality." *Diogenes* 45:1–25.

Berger, Peter, and Thomas Luckmann. 1967. *The Social Construction of Reality.* Garden City, N.Y.: Doubleday.

Berk, Sarah Fenstermarker. 1985. *The Gender Trap: The Apportionment of Work in American Households.* New York: Plenum.

Bernstein, Basil. 1970. "A Sociolinguistic Approach to Socialization: With Some Reference to Educability." Pp. 26–62 in Frederick Williams, ed., *Language and Poverty: Perspectives on a Theme.* Chicago: Markham.

Blau, Francine D. 1984. "Women in the Labor Force." Pp. 297–315 in Jo Freeman, ed., *Women: A Feminist Perspective*. 2nd ed. Palo Alto, Calif.: Mayfield.

Blumstein, Philip, and Pepper Schwartz. 1983. *American Couples: Money, Work, Sex.* New York: Morrow.

Caplow, Theodore, et al. 1982. *Middletown Families: Fifty Years of Change and Continuity.* Minneapolis: University of Minnesota Press.

Cazden, Courtney B., Vera P. John, and Dell Hymes, eds. 1972. *Functions of Language in the Classroom.* New York: Teachers College Press.

Chalfant, H. Paul, Robert E. Beckley, and C. Eddie Palmer. 1987. *Religion in Contemporary Society* . 2nd ed. Palo Alto, Calif.: Mayfield.

Cherlin, Andrew. 1978. "Remarriage as an Incomplete Institution." *American Journal of Sociology* 84(November):634–650.

Cicourel, Aaron, et al. 1974. *Language Use and School Performance*. New York: Academic Press.

Collins, Randall. 1979. *The Credential Society: An Historical Sociology of Education and Stratification*. New York: Academic Press.

———. 1982. *Sociological Insight: An Introduction to Nonobvious Sociology* . New York: Oxford University Press.

Comte, August. 1853. *The Positive Philosophy*. 2 vols. London: J. Chapman.

Cooley, Charles H. 1922. *Human Nature and the Social Order*. New York: Scribner's.

Crandall, Robert W., et al. 1986. *Regulating the Automobile*. Washington, D.C.: Brookings Institution.

Deken, Joseph. 1982. *The Electronic Cottage*. New York: Morrow.

Derber, Charles. 1979. *The Pursuit of Attention; Power and Individualism in Everyday Life*. Cambridge, Mass.: Schenkman.

Denzin, Norman. 1987. *The Alcoholic Self*. Newbury Park, Calif: Sage.

Dixon, Carol. 1972. "Guided Options as a Pattern of Control in a Headstart Program." *Urban Life and Culture* 3(July):203–216.

Douglas, Mary. 1986. *How Institutions Think*. Syracuse, N.Y.: Syracuse University Press.

Dow James. 1987. "Toward an Understanding of Some Subtle Stresses on Langauge Maintenance Among Old Order Amish of Iowa." *International Journal of the Sociology of Language* 69(January): 322–356.

Dreitzel, Hans Peter. 1972. *Recent Sociology, No 2*. New York: Macmillan.

Durkheim, Emile. 1938. *Rules of the Sociological Method*. The University of Chicago Press.

———. 1947. *Division of Labor in Society*. New York: Free Press.

———. 1951. *Suicide*. New York: Free Press.

———. 1954. *Elementary Forms of Religious Life*. New York: Free Press.

Edelman, Murray. 1977. *Political Language: Words That Succeed and Policies That Fail*. New York: Academic Press.

Elias, Norbert. 1982. *Power and Civility*. New York: Pantheon.

Elias, Norbert, and Eric Dunning. 1986. *Quest for Excitment: Sport and Leisure in the Civilizing Process*. New York: Oxford University Press.

Elkin, Frederick, and Gerald Handel. 1984. *The Child and Society: The Process of Socialization*. New York: Random House.

Ellul, Jacques. 1964. *The Technological Society*. New York: Vintage.

Etzioni, Amitai. 1977. "The Family: Is It Obsolete?" *Journal of Current Social Issues* 14(Winter):4–9.

Faberman, Harvey A. 1980. "Fantasy in Everyday Life: Some Aspects of the Intersection Between Social Psychology and Political Economy." *Symbolic Interaction* 3(Spring): 9–21.

Fass, Paula. 1977. *The Damned and the Beautiful: American Youth in the 1920's*. New York: Oxford University Press.

Ferguson, Kathy E. 1984. *The Feminist Case Against Bureaucracy*. Philadelphia: Temple University Press.

Frank, Arthur W. 1987. "Review Essay." *Symbolic Interaction*. 10(1):295–311.

Freudenburg, William R. 1986. "Sociology in Legis-land: An Ethnographic Report on Congressional Culture." *Sociological Quarterly*. 27(Fall):313–326.

Gaede, Stan. 1977. "Religious Affiliation, Social Mobility, and the Problem of Causality: A Methodological Critique of Catholic-Protestant Socioeconomic Achievement Studies." *Review of Religious Research* 19:54–62.

Galbraith, John Kenneth. 1967. *The New Industrial State.* Boston: Houghton Mifflin.

Gans, Herbert J. 1975. *Popular Culture and High Culture: An Analysis and Evaluation of Taste.* New York: Basic Books.

———. 1979. "Symbolic Ethnicity: The Future of Ethnic Groups and Cultures in America." Pp. 193–220 in Herbert J. Gans, ed., *On the Making of America: Essays in Honor of David Riesman.* Philadelphia: University of Pennsylvania Press.

———. 1988. *Middle American Individualism: The Future of Liberal Democracy.* New York: Free Press.

Garfinkel, Harold. 1967. *Studies in Ethnomethodology.* Englewood Cliffs, N.J.: Prentice-Hall.

Glenn, Evelyn and Roslyn L. Feldberg. 1984. "Clerical Work: The Female Occupation." Pp. 316–336 in Jo Freeman,ed., *Women: A Feminist Perspective*, 3th ed. Palo Alto, Calif.: Mayfield.

Goffman, Erving. 1959. *The Presentation of Self in Everyday Life.* Garden City, N.Y.: Doubleday.

———. 1961. *Stigma: Notes of the Management of Spoiled Identity.* Englewood Cliffs, NJ: Prentice-Hall.

———. 1974. *Frame Analysis: An Essay on the Organization of Experience.* Cambridge: Harvard University Press.

———. 1981. *Forms of Talk.* Philadelphia: University of Pennsylvania Press.

———. 1983. "Interactional Order." *American Sociological Review* 48:1–17.

Glock, Charles, and Rodney Stark. 1965. *Religion and Society in Tension.* Chicago: Rand McNally.

Gordon, David. 1974. "The Jesus People: An Identity Synthesis." *Urban Life and Culture.* 3:159–178.

Gordon, Michael. 1978. *The American Family: Past and Present.* New York: Random House.

Greeley, Andrew. 1989. "Protestant and Catholic." *American Sociological Review* 54:485–502.

Habermas, Jurgen. 1975. *Legitimation Crisis.* Translated by T. McCarthy. Boston: Beacon Press.

Heberle, Rudolf. 1951. *Social Movements: An Introduction to Political Sociology.* N.Y.: Appleton-Century-Crofts.

Hewitt, John P., and Randall Stokes. 1975. "Disclaimers." *American Sociological Review.* (February):1–11.

Higgins, Paul C., and Gary L. Albrecht. 1977. "Hellfire and Delinquency Revisited." *Social Forces* 55:952–958.

Hirschi, T., and R. Stark. 1969. "Hellfire and Delinquency." *Social Problems.* 17:202–213.

Hoffer, Eric. 1951. *The True Believer: Thoughts on the Nature of Mass Movements.* New York: Harper & Row.

Howton. F. William. 1969. *Functionaries.* Chicago: Quadrangle.

Hummel, Ralph. 1987. *The Bureaucratic Experience* , 3rd ed., New York: St.Martin's Press.

Iacocca, Lee, With Sonny Kleinfield. 1988. *Talking Straight.* New York: Bantam.

Ianni, Francis A.J. 1989. *The Search for Structure: A Report of American Youth.* New York: Free Press.

Illich, Ivan. 1971. *Deschooling Society.* New York: Harrow Books.

Inkeles, Alex. 1983. *Exploring Individual Modernity.* New York: Columbia University Press.

Israel, Joachin. 1971. *Alienation from Marx to Modern Society.* Boston: Allyn and Bacon.

Jackson, Elton F., William S. Fox, and Harry J. Crockett, Jr. 1970. "Religion and Occupational Achievement." *American Sociological Review* 35(1): 48–63.

James, William. 1890. *Principles of Psychology.* New York: Holt.

Katchadourian, Herant A., and John Boli. 1985. *Careerism and Intellectualism among College Students*. San Francisco: Jossey-Bass.

Katz, Judith Milstein. 1976. "How Do You Love Me? Let Me Count the Ways (The Phenomenology of Being Loved)" *Sociological Inquiry*. 46:17–22.

Kelly, Alfred H., and Winfred A. Harbison. 1970. *The American Constitution: Its Origin and Development*. New York: Norton.

Keniston, Kenneth. 1968. *Young Radicals: Notes on Committed Youth*. New York: Harcourt, Brace and World.

———. 1977. *All Our Childern: The American Family under Pressure*. New York: Harcourt Brace Jovanovich.

Kinsey, Barry. 1985. "Congressional Staff: The Cultivation and Maintenance of Personal Networks in a Insecure Work Environment." *Urban Life: A Journal of Ethnographic Research* 13(January):395–422.

Lacey, Robert. 1986. *Ford: The Men and the Machine*. Boston: Little. Brown.

Langenberg, Donald N. 1989. "Supporting the Global Scholar." *Academic Computing* (January):12–16.

Lantz, Herman, et al. 1968. "Pre-Industrial Patterns in the Colonial Family in American." *American Sociological Review* 33(June):413–426.

LeMasters, E.E. 1975. *Blue-Collar Aristocrats: Life Styles at a Working Class Tavern*. Madison: University of Wisconsin Press.

Lenski, Gerhard F. 1961. *The Religious Factor*. Garden City, N.Y.: Doubleday.

Lenski, Gerhard F., and Jean Lenski. 1978. *Human Societies: An Introduction to Macrosociology*. New York: McGraw-Hill.

Levine, Donald N. 1985. *Flight from Ambiguity*. Chicago: Unversity of Chicago Press.

Linton, Ralph. 1936. *The Study of Man*. New York: Appleton-Century.

Lofland, Lynn. 1973. *World of Strangers*. New York: Basic Books

Lyman, Stanford, and Marvin Scott. 1968. "Accounts." *American Sociological Review*. 33 (February): 46–62.

——— 1970. "Coolness in Everyday Life." Pp. 145–158 in Lyman and Scott, *A Sociology of the Absurd*. New York: Appleton-Centruy-Crofts.

——— 1989. *A Sociology of the Absurd*. 2nd ed. Dix Hills, N.Y.: General Hall.

Lynd, Robert, and Helen Lynd. 1929. *Middletown: A Study of Modern American Culture*. New York: Harcourt, Brace and World.

McNamara, Patrick H. 1974. *Religion American Style*. New York: Harper & Row.

Maisel, Robert 1974. "The Flea Market as an Action Scene." *Urban Life and Culture* 2:488–505.

Marx, Karl. 1971 (1872). *Capital: A Critique of Political Economy*. Chicago: C.H. Kerr.

Mayhew, Leon. 1984. "In Defense of Modernity: Talcott Parsons and the Utilitarian Tradition." *American Journal of Sociology* 89 (May):1273–1305.

Mead, George H. 1934. *Mind, Self and Society*. Chicago: University of Chicago Press.

Mehan, Hugh, and Houston Wood. 1974. *The Reality of Ethnomethodology*. New York: Wiley.

Merton, Robert K. 1957. *Social Theory and Social Structure*. Glencoe, Ill: Free Press.

Michels, Robert. 1959. *Political Parties: A Sociological Study of Oligarchical Tendencies of Modern Man*. New York: Free Press.

Mills, C. Wright. 1951. *White Collar*. New York: Oxford University Press.

———. 1959. *The Sociological Imagination*. New York: Oxford University Press.

Mintz, Morton, and Jerry S. Cohen. 1971. *America, Inc.: Who Owes and Operates the United States*. New York: Dial Press.

Mitchel, Arnold. 1981. *The Nine American Life Styles* . New York: Macmillan.

Molotch, Harvey L., and Deirdre Boden. 1985. "Talking Social Structure," *American Sociological Review* 50(June): 273–288.

Murdock, George. P. 1935. "Comparable Data on the Division of Labor by Sex." *Social Forces*: 551–553.

Muson, Howard. 1982. "Getting the Phone's Number." *Psychology Today* (April):42–49.

Naisbitt, John. 1982. *Megatrends: Ten Directions Transforming Our Lives*. New York: Warner Books.

Nash, Anedith. 1987. "Five Acres and a Truck: Symbolism in Suburban American." Paper delivered at Midwest Sociological Society, Chicago, April.

Nash, Jeffrey E., and James M. Calonico. 1974. "Sociological Perspectives in Bernstein's Sociolinguistics." *The Sociological Quarterly* 15(Winter):81–92.

Nash, Jeffrey E., and David W. McCurdy. 1989. "Cultural Knowledge and Systems of Knowing" *Sociological Inquiry* 59(May): 117–126.

Nelson, Joel I., and Chapman Tsui. 1986. "Employment Trends in Post Industrial Society." *Sociology of Rural Life* 8(Spring): 3.

Nolan, Tom. 1976. The Family Plan of the Latter-day Osmonds." *Rolling Stone* (March):46–49.

Ogburn, William. 1927. *Social Change with Respect to Culture and Original Nature*. New York: Viking.

Pattison, Robert. 1982. *On Literacy: The Politics of the Word from Homer to the Age of Rock*. New York: Oxford University Press.

Parsons, Talcott. 1937. *The Structure of Social Action*. New York: McGraw Hill.

———. 1951. *The Social System*. Glencoe, Illinois: The Free Press.

———. 1959. "Some Problems Confronting Sociology as a Profession." *American Sociological Review* 4(August): 543–550.

———. 1971. *The System of Modern Societies*. Englewood Cliffs, N.J.: Prentice-Hall.

Peek, Charles, Evans W. Curry, and H. Paul Chalfant. 1985. "Religiosity and Delinquency Over Time." *Social Science Quarterly* 66:120–131.

Perrolle, Judith A. 1987. *Computer and Social Change: Information, Property and Power*. Belmont, Calif.: Wadsworth.

Piven, Frances F., and Richard A. Cloward. 1971. *Regulating the Poor: The Functions of Public Welfare*. New York: Pantheon.

Redfield, Robert. 1960. *The Little Community: Peasant Society and Culture*. Chicago: University of Chicago Press.

Riesman, David, With Reuel Denney and Nathan Glazer. 1950. *The Lonely Crowd*. New Haven, Conn.: Yale University Press.

Robbins, Thomas, Dick Anthony, and James Richardson. 1976. "Theory and Research on Today's 'New Religions'." *Sociological Analysis* 37:95–122

Rokeach, Milton. 1960. *The Open and Closed Mind*. New York: Basic Books.

Roof, Wade Clark, and William McKinney. 1987. *American Mainline Religion*. New Brunswick, N.J.: Rutgers University Press.

Rosenthal, Robert. 1968. *Experimenter Effects in Behavioral Research*. New York: Appleton-Century-Crofts.

Rosenthal, Robert ,and K. L. Fode. 1963. "The Effect of Experimenter Bias on the Performance of Albino Rats" *Behavioral Science* 8(July):183–189.

Rosenthal, Robert and L. Jacobsen. 1967. *Pygmalion in the Classroom*. New York: Holt, Rinehart and Winston.

Rosow, Irving. 1966. "Forms and Functions of Adult Socialization." *Social Forces* 3:35–45.

Schroyer, Trent. 1970. "Toward a Critical Theory for Advanced Industrial Society." Pp. 569–581 in Hans Peter Dreitzel, ed., *Recent Sociology No. 2*. New York: Macmillan.

Schutz, Alfred. 1971. *Collected Papers II: Studies in Social Theory.* The Hague: Martinus Nijhoff.

Schwartz, Morris S. 1976. "Notes of the Human Dimension." *Sociological Inquiry* 46(3–4):197–205.

Sebald, Hans. 1984. "New-Age Romanticism: The Quest for an Alternative Lifestyle as a Force of Social Change." *Humbolt Journal of Social Relations* 11(2):106–127.

Selznick, Philip. 1966 (1949). *TVA and the Grass Roots.* New York: Harper & Row.

Simmel, George. 1950. *The Sociology of Georg Simmel.* Edited by Kurt H. Wolff. New York: Free Press.

————. 1986. *Schopenhauer and Nietzsche.* Translated by Helmut Loiskandl, Deena Weinstein, and Michael Weinstein. Amherst: University of Massachusetts Press.

Singer, Benjamin D. 1981. *Social Functions of the Telephone.* Palo Alto, Calif.: R & E Research Associates.

Sklare, Marshall. 1971. *America's Jews.* New York: Random House.

Skolnick, Arlene S., and Jerome H. Skolnick. 1986. *Family in Transition: Rethinking Marriage, Sexuality, Childrearing and Family Organization.* Boston: Little, Brown.

Smith, Mark C. 1984. "From Middletown to Middletown III: A Critical Review." *Qualitative Sociology* 7(4):327–336.

Smith, Tom. 1984. "America's Religious Mosaic." *American Demographics* 6(June):19–23.

Spradley, James P. 1988 (1970). *You Owe Yourself a Drunk: An Ethnography of Urban Nomads.* New York: University Press of America.

Spradley, Jame P., and David W. McCurdy. 1980. *Anthropology, The Cultural Perspective.* New York: Wiley.

Stark, Rodney. 1984. "Religion and Conformity: Reaffirming a Sociology of Religion." *Sociological Analysis* 45:273–282.

Stein, Peter J., ed. 1981. *Single Life: Unmarried Adults in Social Context.* New York: St. Martin's Press.

Stinchcombe, Arthur L. 1973. "Formal Organizations." Pp.23–66 in Neil J. Smelser, ed., *Sociology: An Introduction.* New York: Wiley.

————. 1974. "A Parsonian Theory of Traffic Accidents." *Sociological Inquiry.* 45(1):27–30.

Stonequist, Edward V. 1937. *The Marginal Man.* New York: Scribner's.

Strauss, Anselm. 1978. *Negotiations: Varieties, Contexts, Processes and Social Order.* San Francisco: Jossey-Bass.

Sumner, William Graham. 1959 (1906). *Folkways.* Boston: Mentor.

Terkel, Louis (Studs). 1984. *Working: People Talk about What They Do All Day and How They Feel About What They Do.* New York: Pantheon.

Troeltsch, Ernst. 1931. *The Social Teaching of the Christian Churches.* New York: Macmillan.

Trudgill, Peter. 1983. *Sociolinguisitics: An Introduction to Language and Society.* New York: Penguin.

Turkle, Sherry. 1984. *The Second Self: Computers and the Human Spirit.* New York: Simon and Schuster.

Useem, Michael. 1989. *Liberal Education and the Corporation: The Hiring and Advancement of College Graduates.* Hawthorne, N.Y.: Aldine de Gruyter.

Veblen, Thorstein. 1918. *The Higher Learning of America.* New York: B.W.Huebsh.

Wandersee, Winifred D. 1988. *On the Move: American Women in the 1970's.* Boston: Twayne.

Weatherford, J. McIver. 1981. *Tribes on the Hill.* New York: Rawson, Wade.

Weber, Max. 1958. *Protestant Ethic and the Spirit of Capitalism.* New York: Scribner's.

————. 1961. "The Three Types of Legitimate Rule." Pp. 4–18 in Amitai Etzioni, ed., *Complex Organizations.* New York: Holt, Rinehart and Winston.

Weigert, Andrew J. 1983. "Identity: Its Emergence within Sociological Psychology." *Symbolic Interaction* 6(Fall):183–206.

Weigert, Andrew J. and Ross Hastings. 1977. "Identity Loss, Family and Social Change." *American Journal of Sociology* 82(6):1171–1185.

Weil, Frederick D. 1985. "Education and Liberalism." *American Sociological Review.* 50(August): 458–474.

Whyte, William. 1956. *The Organization Man.* New York: Simon and Schuster.

Wiley, Norbert. 1967. "America's Unique Class Politics: The Interplay of the Labor, Credit and Commodity Markets." *American Sociological Review* 32(August): 529–541.

Williams, Frederick. 1982. *The Communications Revolution.* Beverly Hills, Calif.: Sage.

Williams, Robin M. 1960. *American Society: A Sociological Interpretation.* New York: Knopf.

Wolfe, Tom. 1980. *In Our Time.* New York: Farrar, Straus and Giroux.

Wood, Michael R. and Louis A. Zurcher Jr. 1987. *The Development of the Post Modern Self: A Computer Assisted Comparative Analysis of Personal Documents,* New York: Greenwood Press.

Woodward, Bob, and Carl Bernstein. 1974. *All the President's Men.* New York: Simon and Schuster.

Wrong, Dennis. 1961. "The Oversocialized Conception of Man in Modern Society." *American Sociological Review* 26:183–193.

Yankelovich, Daniel. 1981. *New Rules in American Life: Searching for Self-fulfillment in a World Turned Upsidedown.* New York: Random House.

Yinger, J. Milton. 1957. *Religion, Society and the Individual.* New York: Macmillan.

Zaretsky, Eli. 1976. *Capitalism and the Family and Personal Life.* New York: Harper & Row.

Zicklin, Gilbert. 1973. "Communal Child-rearing: A Report on Three Cases." Pp. 176–211 in Hans Peter Dreitzel, ed., *Recent Sociology No. 5: Childhood and Socialization.* New York: Macmillan.

Zurcher, Louis. 1977. *The Mutable Self: A Self Concept for Social Change.* Beverly Hills, Calif: Sage.

———. 1982. "The Staging of Emotion: A Dramaturgical Analysis." *Symbolic Interaction* 5 (Spring):1–22.

Name Index

Subject Index